SOCIAL WELFARE POLICY

SOCIAL WELFARE POLICY

A Research and Action Strategy

W. Joseph Heffernan
University of Texas

Longman
New York & London

Social Welfare Policy: A Research and Action Strategy

Longman, 95 Church Street, White Plains, N.Y. 10601

Associated companies:
Longman Group Ltd., London
Longman Cheshire Pty., Melbourne
Longman Paul Pty., Auckland
Copp Clark Pitman, Toronto

Senior editor: David Estrin
Production editor: Linda Witzling
Cover design: Michelle Szabo
Text art: Fine Line Inc.
Production supervisor: Richard Bretan

Library of Congress Cataloging-in-Publication Data

Heffernan, W. Joseph.
Social welfare policy : a research and action strategy / by W. Joseph Heffernan.
p. cm.
Includes bibliographical references and index.
ISBN 0-8013-0546-2
1. Public welfare—United States. 2. Public welfare—Research—United States. 3. United States—Social policy. I. Title.
HV95.H393 1991
361.6'1'0973—dc20 91-28269
CIP

1 2 3 4 5 6 7 8 9 10-MW-9594939291

To Linda

Contents

Acknowledgments

Many students and colleagues have read and commented on early drafts of this work, too many to acknowledge properly. At various stages in its preparation, Mary Ellen Burns, Sarah Sutton, and Linda Heffernan read the entire manuscript. All made both gentle and forceful suggestions for modifications. I am indebted to them for taking the time from their activities to help. Kelly Larson and Belinda Boon provided more than word processing and manuscript organizing and faxing assistance. I also wish to thank David Estrin, Linda Witzling, Marcy Gray, and a copy editor whose name has been withheld from me for our mutual protection during the production process. All of the above have saved me from more embarrassing errors than I would like to admit. Robin McCullough, Charlotte Gardiner, and Sheri Weaver provided assistance at the stage of proofreading and fact checking.

PART **1**

A Logic of Social Wefare Policy

This text looks at ways our governmental and voluntary agencies take action—or fail to take action—in response to a wide variety of social welfare problems in the United States. The specific focus is on the role of social workers in the process of shaping public policy and voluntary agency responsibilities. The first part is divided into four chapters which serve as an introduction to the extensive literature on conceptions of the welfare system and the policy process. The first chapter provides some views on the parameters of the social welfare system. The distinctions identified in this chapter emphasize the substance, goals, and content of social welfare programs. The second and third chapters review alternative models used by professionals to explain how choices are made about what society ought, and ought not to do in response to pressing social needs. The central theme is the understanding of the political context of social welfare choices. The fourth chapter diverges slightly to review the economic context of the political choices.

CHAPTER 1

The Scope of Social Welfare Programs

It is easy to say that a welfare state is one in which public policy is predominantly concerned with the welfare of its members, but this does not provide us with any insight into the nature of welfare.

William A. Robson

RELEVANCE OF POLICY STUDIES TO DIRECT PRACTICE

This book about the analysis, implementation, and evaluation of social welfare policy in the United States is written from the perspective of the social worker. Observations about the structure and the study of social welfare have a clear and direct relevance to planners, administrators, and researchers. However, these are not the people responsible for implementing social programs at the street level, where social worker and client interact directly. For most graduate students in social work, the first job will be at the level of direct practice—delivering social welfare services in direct interaction with clients. It is the client with a presenting problem with whom the social worker interacts. It is the presenting problems, in their many manifestations, to which social policies are designed as a response. It is the social worker at the street level who hears first what clients think and feel about these policies.

Rarely is the direct practice social worker called upon to deliver testimony before a congressional or state legislative committee, or to be present when the cabinet officer is designing administrative directives. Yet caseworkers and other direct practitioners do play vital roles in the formulation and shaping of policy because they are the vital link in the flow of information from client to policymaker and from policymaker to client. As a result, street-level bureaucrats in both public and private agencies exercise a broad range of discretion on the ways in which policies are shaped and delivered.

The flow of realistic information from client to policymaker and the heightened sensitivity of policymakers to clients' circumstances can best be accomplished when caseworkers both appreciate and understand the opportunities and the limits of the American policy-making process.

Because the direct practitioner's major functional role is far removed from the "decision point" in broad comprehensive policy, students sometimes think that time spent in policy courses could be more effectively devoted to the development of practitioner skills. I believe the reverse is true. It is precisely because policymakers have so little understanding of the impact of policy on clients that practitioners need to have an understanding of the limits and problems of the policymakers. The social worker called upon to implement particular kinds of decisions needs to understand that, for the most part, regulations are not made with indifference to the welfare of clients. Social workers also need to understand the policy processes so that they can effect change when policymakers have been ill informed or have acted capriciously. Only by understanding the range of choices that are economically efficient and politically feasible, while still being responsive to the underlying social problem, can social workers do this successfully. Proposed alternatives to a flawed policy must take into account what the current policy offers, as well as the values, both implicit and explicit, in the alternatives. Even social workers who do not impose their own values on the clients they serve often use only their own values in judging social policies. It is easy to dismiss supply-side economics as a pretext for securing the wealth of the very rich at the expense of the rest of society. It is also easy to dismiss spending on some social programs as "throwing money at a problem" in order to buy votes. The political and economic considerations that best explain distributions of wealth and income are far more complex than the rhetoric of either the right or the left would suggest.

APPROACHES TO THE STUDY OF SOCIAL WELFARE

No single policy perspective is inherently superior to others and the modes of investigation of these perspectives are not entirely separable. There is considerable room for reasonable disagreement about what should be known and how to act. To understand and act intelligently about issues of social policy we must ask a series of basic questions that will vary from one situation to the next. There is a basic framework for the questions. The central one is, "What ought I to do in order to promote a better set of social welfare programs and policies?" This demands attention to the question "How and why have policies turned out as they are?" Yet other questions have to be addressed: "What would be a better set of programs and policies?" "How do I know (or think) it would be better?" More generally, the question is, "What distinguishes the best from the worst?" Three basic approaches are commonly used to seek answers to these interrelated questions: What ought to be done to change things requires a focus on the *political process*; how and how well things are done now demands a focus on the *performance* of the social welfare system; and finally, to discover the norms with which to judge welfare services and policy calls for a *normative* focus.

Studies of the process focus on the dynamics of the policy process with specific regard to economic, social, and political forces that shape both the realistic options and the choices that are made within the constraints of the political system. The conceptual frameworks borrowed from political science and economics are used to focus on the manner in which the input variables of the political process are transformed into the outputs of a formal set of social welfare institutions.

The performance perspective has a focus on the institutions of the social welfare system itself. Essentially descriptive studies are used so that the student is informed about the current shape of mental health institutions, foster care practice, adoption policies, and so on. One thought behind this approach is that the student can best help clients by knowing what the institutions do and how they do it. Another is that, should we seek to change things, we need first to know something about the way things are now.

The third perspective is normative and evaluative. The normative approach examines the social welfare system in a clearly nonneutral frame of reference. It asks essentially ethical questions about performance. A fundamental purpose of evaluation in one sense is to measure the degree to which programs have attained their goals. Evaluative research measures the performance both qualitatively and quantitatively. Two types of evaluative questions are asked: (1) "What are the observable consequences that can reasonably be attached to the introduction of a particular program? (2) "What are the effects of social policy on the citizen and the political system?" In the first approach the effort is basically to measure preprogram and postprogram conditions and to isolate the programs' impacts on those differences.[1] In the second approach the effort is to make more explicit the central ethical dilemmas implicit in how a social welfare system is to be structured.[2]

This text focuses on the policy process perspective. Specifically, it looks at the role of the social worker in the development of social welfare policy. The intent is to provide a practical framework for social work students as they prepare for their role as advocates, analysts, researchers, and implementers of American social welfare policy.

GOAL-ORIENTED DEFINITIONS OF SOCIAL WELFARE

The goals of social welfare systems may be viewed from several levels of abstraction. One perspective is that of basic goals. Kenneth Boulding defines social welfare policy as those aspects of domestic public policy that focus on the degree to which public programs can encourage integration of individuals and groups into the whole of society.[3] T. H. Marshall describes social welfare as those policies of government that have as their intent the provision of income protection, health, and other essential services.[4] Richard Titmus describes social welfare policy as an integrated system concerned with fiscal welfare, occupational welfare, and the general welfare of individuals. The latter has as its intent the provision of education, health, housing, income security, and personal social services.[5] The common feature of these definitions is that they describe the social welfare system in terms of its goals.

The complex matrix of social welfare goals is further discussed by Michael Hill and Glen Bramley.[6] They show that even if a clear goal or set of goals could separate social welfare policy from other domestic policy endeavors, the aim of social welfare would still be unclear, and that in the real world, people who cooperate to pass a law may have different subjective goals. Members of legislative bodies who vote for a law may have no intent beyond placating particular constituents. A Housing and Urban Development (HUD) official may fund public housing projects as payment for past political favors. A local community may seek the housing project because it will create jobs in the construction industry and/or provide an outlet for investment opportunities. Another purpose could be that locating public housing in a particular area might promote—or retard—the pattern of residential segregation. Some who support the legislation may be more concerned with its impact on residential segregation than its effect on the supply of adequate and affordable housing. Any complex law is a compromise among many interested parties. The blunt political fact is that laws have many purposes—some manifest, some latent, some acknowledged, and some vehemently denied. In this frame of reference, to judge social welfare laws by the standard of intent is simplistic. Often the expressed intent, the manifest intent, and the latent intent are quite different.

A further difficulty of judging policy by its intent stems from the interrelatedness of all aspects of public life in a complex society. There is a rough distinction between foreign policy and domestic policy. Yet it is clear that defense expenditures strain resources that could be used for domestic ends, and that a trade boycott disrupts domestic distribution of goods and services. The problem of separating the various components and consequences of domestic policy is even more difficult. Social welfare ends are promoted or retarded as a consequence of policy shifts throughout the whole of government, not only as a result of what is done by welfare-oriented programs.

FUNCTION-ORIENTED DEFINITIONS OF SOCIAL WELFARE

One of the most cherished ideals of Western civilization is that all members of society should fare well. Clearly, however, not all members of society enjoy the same level of existence. All human societies organize themselves so that members of that society might fare well, but not necessarily equally so. Sometimes the organization of the society is structured around exploitation of some citizens by others. Deliberate exploitation, when practiced, may be masked in a variety of ways. Denying the full humanity of certain populations is often an excuse for what might appear to another person to be clear exploitation. A law that restricts the mobility of recipients of relief might be designed to equalize among various units of government the cost of distributing that assistance; the same law might also have the effect of securing a stable, low-wage labor force.

Social goals exist on many levels of generality. At the most general level, a society seeks to maximize societal benefits and minimize social costs while assuring all some basic social minimum. Often the concern is not the net social cost but who pays the social costs. The presumption is that all social organizations are created to carry on the essential social functions in pursuit of a general social welfare; the reality might be very different. In a very specific sense, laws of social welfare use public sanctions and taxes to encourage or discourage behaviors that have impacts on the minimum standards and the opportunity structures for all persons. Minimum wage laws restrict the freedom of contracts for a larger social purpose. Taxes on alcohol for human consumption have the dual goal of raising revenues and discouraging consumption. Establishing benefit schedules for those receiving Aid to Families with Dependent Children (AFDC) affects the security and opportunities of many families, not just those on welfare.

Social goals do not exist in a political vacuum. In the American political system, two value systems, the liberal and the conservative, complement one another as social welfare organizations are shaped and transformed.[7] Liberal values are oriented toward (1) having the government play a more dominant role in meeting social problems; (2) promoting greater equality of opportunity if not of income or wealth; and (3) having consumers, workers, and program participants play more active roles in social decisions. Conservative values are oriented toward (1) using the power of the marketplace to prevent the occurrence of social problems; (2) placing a greater reliance on family, church, neighborhood, and voluntary institutions to soften the consequence of societal or individual failure; and (3) justifying the presence of inequality based on merit and inheritance but minimizing the opportunity for that inequality to perpetuate itself. In either value context, or in a merged context, social institutions must be structured to allow for the accomplishment of the essential social functions.

The listing of essential social functions is largely a matter of judgment for setting specificity in any particular investigation. For our purpose, the essential social functions are (1) procreation, child rearing, and socialization throughout the life cycle; (2) production and distribution of goods and services; and (3) authoritative allocation of rules and values. In this formulation the three primary institutions of society are the family, the market, and the political system. These three primary systems are organized in a number of ways and they further interact to generate a number of specialized subsystems such as the health care system, the educational system, the alternate child care system, and others. The social welfare system is one such subsystem, consisting of formal and informal structures created to guarantee minimal standards for health, education, income security, and personal social service.

The various primary and specialized subsystems are illustrated in Table 1.1.

Functional diffusion across agency lines prevents an analysis that would assign responsibility of educational needs to schools, health problems to hospitals, or welfare

TABLE 1.1 A Social Systems Perspective

Primary Systems	Principal Function
Family	Procreation, care, and socialization through the life cycle
Market	Production, distribution, and allocation of goods and services
Political	Establishment and enforcement of rules of common conduct
A Sample of Specialized Subsystems	**Principal Function**
Education	Transmission of skills and values
Health	Prevention of illness and care for individuals when it occurs
Social Welfare	Guarantee of minimal standards for health, education, income security, and provision of essential social service to provide equality of opportunity

to welfare agencies. Real human problems do not present themselves in such neat and limited forms, nor do the problems occur in isolation of a host of contributing factors, which themselves cross functional lines. Health care professionals work in public and voluntary agencies as well as in profit-oriented programs. In each they use clinical and preventive techniques to enhance the health of individuals. Community health programs require governments to encourage healthful habits and to prohibit certain forms of behavior thought to be harmful to the physical and mental health of individuals. Clinical health and community health are not separable spheres but are part of a single continuum. Most health programs cross family, market, and government lines. These same lines are crossed by social workers and social welfare programs. Social welfare programs always interface with other social institutions. The school program that responds to the special needs of pregnant students is at once a health, educational, and welfare program. The value constraints of each of the primary systems and the structures of the interconnected subsystems affect the way the programs take shape. Effective social policy must mediate the values and the constraints of the dominant society and the various social institutions as well as the needs of the clients in the social policy decision-making process.

DECISIONS ABOUT SOCIAL WELFARE PROGRAMS

The vagueness of distinctions and the imperceptible merging of functions does not mean that these distinctions are not important. Just as the colors of the rainbow establish a spectrum, so do the elements of each subsystem shape a social system. In order to establish a single framework for social welfare programs this text is structured around Lawrence Friedman's formulation of the distinctive elements of social welfare programs. In Friedman's framework, social welfare programs have three distinctive elements: (1) They establish a minimum standard; (2) they identify eligible population(s) for whom these standards are applicable; and (3) they establish specific procedures for the delivery of the service, benefit, and/or other requirements specified in the standard.[8]

A public social welfare program is created when a legislature or administrative agency establishes funding authorizations and regulations for public spending and/or use of public authority to obtain one or more elements described above. Programs and agencies are also the result of voluntary cooperation outside the public sector. Funding for private activity is, indirectly, public funding, as the gifts are partially tax sheltered by regulations of the internal revenue code. Voluntary social agencies are sometimes established to forestall a public intervention and sometimes emerge as a consequence of what some citizens view as a public failure. Simply because an agency is voluntary does not mean that its policies and programs are shaped outside the mainstream of American politics.

In both the public and voluntary sectors, two polar conceptual frameworks illustrate the nature of social welfare programs. In one view social welfare programs are to be responsive only to failures and/or temporary breakdowns in the healthy operation of the primary systems, that is, market, family, and political systems or one of their specialized subsystems. This view, known as the *residual approach,* contains an implicit assumption that standards are ideally set by the healthy operation of the primary social systems. When public programs and voluntary charitable agencies establish their artificial benefits the results are sometimes self-destructive or sometimes just inefficient, but they never work as well as the natural primary system. Social welfare programs ought to form a safety net and come into operation only when there is a lapse in the way the primary systems function. Families should care for children. Family systems fail for many reasons, however, and thus there is a need for a backup system in the form of adoption and foster care. The foster care system should not replace, compete with, nor undermine the healthy functioning of the family. In general, the corrective social welfare institutions should be structured to have minimum impact on the normal operations of family and market institutions and the political systems. In the residual perspective the social welfare system is a special kind of subsystem. While other systems—health, education, transportation, and so on—have specialized responsibilities, the social welfare system is expected to function only when some other system fails.

Alternatively, the *institutional approach* rests on the belief that in complex interdependent societies social welfare programs have a normal specialized function in an integrated society. Just as the prevailing belief now is that the family cannot educate its own young as well as a formal education system can, society believes that formal systems of child care, social insurance, and the like need to be permanent and structured parts of a social system for meeting individual needs throughout the life cycle.

A problem is seen as *residual* when it is the consequence of the occasional, yet inevitable, lapse of a primary system from its normal healthy operation. A problem is seen as *institutional* when it occurs under any conceivable social arrangement because it is part of the irreducible imperfection of society. Many social welfare policy debates focus on whether a specific problem is mainly residual or institutional.[9] A residual or institutional response often reflects residual or institutional conceptions of the problem. Irregular short-term unemployment is an expected part of a dynamic economy. A specialized subsystem of unemployment insurance can be structured to fill the gap in income that results. Persistent, long-term unemployment is a reflection of a deeper problem in the economy. The response should be carefully crafted so that aid to those outside the labor force for long periods of time is not seen as a regular way of doing business.

One aspect of this debate is the degree to which one believes that individual fault and individual behavior perpetuate the problem. If the individual is at fault, then the response should be residual so as not to encourage the behavior of individuals that causes the problem. However, when there is a demonstrated limit to the capability of the primary or specialized subsystem to prevent the occurrence of a problem, then formal institutional social welfare programs are required. Individual fault and social responsibility are only two of the questions to be faced. The mores and belief patterns of the dominant culture dictate how the social response should be structured.

The provision of alternate child care arrangements was seen as residual. Only a few years ago the normal care pattern was that provided by the mother or some other relative in the child's own home. Any effort to ease this responsibility would weaken the family. Today the emphasis is on the nuclear, as opposed to the extended, family, and there is a high rate of mothers now working outside the home. Thus other child care arrangements are seen as a requisite of a society concerned with the welfare of children and the realistic opportunity for women to contribute in ways other than as child rearers. At one point the dominant cultural perspective was that the day-care function should be structurally residual. Beliefs about work, gender roles, and economic factors have shifted the dominant view into an institutional mode. As both views are still present, the policy debate about the shape of alternate day care has become very difficult.

Although it might appear that the residual and institutional perspectives are antithetical, in the practice of American social welfare, the response often exhibits a blending of approaches. It is true that most social problems have social solutions, but it is also true that most social solutions have social costs. Making decisions about who should pay and who should benefit when neither the costs nor the benefits of social problems and social programs are clear is largely a function of the social perspective or ideology.

CENTRAL FUNCTIONAL ISSUES

Various typologies have been developed to assist in explaining the dynamics of the policy process as distinct policy questions raise different kinds of social, political, and economic issues and therefore invoke distinct political dynamics in the policy-making and implementation process.[10] Peggy and Richard Musgrave, a husband and wife economics team, distinguished in their typology by delineating three central, functional, economic planning roles of the state, described below:

1. The *allocative function* is concerned with use of a society's goods and resources so that the maximum social benefits can be obtained.
2. The *distributive function* has to do with the distribution of the goods and services among the households in the society.
3. The *stabilization function* relates to the stability of the economy so that both allocative and distributive choices can be made with a sense of a stable future into the next generation.[11]

By way of contrast, political science has an alternative approach that was developed by the political scientist Theodore Lowi. He classified policies as follows:

1. *Distributive policies* by which the government distributes a commonly held resource; an example is nineteenth-century land policies.
2. *Redistributive policies* by which the government deliberately alters the economic distribution that has been generated by market forces. The tax and benefit laws in the Old Age Survivors and Disability Social Insurance Program are an example of this function.
3. *Regulatory polices* by which the government dictates the ways that market forces can allocate resources. An example is the rules to govern adoptions in general.
4. *Constituent policies* by which the government sets up special rules for the formulation and/or reformulation of the policy and designates responsibilities to various branches and divisions of government. An example of this is the 1987 Indian Child Welfare Act, which established special review procedures in child welfare cases involving American Indian children.[12]

TABLE 1.2 Typologies of the Political and Economic Functions of Governments

	Economic Functions		
	Allocative (1)	Distributive (2)	Stabilization (3)
Political Functions			
A. Distributive		X	
B. Redistributive	X	X	X
C. Regulative		X	
D. Constituent Policy		X	

By establishing a two-dimensional typology combining the insight of Lowi and the Musgraves, we can classify public and voluntary social welfare programs by their economic and political functions at the intercepts indicated in Table 1.2. Social welfare programs are seen most often, but not exclusively, at the intercepts marked in this table.

CENTRAL DESIGN ISSUES

An understanding of the economic and political function of a social welfare policy helps one to frame the design issues that must be considered in establishing a social program. Lawrence Friedman's framework is the most useful, simply because it directs attention to the features that need to be considered in the establishment, implementation, and evaluation of social programs.

Table 1.3 shows the dominant questions that must be resolved for each welfare program. These are the critical questions that need to be asked of all programs: (1) What constitutes the standard by which the benefit/service is defined? (2) Who should benefit? (3) What agencies of society should operate the program?

An expression often used among those concerned with the development of specific legislative proposals suggests that "the devil is in the detail." An awareness of the devilish details applies to the ends that are sought and the means that are selected. There is an inescapable necessity of choice. Just a few of the considerations that apply are discussed next.

TABLE 1.3 Basic Parameters of Choice about Social Welfare Programs

Standard	
Curative	Preventive
Minimal Standards	Restore original condition
In Kind	Cash
Define the Population of Recipients	
Categorical	Universal
Who Should Operate the Program	
Nonprofit	Public
Local and/or State	Federal

STANDARDS FOR SOCIAL WELFARE PROGRAMS

There is a very strong connection between the welfare benefit standards used and one's understanding of the circumstance of the need. Curative programs are designed to respond after a crisis has occurred; preventive programs are designed to minimize the likelihood that the crisis will occur. There is a general bias in favor of programs that are preventive rather than curative. However, given the complexity of society, it often makes sense to wait to see whether something is broken before fixing it. A complex and cumbersome system could be established to prevent all unemployment. In the United States and in most Western countries we have chosen to use macro-economic strategies to keep unemployment to a minimum but have also set up a program of unemployment compensation to provide for the circumstance once it occurs.

The establishment of the standard is central to welfare choice. In some cases the standard is set by a conception of what is required for basic maintenance; in others the standard is set to restore the prior condition after the social need occurs. Often, when the individual is seen as culpable in establishing the condition of need, benefit levels are deliberately structured to be at or near some social minimum so as to discourage certain forms of social behavior. When programs are based on an assumption of culpability, when in fact no such culpability is present, the result is that some citizens suffer needlessly. Low levels of AFDC benefits are sometimes thought to discourage both illegitimate births and the breakup of families. The reality is, in fact, far more complex than that simplistic assumption.[13]

Typically, one begins with the assumption that for goods and services the best mode of distribution is through the ordinary marketplace; thus, benefits are best distributed by cash. Sometimes, however, for various political and economic reasons, a desire to control the population of potential recipients dictates that the benefits be distributed in kind. Medical benefits are distributed by Medicaid, while food is distributed by food stamps. There is a complex of historical, political, and administrative considerations that dictate the selection of the in-kind substitute for cash redistribution and which need to be explored in each case.[14]

THE RECIPIENT POPULATION

One of the most persistent questions in the design of social welfare programs is whether the aid should be targeted to a specific subpopulation in need or provided in the same way for all. "Helping the needy and not the greedy" is a catch phrase that reflects a desire to help different people in different circumstances differently. The social welfare planner typically finds that it makes sense to design unique welfare programs for well-defined categories of persons in need. The income security needs of the aged, the single parent, and the unemployed are quantitatively and qualitatively different. A specific strategy designed for one group might be totally undesirable for a second group. We may wish to encourage the aged to leave the labor force while encouraging the younger unemployed to do all they can to find jobs. Having one program for both would not make sense. Political difficulties, however, immediately arise. As a society, we clearly do not want to aid equally all those in need. Once a category of persons is separated out for purposes of planning, that group is subject to political speculation. Senior citizens, because of their organized political power, their specific historical conditions, and the beliefs we hold about individual responsibility, are almost certain to be aided more generously than, say, unwed mothers or recovering addicts, both of whom are seen as being more responsible for their conditions of need.

WHO SHOULD OPERATE THE PROGRAM

Whether the administration and funding of an aid program should be in the public or voluntary sector is also addressed in terms of both goals and issues of political feasibility. Historical circumstance plays an important part in such decisions. A prison system, because it denies freedom to individuals, needs to have public authority. In recent years, however, some states have turned their prison operations over to contracted agencies, both voluntary and profit oriented. The politics of abortion also demands that much of the work in counseling and/or education about abortion is best accomplished in voluntary agencies. Dramatic differences in the social responses to need are often a function of the public versus voluntary charter of the agency providing the assistance.

The federal/state issue is similarly complex. One question revolves around the desirability of interstate flexibility as contrasted with a desire for equal treatment across state lines. The level of government delivering the service, the level of government paying for the service, and the level of government regulating the service often take on as much significance as the policy debate itself. The concept of federalism of national standards adapted to local conditions is often frustrated on the altar of naked political power conflicts.

In 1982, David Stockman, director of President Reagan's Office of Management and Budget (OMB), presented to the Senate Finance Committee the administration's case for greater reliance on the states. In so doing, he created a new adjective for federalism. In Stockman's perspective we had moved to "fragmented federalism." In his view the nation had shifted from the traditional "dual federalism," by which each government had well-defined and separate responsibilities, through a period of "cooperative federalism," in which a few specific functions were shared, to the current "fragmented federalism," where there is decisional overload at the national level. He argued that mayors and governors were not judged by their policies or their performances at home, but by their capacity to attract federal grant monies. He claimed that the system distorts judgments about both political merits and social needs for changes in social welfare programs. Stockman summarized his argument as follows:

> Concern has been expressed about the willingness and the ability of the states to take care of the disadvantaged [within their borders]. . . . On this point we should recognize that there are cliches and there are realities and one reality is that the same electorate which chooses the President and Congressmen also elect governors, mayors and state legislators. There is no reason to believe that in the year 1982 the American people have two minds, two hearts and two agendas regarding the responsibility of government to meet basic social needs.[15]

Presenting an earlier case for the role of the national government, Paul O'Neil, director of President Ford's Office of Management and Budget, said:

> The needy population is not uniformly distributed among the states. Second, the financial capacity to aid the needy is not distributed in relation to where the needy live, [and] third, the federal government provides such a large share of the financial support of the existing programs that it is difficult to see how it can extricate itself . . . [without massive disruptions in the AFDC system].[16]

Taking a third path, which focused attention on the political history of reform efforts, Dick Nathan, OMB chief for Nixon, came to the same conclusion:

> The idea of a block grant for AFDC [turns] the clock back, isolate[s] the most controversial and vulnerable group of welfare recipients. It could result in higher concentrations of the poor in states with the most adequate benefits. The fact that people and jobs move in a free society is the underlying reason why the burden of financing welfare benefits should be shared on a equitable basis by the society as a whole.[17]

Each of these seemingly objective statements about a federal system of sharing national and state responsibilities was made in support of specific legislation. It has been suggested that the debate was not about federalism at all but was instead about distributive policies. Turning responsibility to the states was simply a device for escaping the responsibility to act.[18]

FINDING THE SHAPE OF SERVICE ISSUES

The distinctions above emphasize the substance and content of social welfare programs that focus on the provision of resources, in cash or in kind, to the populations that benefit from social welfare programs. In terms of dollars spent, this transfer of resources is the larger portion of social welfare expenditures. In terms of hours spent by social workers in direct practice, the larger portion of time is spent in the delivery of services. The policy concerns with social services clearly involve the issues of which populations are to be served and who should operate the programs. Questions in the service sector are essentially the same as those in the benefit sector. Service programs tend to be debated around the issue of public versus voluntary versus corporate sector responsibility.

CONCLUSIONS

Policy choices involve a complex political dynamic for which there is no one correct response. All policy choices are endowed with complex historical antecedents, and all reflect distinct beliefs about the shared standards a society should have for its people. Our understanding of the choices can best be served by abandoning the assumption that there is one best way to help a particular group. Rather, it is important that the social worker be able to understand the context of the policy debates. Conflicts over the future directions of social welfare programs can be better understood when the critical functions of the social welfare program are specified, the central design issues are made explicit, and the political circumstances are made clear.

A somewhat more cynical perspective is that policy analysis is not politically neutral. The proposition in politics is that policy decisions involve bargaining among participants who not only have different real interests but also very different perceptions of reality. That which purports to be analysis is but another component of the conflict of power. He who defines the debate wins the debate.

NOTES

1. Robert Schalock and Craig Thornton, *Program Evaluation* (New York: Plenum, 1988).
2. Frank Fischer and John Forester, eds., *Confronting Values in Policy Analysis* (Newbury Park, CA: Sage, 1987).
3. Kenneth E. Boulding, "The Boundaries of Social Policy," *Social Work* 12, no. 4 (1967): 3–11.
4. T. H. Marshall, *Social Policy* (London: Hutchinson University Library, 1955).
5. Richard Titmus, *Essays on the Welfare State* (London: Urwin University Books, 1958).
6. M. Hill and G. Bramley, *Analyzing Social Policy* (London: Basil Blackwell, 1986), chap. 1.
7. In popular political discourse the terms *liberal* and *conservative* are often used for their popular appeal rather than their descriptive merit. Nonetheless, the terms retain a certain utility as a shorthand expression for views about the way governments can use or abuse power in responding to social problems.
8. Lawrence Friedman, "Social Welfare Legislation: An Introduction," Discussion Paper (Madison, WI: Institute for Research on Poverty, 1968), pp. 17–68.
9. Charles Frankel, *The Democratic Prospect* (New York: Harper & Row, 1962), chap. 12.
10. Hill and Bramley, *Analyzing Social Policy,* chap. 8.
11. Richard A. Musgrave, *The Theory of Public Finance* (New York: McGraw-Hill, 1959).
12. T. A. Lowi, "Four Systems of Policy, Politics and Choice," *Public Administration Review* 32, no. 4 (1972): 298–310.
13. Irwin Garfinkel and Sara McLandhan, *Single Mothers and Their Children* (Washington, DC: Urban Institution Press, 1986).
14. Sheldon Danziger and Daniel Weinberg, *Fighting Poverty: What Works and What Doesn't* (Cambridge, MA: Harvard University Press, 1986).
15. David A. Stockman, statement issued February 14, 1982, Office of Management and Budget, Washington, DC, p. 1.
16. *Common Sense* (Winter 1980): 27.
17. *Common Sense* (Winter 1980): 10.
18. Timothy Conlan, *New Federalism: Intergovernmental Reform from Nixon to Reagan* (Washington, DC: Brookings Institution, 1988), p. xi.

BIBLIOGRAPHY

Boulding, Kenneth E. "The Boundaries of Social Policy." *Social Work* 12, no. 1 (1967): 3–11.

Common Sense (Winter 1980).

Danziger, Sheldon, and Daniel Weinberg. *Fighting Poverty: What Works and What Doesn't.* Cambridge, MA: Harvard University Press, 1986.

Fischer, Frank, and John Forester, eds. *Confronting Values in Policy Analysis.* Newbury Park, CA: Sage, 1987.
Frankel, Charles. *The Democratic Prospect.* Chap. 12. New York: Harper & Row, 1962.
Friedman, Lawrence. "Social Welfare Legislation: An Introduction." Discussion Paper. Madison, WI: Institute for Research on Poverty, 1968.
Garfinkel, Irwin, and Sara McLandhan. *Single Mothers and Their Children.* Washington, DC: Urban Institution Press, 1986.
Hill, M., and G. Bramley. *Analyzing Social Policy.* Chap. 1. London: Basil Blackwell, 1986.
Lowi, T. A. "Four Systems of Policy, Politics and Choice." *Public Administration Review* 32, no. 4 (1972): 298–310.
Marshall, T. H. *Social Policy.* London: Hutchinson University Library, 1955.
Robson, William A. *Welfare State and Welfare Society: Illusion and Reality.* London: Allen & Unwin, 1976.
Schalock, Daniel, and Craig Thornton. *Program Evaluation.* New York: Plenum, 1988.
Titmus, Richard. *Essays on the Welfare State.* London: Urwin University Books, 1958.

CHAPTER 2

How Policies Are Selected

Political decisions are the collective choices of people who disagree; behind these decisions stands the coercive power of government.

Steven Kelman

Disagreement and power are the two essential elements of political choice. In this context power has two aspects: the power of government to enforce its own political choices, and the power of individuals or groups within the society to influence the choices made by governments. This chapter concerns the second aspect of power.

Traditionally we think of politics as involving governments, but in fact we may observe the dynamics of political choices in schools, nongovernmental agencies, churches, and even the family. Wherever power and disagreement exist there is a political process that structures the way choices are made. Those who seek to influence the choices made need to understand this process.

The phrase "It's all politics" implies that choices are based on power considerations and that reasoned deliberations have nothing to do with them. This book proceeds from an assumption that, in the process of selecting public policies, reason and power do in fact work together.[1] Our specific concern is with the political process within the social welfare system and our primary focus is on the role the social worker plays in this political process.

In Chapter 1 we established that government and private social agencies respond in particular ways to social welfare problems and that those responses result in

1. *provision of essential services* to persons, groups, and communities in need
2. *redistribution* of a great variety of substantive and symbolic benefits
3. *regulation* of behavior of persons and groups

Social workers have an interest in the process of choice and an equal interest in how the political process malfunctions to create a political stalemate whereby no choice is made and a problem festers without response.

MODELS OF PUBLIC CHOICE

One of the essential characteristics of social welfare policies is that they are socially sponsored; thus both governmental and voluntary sector choices can be seen as public policy. Both are part of a political process that can be understood through the use of exemplary models.

Models in social science are structured so that the dimensions of reality are deliberately altered to focus attention on particular aspects of a social interaction. In this case the interactions that surround choices about social welfare policies are examined. A model does not purport to be true or false. Rather, real-world conditions are deliberately oversimplified to allow one to gain an initial comprehension of the process the model represents.[2] As Anthony Downs notes, "The model is not an attempt to describe reality accurately. It treats a few variables as crucial and ignores others which actually have influence."[3] In the models reviewed here, we focus on significant components of choices about social welfare that could easily be overlooked in descriptions of real-world conditions.

INSTITUTIONAL CONTEXT

Political choices are made within an *institutional context.* At the core of the political system are the institutions and personnel involved in the decision-making process. Who will be a member of the select group of decision makers is an unsettled question. Clearly there are formal rules of choice involving the actions of presidents, governors, legislators, bureaucrats, and other members of government who have constitutional authority to act. Understanding choice requires an understanding of the rules of choice as they have been formally prescribed in constitutions and other legal documents.

Further, policy decisions are made in a historical context; policy is most often a continuation of past activity. What has been done in the past fundamentally shapes what will be considered. Most policies are made not by great shifts in direction but by incremental adjustments to policy already in place.

The institutional and historical contexts of public choices are tempered by the shifting distribution of power. Power to make changes is held not only by formal holders of public office but also by vast numbers of private citizens who play vital roles in defining opportunities and making choices. Empirical models of power focus on who actually influences choice. In the main, there are three distinct models of the distribution of power: elitist models, which focus on the influence of the powerful few at the top; pluralist models, which focus on patterns of cooperation and conflict among groups most affected; and neo-elitist models, which focus on the efforts of unrepresented citizens to have their voices heard.

Finally, power, however distributed, must be used in some orderly way to influence choices. In all political systems power is used and decisions are made (or not made) through some more or less systematic process. The essence of politics is not *what* choices are made but *how* they are made.

Thus, the models described in this chapter focus attention on the following aspects of social welfare choices:

1. The *institutional* model directs attention to the reality that each choice is made within an environment in which rules, expectations, and responsibilities are established by historical and functional forces. The dimensions of the institutional constraints on decisions differ within specific institutions, such as Congress and the Department of Health and Human Services. The constant factors remain: Individuals make choices within a context and a structure, and the institutions themselves are the products of prior political choices. Both formal and informal aspects of these institutions prescribe and limit the range of freedom that actors enjoy on the political scene.[4] The institutional structure is a factor that must always be considered. Sometimes, but certainly not always, the institutional structure is the only decisive factor.
2. The *incremental* model focuses attention on public policy as a continuation of past governmental activity. What has been done fundamentally shapes what will be considered. Charles Lindblom presented the incremental model as a critique of the rational perspective on the way policy options were often considered.[5] Lindblom argued that political actors seldom approach a policy choice in terms of a logical problem. In his "rational comprehensive" model, decisions about what to do are perceived as problems of how to achieve maximum social benefit without regard to the winners or losers. As each policy has costs as well as benefits and the distribution of these is normally uneven, some citizens are made better off by a policy while others are made less well off. In the rational model it is only the social net benefit that is critical. The rational comprehensive model employs the central concepts of microeconomics and a logic of choice to establish a common framework of real costs and benefits (see Chapter 3). Lindblom suggested that political actors actually use an alternate framework of "incremental reasoning." Choices are seen as limited by highly specific contextual conditions. Those who make decisions rely on a mode of analysis known as argumentation, a mode of reason characteristic of jurisprudence.
3. The *power* models are focused on the use and distribution of power in the political system. Policy choices are not made in a vacuum; they are tempered by the distribution and application of power within the political system. The power models have three subsystems:
   a. The *elitist* model focuses on the roles of the powerful few who stand at the apex in a triangularly shaped political system. The critical question is who really governs: the people, their elected leaders, or some hidden and powerful few who really control what is going on?
   b. The *pluralist* model draws attention to the diffusion of power among many individuals and groups, and particularly to how economic interest groups use (or fail to use) the power that is presumably available to them.
   c. The *neo-elitist* model focuses attention on the establishment of "situational elites" whereby some citizens place barriers in the way of other citizens who are also attempting to influence choices about social welfare.
4. The *process* model examines policy as the consequence of a series of sequenced activities that governmental personnel and citizens use in searching for the resolution to a problem troublesome enough to require public attention.

The policy process model addresses a complex set of events that shape the actions governments and agencies take (or fail to take) in response to a social problem. The model focuses first on how issues are brought to government, then on the identification, selection, and implementation of one or more solutions. The political process does not end when government acts, however. The objective and subjective impact of governmental action generates new problems and the cycle continues.

INTERACTION OF THE MODELS

Figure 2.1 presents a highly simplified diagram of the interlinkages of factors in the policy process. Around the outer edge of the model are the steps or stages of the policy process. The process model, as we use it, emphasizes that rather than moving sequentially through each stage, decision making is continually mediated through a political environment. Real-world political conflicts do not move step-by-step in orderly fashion. Initiative on some may be blocked for years at a particular stage while others may move through a stage so quickly they appear to have skipped it. Initiatives may fall back and jump forward. Yet generally, there is a sequenced structure to public choice.

An overview of six distinct models is given in the order shown below. A seventh model, the process model, is reviewed in detail in the next chapter so it is only introduced here.

1. Institutional Model
2. Incremental Model
3. The Power Models
   a. Elitist
   b. Pluralist
   c. Neo-elitist

The literature of political science presents many variations and exceptions to all of these models. Our intent here is simply to display the substance of each without

FIGURE 2.1

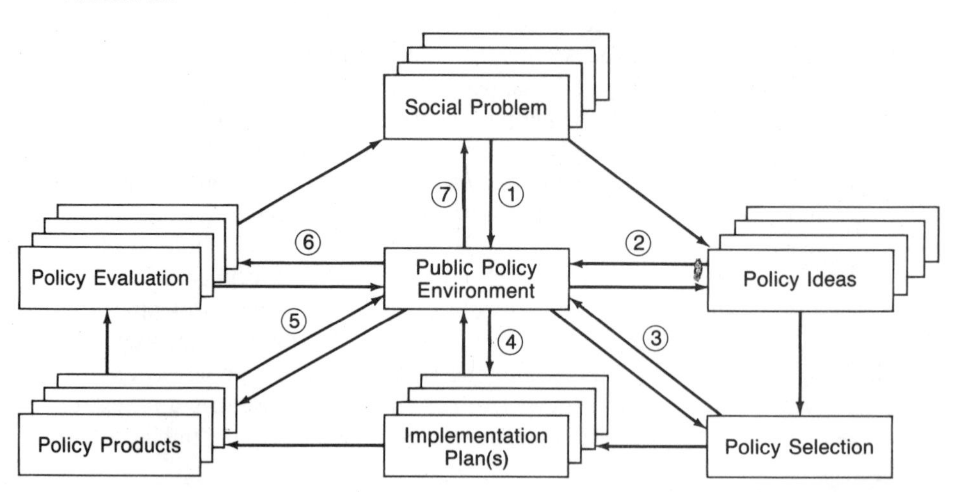

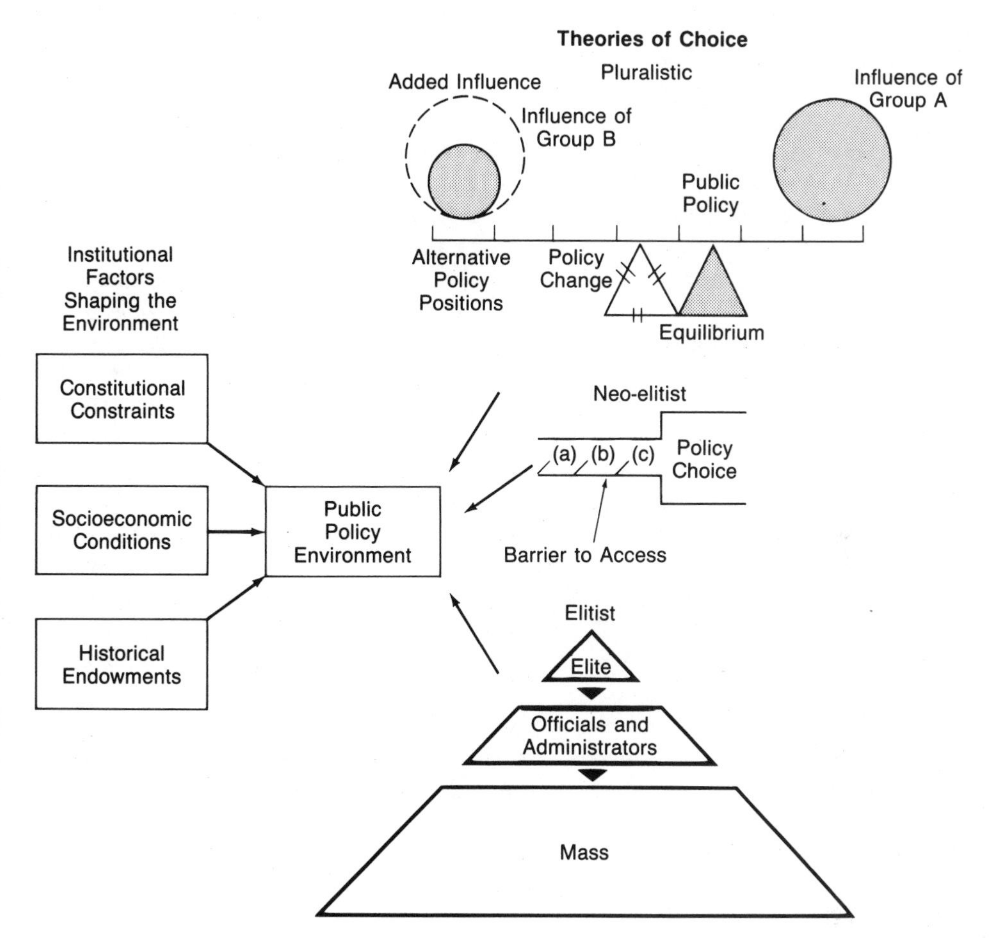

FIGURE 2.2

distorting it. No single model captures the whole of the system, for the political environment is shaped by them all. Figure 2.2 diagrams the three power models to one side of the political environment and those factors that are fundamental in the institutional and incremental models to the other side. Our goal is to demonstrate that the structure of the political environment itself is shaped by all of these elements. The model most productive of insights will vary considerably from case to case or even by stage in a single case.

THE INSTITUTIONAL MODEL: POLICY CREATED BY STRUCTURES OF GOVERNMENT

A formal theory of democracy suggests that choice among policies is the result of majority rule constrained by constitutional provisions designed to protect the minority. Important corollary propositions are that all votes are counted, that the votes of all citizens are equal, and that all citizens are well informed about what is in their best interest.[6] A moment's reflection indicates that these conditions almost never apply. Institutions, both formal and informal, separate political opportunities and political responsibilities in very uneven ways. An institutional perspective is designed to show how the power to act is divided among offices. The central notion of American national government is that the power to legislate belongs to Congress, the power to implement goes to the executive branch, and the courts monitor the constitutionality and legal propriety of the actions of the other two branches.

To understand the "real process" of lawmaking, one must consider these formal rules as well as a wide range of informal rules and practices. Taken together, they all constitute the institutional character of governments. These are the *rules of the political road* by which ideas are transformed into laws and administrative practice. Evidence that the institutions are not fixed and unchanging may be found in the following example. In 1952, 80 percent of the congressional districts gave majority votes to presidential and congressional candidates of the same party. Straight party voting was the clear norm. In 1988, less than 60 percent of the congressional districts gave distinct majorities to presidential and congressional candidates of the same party. The people in more than 40 percent of the districts elected a president of one party and a member of Congress of the other. Such a practice is not a formal part of government, but it fundamentally shapes the institutional character of the way our government works or fails to work. A condition in which president and Congress see themselves as independently responsible to the voters is different from one in which they see themselves as mutually responsible to the voters.

The rules, structures, and practices of government are obviously not neutral to the kind of policies that are adopted. Any set of rules, practices, and formal structures provides advantages to some and disadvantages to others. If there were no systematic differences between the values and beliefs of those advantaged and disadvantaged by the status quo, then the rules of the game would be a neutral guidebook. Clearly, the distribution of beliefs and the distribution of formal authority are anything but random. Understanding not only the rules but also how those rules give advantages and disadvantages to distinct groups in our society, is the first requirement of the political activist. This understanding is particularly necessary for addressing social welfare problems when those affected most are often thought to have the least formal power.

Some believe that there is something unfair about uneven rules. They forget that rules by definition give advantages. A case can be made against deliberate and systematic manipulation in the institutions of politics to benefit a particular few, but making a case for the kinds of rules that ought to govern politics is far more difficult.[7] Sometimes the most important objective of the activist in social welfare is not to change a particular policy but to change the rules of the game. Many of the efforts of the Great Society programs of the Kennedy/Johnson administration were directed to that end.[8] Our concerns ebb and flow with the kinds of rules we want to have and the kinds of decisions we want governments to reach.[9] Although there is an implicit idealism in fairness of the rules, at the same time, "the rightness of decisions" tempers our belief about what rules should apply. Each of us views political conflicts with a unique combination of interest in rules and interest in outcomes. Legitimacy has both a substantive and a procedural component. Understanding formal and informal institutional rules is essential to making pragmatic choices about how to help whom within the social welfare system.

The importance of institutional constraints on choice needs to be understood for both the explanation and achievement of change. Useful institutional study of a particular policy question must meet three stringent requirements: (1) It must show which institutions are involved in the choice; (2) it must delineate how the rules of that institution provide advantages and disadvantages to particular groups; and (3) it must provide a pragmatic guide across the minefield of political institutions.

Such microinstitutional studies are essential in each policy question as it arises. The importance of the microperspective is to emphasize the factors shown on the left side of Figure 2.2.

THE INCREMENTAL MODEL: POLICY AS DICTATED BY POLITICAL HISTORY

The political environment is shaped by practice and custom as well as by constitutional and structural constraints. Each unique policy question is influenced by the political history of that policy issue. The single best predictor of policy next year is policy this year coupled with information about systematic limitations on the opportunities for reform. For example, a number of dynamic factors would be expected to shape a state's AFDC benefit level, but the single most important factor is the level of benefits in prior years. Figure 2.3 plots maximum AFDC benefits for a family of three by state, in current dollars for 1980 and 1990.

One might also think that a state's per capita income, its tax funds available per capita, its unemployment rate, or any of a number of supposedly causal variables would relate closely to the level of AFDC benefits. This is not the case. The significant but much weaker association between current income and current benefits is shown in Figure 2.4.

When one considers both past programs and per capita income, more than 95 percent of the variation in state benefits is explained.[10] The simple truth is that

FIGURE 2.3 AFDC Benefits in the American States, 1980 and 1990 (Maximum Benefits for a Family of Three)

SOURCE: Background material and data on programs within jurisdiction of the Committee on Ways and Means, 1990 edition.

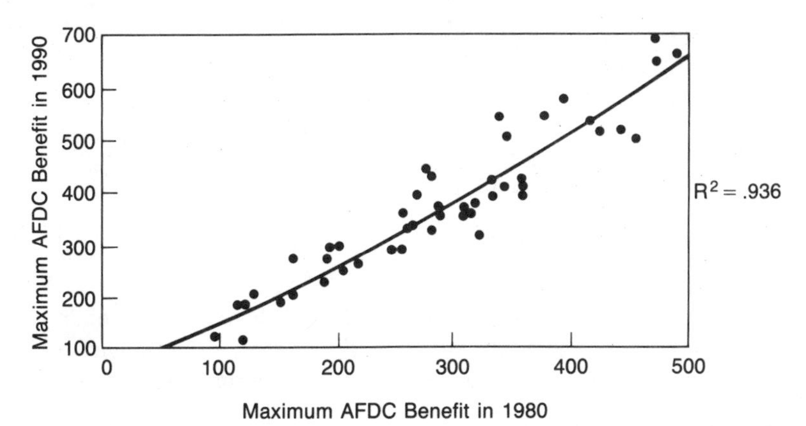

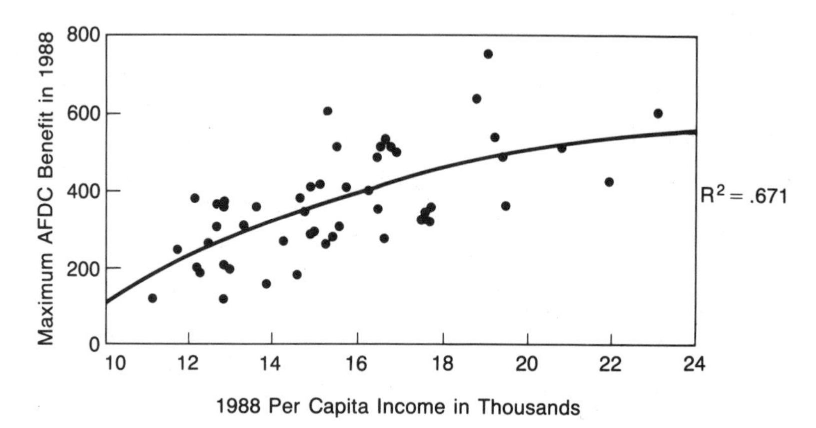

FIGURE 2.4 AFDC Benefit by States and Per Capita Income in Each State, 1988

SOURCE: Background material and data on programs within the jurisdiction of the Committee on Ways and Means, 1990 edition.

opportunities for changing the pattern of benefits in place in a state at a particular time are severely limited. The most feasible aim is to achieve the change by very small increments.

One aspect of the incremental model treats the existing program, policies, and expenditures as a base. Changes are designed to fit with past choices. These changes are typically small when compared to the base for a number of reasons:

1. Programs in place have established constituencies and new programs have none. Citizens will normally invest more of their own political resources to maintain a present benefit than they will to acquire a new one. A new program for welfare may be proposed that would show a net increase of benefits for all the poor, collectively. However, if the new program reduced benefits for some already getting help and provided new benefits to some poor not previously helped, as long as the new benefits were larger than the benefits cut, the net change would benefit the poor as a group but make some of the poor less well off. It is almost certainly true that those to be disadvantaged will strongly oppose the change. The newly aided may not even know about the change, but those adversely effected almost certainly will. The congressional mail bags will fill with "vote no" mail that will not be balanced by "vote yes" mail.
2. Programs in place have incurred "sunk costs" and certainly a large shift will incur large "costs of change." If, for example, new technology, new drugs, and other improvements allow a shift from custodial to community care of large numbers of the mentally ill, the expenditure already made on hospitals, which might have no alternative use, generally retards a shift away from the old practice.
3. Change, by definition, introduces uncertainty. When the predictability of future programs is clouded, public officials, rather than risk change, are likely to stick with existing and known programs whose inefficiencies are familiar.

4. Minor adjustments are politically expedient. Political agreements once obtained are only reluctantly abandoned. Reconsideration of options not only rekindles old political conflicts; it also generates new ones. The axiom "if it ain't broke, don't fix it" is very strong in the political world.
5. Change requires the introduction of a new force. In politics as in physics, a body in motion stays in motion, and a body at rest stays at rest until new force is exerted. So also with public programs. It is politically difficult to overcome these political laws of motion and inertia.

The incremental model does not suggest that no change takes place, only that most changes are *incremental.* The purpose of the incremental model is to emphasize the historical endowments in the lower left of Figure 2.2. In any particular policy study the value of the incremental perspective is the insight it gives into the real parameters of the politically feasible. The concept of incremental change indicates that change is always at the margin of old programs, a reality that calls for a distinct form of reasoning in problem solving.

POWER MODELS: WHO REALLY GOVERNS

Who really governs? Is it the people, their officially designated representatives, or an invisible but very powerful elite? Such questions have been raised by students of government as long as there have been governments. The answers have been given in dispassionate academic monologues and fiery speeches. Only a few persons hold no strong opinion on this subject. As an empirical matter this is far from a settled question. We must consider a variety of distinct models of power to illustrate particular configurations of power. The best evidence is that power may be shaped one way in one issue area and quite a different way on a second issue in the very same community. The following models are archetypes that provide different views of power.

The Elitist Model: Policy as the Preferences of the Few

According to the elitist model, a very few individuals at the apex of our society control the choices that the rest of society think they are making. In its pristine form, elitism argues that society is divided into two classes: the very few who actually govern and the masses who are governed. The two are separated by the agents of the elite who are not strictly members of either class. Gaetano Mosca, an early twentieth-century Italian political theorist, expressed the concept as sharply as anyone:

> In all societies—from societies that are very undeveloped and have hardly attained the dawning of civilization, down to the most advanced and powerful societies—two classes of people appear—a class that rules and a class that is ruled. The first class, always the less numerous, performs all of the political functions, monopolizes power, and enjoys the advantages that power brings, whereas the second, the more numerous class, is directed and controlled by the first, in a manner that is now more or less legal, now more or less arbitrary and violent.[11]

A basic corollary of the elitist model is that the few who govern are interconnected with one another through bonds of kinship, common ownership of property, and intermarriage. In all the many manifestations of this model, the major substantive benefits from government go to these elites; a few substantive, and many symbolic, benefits are presented to the masses as a mechanism of social control.[12]

Numerous authors have used both the expansion of government in the 1960s and the retrenchment of government in the 1980s as proof of elite domination of the decision-making processes.[13] This is not to suggest that the elitist view of power is either certainly true or patently absurd, though a number of books may be found to support either position.[14] In reality, power is unevenly distributed in our society and some individuals and families are very powerful.

The pyramid in the lower right of Figure 2.2 illustrates the elitist model. At the top are a small number of persons, the elite who actually govern. These individuals are self-selected by an intricate mechanism of property ownership, intermarriage, privileged eduction, and gradual absorption into the governing group. They make choices designed to perpetuate their hegemony and to inculcate among the masses values that the elite believe the masses should hold. In order to rise in the system, the minions of the elite demonstrate their loyalty and willingness to comply with the status quo. The masses may in fact be unaware that they are truly disenfranchised. The elite attempt to maintain the myth of majority rule.

A number of students of welfare policy have found the elite model a convenient structure to explain how and why welfare rules serve for the elite. Two leading exponents of this view, Richard Cloward and Francis Piven, have written as follows:

> Relief arrangements are ancillary to economic arrangements. Their chief function is to regulate labor, and they do that in two general ways. First, when mass unemployment leads to outbreaks of turmoil, relief programs are ordinarily initiated or expanded to absorb [the unemployed]; then, as turbulence subsides, the relief system contracts, expelling those who are needed to populate the labor market. Relief also performs a labor-regulating function in this shrunken state, however. Some of the aged, the disabled, the insane, and others who are of no use as workers are left on the relief rolls, and their treatment is so degrading and punitive as to instill in the laboring masses a fear of the fate that awaits them should they relax into beggary and pauperism. To demean and punish those who do not work is to exalt by contrast even the meanest labor at the meanest wages. These regulative functions of relief, and their periodic expansion and contraction, are made necessary by several strains toward instability inherent in capitalist economies.[15]

A number of authors take the opposing view that the elitist model is little more than a demonstration of self-fulfilling prophecy.[16] Our concern here is not with the explanatory power of elitism for a generalist perspective but rather as an explanation of how an elite perspective can inform a particular policy study. In any investigation of the stakeholders in a policy choice some attention must be given to those who are presumed to be much more than ordinarily powerful. Clearly, owners of corporations are concerned with taxes and wage levels, politicians with reelection, and bureaucrats with keeping their jobs. It would be naive to assume that such considerations do not apply, but far too cynical to assume that these are the only considerations that matter. An investigation into a particular policy study should identify the holders of extraordinary power, the control mechanisms they use, and the opportunities for intervention open to the elite that are available in each case. There is, too often, a tendency to find an elitist conspiracy under every rock. The elitist approach to American policy-making is often argumentative rather than empirical and analytical. It almost assumes the existence of a "ruling class" whose interests are served by the policy-making process.[17]

The Pluralist Model: Government by the Many

The dominant political doctrine in the United States today is pluralism. According to this notion, enlightened self-interest guarantees good government. The pluralist conception of self-interest is not brutal selfishness but an informed concern that leaves room for altruism. The central doctrine of pluralism is that while power may not be evenly distributed it is highly diffuse. To be sure, those with shared values do link together in interest groups to press for their own views. That this does not create a monolith of power is due to the multiplicity of overlapping memberships in interest groups. These overlaps may make us allies on one issue and opponents on a second one. Further, varying intensity in levels of interest with regard to particular issues serves to mediate concentrations of power. On any particular issue on any particular day there is a distribution of power and a distribution of intensity.

The power to influence a governmental choice is a function of many things: time, money, access to authoritative figures in their institutional settings, numbers of persons with shared values, and skill in using these instruments of power. In addition, the intensity of individual feelings about an issue tends to emerge from a set of dynamic considerations. A cardinal assumption of pluralism is that a commitment to use power is a measure of the intensity of concern with the issue. This assumption is important because most power resources are diminished by use. For example, you may credibly threaten to vote against your congressman only so many times.

Political demands to act are measured by formal decision makers as some derivative of power and intensity in each distribution. If the power/intensity derivative of those supporting the status quo is far greater than the power/intensity derivative of those asking for change, the status quo is registered as current public policy. Should dynamic shifts in power distribution cause a shift in the equation to the opposite direction, then a shift from status quo to new policy will be registered. The least desirable condition is one in which the desire for change is almost exactly equal to the desire for the status quo, with deep feelings and high intensity on both sides. This condition tends to produce political stalemate. If the issue is important enough, this stalemate can threaten the ability of the political system to function and register choice. This impasse has occurred once in our history and precipitated the Civil War. The political system could not mediate the simultaneous demands to continue and to abolish slavery. Approximately 100 years later the decision to continue or to end the war in Southeast Asia almost precipitated a similar breakdown in the political system. Only a few years ago there were those who suggested that the conflict over the abortion issue could threaten the capacity of the political system to mediate among citizens. Perhaps because of that very threat, public officials on both sides of the issue seek to compromise while activists on both sides work to prevent any compromise.

How the Power Conflict Works. **Power to demand action from government is some function of a group's numbers, wealth, status, access to information and decision makers, the number of groups in a coalition, and so on. The determinants of power may shift from one condition to the next. This function of power in favor of the status quo is labeled "Ps."**

The willingness to use power in any particular conflict is some function of the awareness of the real results of the policy shift, the importance of that shift to the group, the stability of the group, their sense of permanence as a group, and many other factors that also change over time. The function of the willingness to use power to save the status quo is labeled "Ws."

The power and willingness to use power of those seeking change are labeled Pc and Wc.

In any particular conflict the relationship between (Ps) (Ws) on the one hand and (Pc) (Wc) on the other will take one of the following forms:

When $(Ps)(Ws) > (Pc)(Wc)$ the status quo is retained.
When $(Ps)(Ws) < (Pc)(Wc)$ change occurs.
When $(Ps)(Ws) = (Pc)(Wc)$ a political stalemate occurs.

For example, should the National Association of Social Workers (NASW) and the American Medical Association (AMA) be in conflict over an issue about which both were equally committed, there is little doubt that the AMA would win. However, the situation would be different if the issue were one to which the NASW was deeply committed while the AMA cared to some degree, or was perhaps only mildly opposed, or even had conflict within its own ranks. If the NASW were willing to commit its smaller political resources while the AMA withheld its power for other battles, then the less powerful interest group might win. Such a condition did occur in many state legislatures in the fight to allow insurance payments to private practice social workers functioning without direct medical supervision.

In other examples, the National Rifle Association is a powerful interest group, not because of its inherent power—the resources of its members are rather meager—but because on the issue of gun control its members are deeply committed. The fight over abortion rights is intense because of the conviction on both sides and the willingness of those in favor of and those opposed to abortion rights to commit resources in the legislative, judicial, and executive branch conflicts on this question.

The political system registers the conflicts and takes note of how power is used. Out of that conflict a winner emerges. Central to pluralism is the belief that the political system is a marketplace of ideas regarding how the government is to act. The central proposition is not that the ideas are good or bad, right or wrong, but that ideas are to be heard and when the conflict does not register a clear winner the opportunity for compromise arises. Pluralism is sometimes presented as a normative prescription of how the political system ought to work[18] and sometimes as a descriptive paradigm for the way the system really works.[19] It is most useful to the student as an abstract model for obtaining insights into how particular past political conflicts were resolved and a kind of topological map of a projected conflict.

The pluralist model is illustrated in the upper right of Figure 2.2. In the study of a particular policy the researcher must pay attention to the identity of likely stakeholders in a political conflict, the sources of their power, the intensity of their willingness to use that power, and the opportunities for formal decision makers to mediate the dispute.

The Neo-elitist Model: Those Outside the Loop

Attention so far has been on those issues that are brought to the notice of governments. In most disputes both sides have the capacity to bring their case to government and to allow the political system to resolve the conflict. Other issues of vital concern to some citizens are never mediated because they are not addressed by the political system. It takes power and opportunity to place an issue on the agenda of government. Sometimes those who are able to do so place deliberate roadblocks in the way of others who would bring a grievance to open debate.

A nondecision is different from a negative decision. It results from the deliberate attempt to exclude a group from the arena of public choice. Not making a decision can be as important as making one. For example, there may be a political conflict over the level of AFDC benefits and a decision is made not to increase them to keep pace with inflation. That is a political decision. A nondecision occurs when what is presumably an important issue, such as this, is simply not considered. In one case a decision is made not to increase benefits; in the second the question is not even brought up for debate. In both cases AFDC benefits remain flat in nominal terms and fall in inflationary terms. How then does one know when a nondecision has occurred? The answer is that a nondecision is not a nonevent. In the model, a nondecision is the product of intentional efforts to place a barrier between those who seek a decision from government and the formal government's hearing of the complaint or request for change. It is diagrammed in the middle on the right of Figure 2.2. The three critical barriers are community values, information, and the procedural door to the political arena itself. These barriers are well known to clients in the social work community. If a particular question is labeled as contrary to community values it does not receive attention. Thus issues may be branded as the products of outside agitators, a tactic used in the civil rights struggle. In an earlier time issues were marked as "communist inspired" to discredit their standing as legitimate public concerns. The list of pejorative tactics used to define an issue as illegitimate is nearly endless.

A second barrier to policy debate is control over the flow of information. When I worked for a presidential commission I was amused to find that my secretary routinely stamped all papers top secret, including even requests for travel reimbursement. The presumed idea was that the less people on the outside knew, the better off "we" (i.e., those of us on the inside) were. The list of techniques used to keep relevant information out of the hands of the public is sometimes humorous and inconsequential and sometimes devastatingly threatening to the very foundations of a democratic society.

The third principal barrier is the real symbolic door to the arena of choice. Only congressmen, former congressmen, and pages can walk through the real door to the floor of the room where Congress is in formal session. The symbolic door is closed by creating an unnecessarily complex path to the place where choice can occur. It is hardly inconsequential that a simple one-page request for reviews of Old Age Survivors Disability Insurance (OASDI) benefit payment levels are on the front counter or at least required by law to be "clearly visible and available" at every Social Security office in the land. By contrast, and though the practice varies highly from state to state, request for review of an AFDC benefit is almost always more cumbersome and expensive in time and resources. Failure to provide a place and a procedure for quick and easy review of public choice—or to sequester the place where new decisions are made—is an effective mechanism for discouraging petition.

As a descriptive tool, the neo-elitist model leaves much to be desired. In any particular policy study it is useful for the student to look at the barriers to decision making, how they are erected and how they might be overcome. The neo-elitist model focuses attention on the placement of barriers to full participation by all who are concerned.

Process Model: Policy as a Product of Its Process

One of the most fascinating aspects of the study of politics is the seemingly endless pathways from citizen discontent to public policy. Too often the process itself is seen as the essence of choice in politics. The policy model is so complex and so central to our discussion that the entire next chapter will be devoted to it. The theme of the stages of the process is also continued in Part Two where a full chapter is devoted to the social worker's role in each stage of the policy process.

All models are abstractions and contain deliberate distortion designed to focus attention on particular aspects of a highly complex and dynamic process. The models described in this chapter are congruent with reality in the sense that attention is focused on particular aspects of real situations. They are not intended as descriptions of the total reality of any situation but as the means for explaining how a problem is turned into a public program.

Policy never emerges in only one way. The models illustrate factors to be considered in each unique case. For the social worker in the field who is seeking to alter a policy in a particular way, the models cannot be a complete guide. They can, however, alert the social worker to the elements that need to be considered in developing an understanding of how choices are made with regard to specific issues.

NOTES

1. For a classic treatment of the relationship between power and reason, see Aaron Wildavski, *Speaking Truth to Power* (Boston: Little, Brown, 1979). The debate today has somewhat different dimensions: see Robert Reich, *The Power of Public Ideas* (Cambridge, MA: Ballinger, 1988).
2. E. J. Meehan, *The Theory and Method of Political Analysis* (Homewood, IL: Dorsey, 1965).
3. Anthony Downs, *An Economic Theory of Democracy* (New York: Harper & Row, 1957), p. 3.
4. Steven Kelman, *Making Public Policy* (New York: Basic Books, 1987), p. 14.
5. Charles E. Lindblom, "The Science of Muddling Through," *Public Administration Review* 19 (Spring 1959): 79–88.
6. David Braybrooke and Charles Lindblom, *A Strategy of Decision* (New York: Free Press, 1963).

7. Those interested in the normative debate about the propriety and consequence of alternate rules of politics should read Reich, *The Power of Public Ideas.*
8. John H. Ehrenrich, *The Altruistic Imagination* (Ithaca, NY: Cornell University Press, 1985), chap. 6.
9. Kelman, *Making Public Policy,* chap. 9.
10. Joseph Heffernan, "The Problem of Federalism in the Welfare Reform Debate," *Journal of Sociology and Social Welfare* (December 1988): 3–26.
11. Gaetano Mosca, *The Ruling Class,* trans. Hannah Kahn (New York: McGraw-Hill, 1939), p. 50.
12. Murray Edelman, *The Symbolic Uses of Politics* (Urbana: University of Illinois Press, 1964).
13. Kelman, *Making Public Policy,* chap. 11.
14. For an incisive review of the arguments for elitism and its companion model, pluralism, see Nelson Polsby, *Community Power and Political Theory* (New Haven, CT: Yale University Press, 1980).
15. Richard Cloward and Francis Piven, "Regulating the Poor" in *Social Problems,* eds. Williamson, Boren, and Evans (Toronto: Little, Brown, 1974), p. 483.
16. Peter Bachrach and Morton Baratz, *Power and Poverty, Theory and Practice* (London: Oxford University Press, 1970), chap. 2.
17. Brian Hogwood and B. Guy Peters, *Policy Dynamics* (New York: St. Martin's Press, 1983).
18. Kelman, *Making Public Policy,* chap. 10.
19. Reich, *The Power of Public Ideas,* chap. 6.

BIBLIOGRAPHY

Braybrooke, David, and Charles Lindblom. *A Strategy of Decision.* New York: Free Press, 1963.

Committee on Ways and Means, U.S. Congress. 101st Congress, 2nd session, WMCP 101-29, 1990.

Downs, Anthony, *An Economic Theory of Democracy.* New York: Harper & Row, 1957.

Heffernan, Joseph. "The Problem of Federalism in the Welfare Reform Debate," *Journal of Sociology and Social Welfare* (December 1988): 3–26.

Kelman, Steven. *Making Public Policy.* New York: Basic Books, 1987.

Meehan, E. J. *The Theory and Method of Political Analysis.* Homewood, IL: Dorsey, 1965.

Reich, Robert. *The Power of Public Ideas.* Cambridge, MA: Ballinger, 1988.

Wildavski, Aaron. *Speaking Truth to Power.* Boston, MA: Little, Brown, 1979.

CHAPTER **3**

An Overview of the Policy Process

Politics in Washington is a continuous contest . . . knowing the Rules of the Game is crucial to success.

Hedrick Smith

This book examines how the political system responds, and fails to respond, to problems for which social workers have professional responsibility. Most social workers are interested principally in the substance of these problems. They are concerned with the nature of the problems themselves, how they have evolved, the value contexts in which the problems are perceived, and ultimately, the opportunities for political intervention. An understanding of that reality requires an understanding of the policy process.

Lasswell's seminal depiction of policy science as being simultaneously concerned with both *knowledge of the policy process* and *knowledge in the policy process* remains valid.[1] It is axiomatic to say that what you would change, you must first understand. The range of understanding required for a comprehensive policy investigation is broad. The spectrum of policy studies reflects the enormity of the task. The social worker involved at the policy level must provide insight and information about the social problem that will meet the demands of scientific scrutiny. That information must be presented in the context relevant to the political decision maker who must rely on the experts for valid, reliable, and politically relevant summations of the social problems under investigation.

Following a model similar to that developed by Hogwood and Gunn, we suggest that a policy study has both horizontal and vertical dimensions (see Table 3.1). Horizontally, policy studies reflect the complex sequence of events that occurs as a government takes action on social conditions. In this text, the horizontal dimension is presented as a logical progression of events. The vertical plane focuses on the various research strategies used during different stages of that evolution. Study procedures range from reviews of the behavioral roles and expectations found in their institutional

TABLE 3.1 The Vertical and Horizontal Dimensions of Policy Study

The Horizontal Dimension	**The Vertical Dimension**					
	Problem Formulation	***Policy Selection***	***Policy Adjustment***	***Implementation***	***Evaluation***	***Policy***
Political Behavior and Case Studies	X	X	X			X
Descriptive Studies of Institutions		X	X	X		
Program Descriptions			X	X	X	
Impact Analysis of Programs in Place				X	X	X
Simulations to Estimate Consequences of Policy Actions Under Consideration				X		

SOURCE: Brian W. Hogwood and Lewis A Gunn, *Policy Analysis for the Real World* (Oxford, England: Oxford University Press, 1984).

context to simulated analyses of core policy interventions. In this chapter, and in the sections that follow, the principal focus is on the horizontal plane.

It is important at the outset that the investigator select the stage, or stages, of the policy process that will be investigated. Simultaneously, the investigator must select the research strategy that is most consistent with the intent of the investigation, the research budget, the time constraints that will apply, and the form of data that is most likely to be available. The cells with an X in Table 3.1 link most frequently used research strategies with the stages of the process.

To analyze a policy one starts with the initiatives: how social workers and others play a role in shaping it, what opportunities are effectively seized, and what opportunities are often missed. A number of questions must be asked:

1. What were the perceptions of the problem to which this policy action was a response?
2. What ideas were presented as ways of dealing with this problem?
3. How did the formal institutions of government evaluate the diverse items of evidence and select between competing proposals for action?

Once the legislative choice is made the law will not be self-implementing. Attention will then shift to the planning and evaluative activities that follow the adoption of a law. Proceeding with the sequential analysis from implementation to evaluation we ask:

4. How have plans been made to put the new law into practice? To what extent, if any, do the plans redirect the purpose of the law?
5. Who has set up procedures to monitor the impact of the law and how reliable are these procedures?
6. Considering the diverse beliefs about what the new policy has done, how have these beliefs generated within the political system new perceptions of the problem and demand for a new policy cycle?

This frame of reference indicates that first, policy is concerned with a series of choices. Second, the choice is by individuals with political responsibilities, whether or not they are office holders. Third, the choice is concerned with both means and ends. Fourth, policy is contingent on a specified situation and context. The policy process moves forward as commitments to use resources in particular ways shape subsequent stages. There are significant feedback loops. Diagrammatically the process has been sketched in many ways; for our purposes it can be structured as shown in Figure 3.1.

The process perspective emphasizes the critical interactions not only within each phase of the policy process but also between phases of the process. Real policies do not move in easy sequence. Each phase forces at least some reassessment of its predecessor stage. The list of real-world variations to the logical sequence is nearly endless. The sequenced model should not be seen as a straitjacket, which may imply a causal connection when in fact none may exist.

The substance of the problem and the substance of the process of choice are not totally distinct. In each substantive area important process generalities become clear. The politics of health are not identical to the politics of education. Within our own area, the politics of social welfare, policies for children evolve differently from policies for the aged. The critical concepts involved in developing a system for a policy study focus on an endless and iterative set of relationships as a policy evolves.[2]

Studies of process have tended to focus on the politics of choice in both institutional and behavioral perspectives. Some inquiries focus on the institutions themselves, such as Congress, the presidency, the federal system(s), and so forth. In these inquiries the center of attention is on the institution itself as a policy develops. Lynn's study of the presidency in a two-decade search for federal welfare policy is illustrative of

FIGURE 3.1 The Political System as a Process

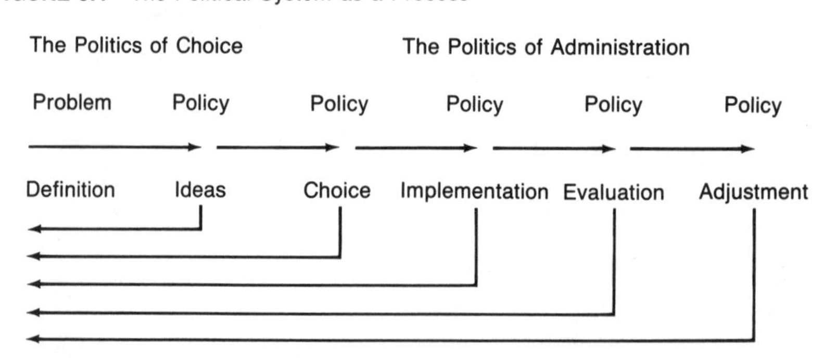

one such institutional perspective.[3] Other inquiries have focused on the behavior of formal and informal groups as a policy is shaped within an institution. Kenneth Bowler's insightful account of the legislative failure of Nixon's Family Assistance plan is a prime example of such group pressure.[4] From a more general point of view, in recent years increasing attention has been given to the process as process. This perspective views the process as a set of interconnected activities in what John Kingdon has called "a policy stream."[5] The metaphor of a stream is useful; we watch a constant stream and observe the dynamic of a log floating down the stream, aware that this log and others are shaping the dimensions of the stream at the same time the stream is propelling the log.

For the purpose of his exposition, Charles O. Jones grouped the activities associated with the process into eleven functions which in turn can be categorized by their place in government structure and by their end product. This conception is shown in Table 3.2.

Gilbert and Specht compared various models generally available in the literature of social work. They established their own parameters by listing a set of stages in the process and linking each to traditional professional social work roles. Table 3.3 is a reproduction of their tabular presentation of stage and function.

The number of stages specified and the labels placed on each stage in the process are generated by the purposes to be served by the investigation. In this text the central attention is given to understanding legislative and/or administrative choices and the roles played by social workers' tasks as policy is developed and put into place. Thus the process, as shown in Table 3.4, is divided into six stages and then subdivided into various items that the social worker must consider in the development of a comprehensive policy research statement.

TABLE 3.2 The Policy Process: A Framework for Analysis

Functional Activity	Categorized in Government	Potential Product Perception/Definition
Aggregation Organization Representation Agenda Setting	Prelegislative Problem to Government	Demand Access Priorities
Formulation Legitimation Budgeting	Legislative Choice by Government	Programs & Budgets
Implementation	Bureaucratic Formal Actions by Government	Varies (services, payments, facilities, controls)
Evaluation Adjustment Termination	Postbureacratic Problem Back to a New Prelegislative Stage	Varies (justification, recognition, change or solution)

SOURCE: Adapted from Charles O. Jones, *An Introduction to the Study of Public Policy* (Monterey, CA: Brooks Cole, 1984), p. 29.

TABLE 3.3 Professional Roles and Policy Formation

Stage	Professional Roles
1. Identification of Problem	1. Direct Service
2. Analysis	2. Research
3. Informing the Public	3. Community Organization
4. Development of Policy	4. Planning
5. Building Public Support	5. Community Organization
6. Program Design	6. Planning and Administration
7. Implementation	7. Direct Service
8. Evaluation and Assessment	8. Research and Direct Service

SOURCE: Neil Gilbert and Harry Specht, *Dimensions of Social Welfare Policy,* 2nd edition (Englewood Cliffs, NJ: Prentice-Hall, 1986), p. 19. Reprinted by permission.

TABLE 3.4 The Stages of the Policy Process and the Items to Be Considered in a Policy Research Statement

Stage	Items of a Policy Research Statement
1. Problem Definition	Needs Assessment Goal Articulation
2. Policy Formulation	Design of Action Strategies Useful for Altering Consequence
3. Policy Selection	The Identification of Stakeholders The Identification of Decision Makers
4. Implementation	Policy Planning Problems Program Planning Problems
5. Evaluation	Empirical Evaluations Normative Evaluation
6. Policy Adjustment	Recommendations for Policy Maintenance Policy Adjustments Policy Termination

In this chapter we will follow the stages as they occur while the process of a policy unfolds. The sequenced process described here is merely representative of what can be a highly idiosyncratic political reality. In the next section of the book we will explore in more detail each functional stage in the policy process and the nature of policy research statements for each stage.

PROBLEM DEFINITION

The policy process begins with the awareness of a problem. Specifically, a problem exists politically when policies are seen as failing to cope in a satisfactory manner. From a political perspective a problem is one that touches a significant number of people or a number of significant people and about which a case has been made that a change by the government will improve things. There is no political poverty problem in a society that sees poverty as "just the way things are" or that the poor somehow deserve their condition. When there is no technology for control there is no need for policy. A society may have a hurricane warning policy and a hurricane evacuation policy, but no society, so far, has a policy to control hurricanes. For a problem to become a political problem, a politically significant mass must come to believe that new actions by government or cessation of current actions by government would make things better. The same process may occur outside government when those involved in an agency or institution come to believe that their agency, church, or family should do, or stop doing, certain things.

Political problems may emerge as a function of new circumstances or technology. For example, the identification of biological fathers has been a political problem for centuries in child welfare policy. With the development of deoxyribonucleic acid (DNA) technologies, parental identification has become almost 100 percent accurate. This certainty, however, has generated demands for the use and control of the new technology. Another way problems may become politically significant is by shifts in political power among stakeholders. The Voting Rights Acts of the 1960s produced diverse and curious impacts on the political perception of the poverty problem.[6] It would be naive not to realize that a large number of low-income citizens suddenly becoming voters had an impact on the way the political system responded to poverty.

New political problems also emerge when there is a shift in the values or criteria by which options are ranked. The dramatic shifts in attitudes toward premarital sexual behavior and family responsibilities have altered beliefs about the abortion policy. All these examples suggest that shifts exogenous to the political world do fundamentally alter initial perceptions of what constitutes a political problem.

Some serious problems about which the government could act never appear on the political agenda. Other apparently trivial problems receive considerable governmental attention. Typically, for an uncomfortable social fact to become politically significant—to acquire status as a political problem—a long period of incubation is required.

In the "problem stage" of the policy process, various groups articulate their needs and identify specific goals. Needs and goals are not identical. Needs tend to be ordered in some systematic fashion, traceable in one way or another to Maslow's seminal hierarchical structure. One articulates a goal with a concept of need in mind, but with cognizance of available political and economic resources. To illustrate this division between needs and goals, people need jobs for a wide variety of psychological, social, and economic reasons; a goal of full employment is but one expression of a conviction that government should commit its resources in a particular way to respond to everyone's "need" for jobs. Alternatively, jobs could be valued only for the income they produce, thus the cost of direct welfare is compared to the cost of training, job placement, and other activities required for full employment. In a harsher environment one might think of the "need to ration jobs," that is, to use public policy to decide who should work. It is clear that the definition of the need establishes the goals sought. To some persons the need to encourage work is as important as the need for income. For others, pushing people off welfare and into dead-end jobs is counterproductive.

Problem definition in its first stage refers to a process by which a perceived difficulty, opportunity, or unwanted trend is *recognized as politically significant,* and is subsequently *interpreted* by distinct groups or actors as relating to their "cognitive maps"[7] for political activity. Problem perception is a highly subjective process. Distinctly different conceptual lenses are always in use when a problem is perceived as a political one.

The essential points are these:

1. Many problems result from the same event or opportunity.
2. Few problems have an objective reality amenable to discovery in the mode of a natural science. The very act of definition sets a course of action for the policy stream. Policies often fail simply because of the way the problem definition emerges politically. Services to the developmentally disabled were defined as a failure of the educational system. The dimensions of that policy process would surely have been different if the failure had been defined as occurring within the health system. A developmental disability therapist may well argue that it is a health as well as an educational problem, but the political definition sets the course of the policy response.
3. Distinct groups have distinct capacities to give their definition privileged or even official status, while other groups have no opportunity for their definition to enter into political discussion. The definition of a problem shapes and is also shaped by groups organizing around the problem. David Truman's seminal work on group processes in politics speaks to this point.[8] Many factors contribute to a group's desire to have its definition of a problem accepted, such as (1) the group's degree of cohesion, (2) its expectation of permanence, (3) its internal division of labor, and (4) its formalized value system. The list could also include attributes of power of various social groups, such as numbers, wealth, access to media, and access to public officials.

In a survey parents were asked what their response would be if there were no school crossing guard at a dangerous intersection their child had to cross. Low-income parents responded as if this were a neighborhood problem and suggested informal means of setting up a guard system. Middle-income parents responded in terms of the political process: petitions to the school board, the principal, and so on. High-income parents spoke in terms of political access saying, "I would call John or Joan," giving the name of responsible officials. Each group was not only expressing a perception of the problem but also reflecting their previous experience with similar problems and the political process.

What is important to one group attempting to define a problem and place its goals on the political agenda of society is not necessarily important to a second group. For social workers, the central role is often to organize the constituency, to raise their consciousness level, and to teach the groups to define a problem in political terms.

There is a critical and central tension involved in the definition of the problem. *Problem definition is expected to arouse the passions of the stakeholders and to provide a semantically clear specification of needs, values, and constraints.* Wolman characterized this tension very well:

> Too frequently rhetoric is substituted for adequate conceptualization resulting in vagueness and lack of direction throughout the entire formulation process. The end

result is perceived to be a program which has failed to solve the problem even though no one is quite certain what the problem is. . . . Thus problems frequently appear on the decision making agenda without having been adequately conceptualized or thought through.[9]

The critical task facing the analyst is that a problem must be placed in a political context, even though it has no objective reality in the scientific sense. A clearly worded analytic frame of reference may indeed provide the critical political breakthrough allowing a consensus to be achieved. The problem statement ought to reflect an awareness of the reality of the dispute. Too often it appears as merely a wish list of some constituents. Too often the problem statement, by the bias of its own rhetoric, denies the legitimacy of any alternative policy perspective. While this one-sided presentation may mobilize support, it may also close the opportunity for discussion and compromise. To consider all abortions murder or to suggest that a woman who is carrying a fetus is the sole judge of whether an abortion is to be performed may serve recruitment needs in a political battle but may also create a false dichotomy of choices available to society.

POLICY FORMULATION

We suggested that a considerable period of gestation is necessary for a social problem to become politically significant. Often, governments become concerned with a problem and its ramifications long after the optimum time for intervention. This is most certainly true in the field of foreign affairs,[10] and is also the case in domestic policy. All significant political groups now favor legislation to protect the abused spouse, but domestic violence was dealt with outside the political arena as recently as the 1970s. Civil and criminal law was clearly inadequate but this inadequacy alone was not sufficient to put the question on the agenda of either the states or the nation.[11]

Candidates for office often present their agenda as one of new ideas, yet most ideas around which political battles take place have existed for a considerable time. Focusing on political conflicts disguises the critical necessity not only for mobilizing support but also for generating policy ideas if one is to facilitate policy choice. To operate successfully in this arena one must understand those environmental circumstances that stifle the identification of creative options and must recruit into the political process people capable of creative thinking.[12]

Too often there appears to be a permanent mismatch between what is rational in terms of program analysis and what is rational in the view of administrators and elected officers. When George McGovern attempted to present abstract ideas about how the tax and transfer system might be reformed simultaneously, the response was a political disaster that nearly cost him the presidential nomination in 1972.[13] More recently, ideas about reforms in mental health policy systems have run afoul of local political demands. The decision to close down large residential hospitals—often the major "industry" of one town—and to substitute many community-based out-patient programs, may place local economic interest and current mental health policy in conflict with one another.

Policy ideas represent the search for creative thoughts about how governments might commit resources in responding to problems. This is the prescriptive level of analysis. The attractions of a consensus are clear if you are in the business of making policy prescriptions. Unfortunately, the consensus rapidly disintegrates as ideas for problem resolution are articulated, particularly as the downside consequences of each idea are made explicit. The process of articulating a set of policy ideas is inordinately complex. This is particularly true in the political world where conflicts over power, abused egos, hidden motives, and many other aspects of decision making confound the rational process. So much attention is given in the daily press to those forces that detract from the role of ideas in government that the casual observer sees politics and rationality as incompatible. Yet policy ideas are often presented as if this were a rational world in which individuals and groups know what they want, are creative about the problem-solving process, have full information about the problem, and are aware of and are not embarrassed by their criteria of choice.

Such a rational model would look something like this. Each group of like-minded citizens would first examine their priorities and rank them (P1, P2 . . . Pn). The options available would be specified (O1, O2 . . . On). The options would then be judged according to some clearly specified criteria (C1, C2 . . . Cn). Some options would be rejected as incompatible with the central criteria and a limited set of new options would emerge. These options would be reevaluated according to the basic priorities and a decision would be reached about which options to support and in what order. Groups would enter the political arena with a reasonably well-established agenda.

In fact, real political conflict is far more complex. In the process of finding our priorities, specifying options, and estimating consequences, a series of divergent political battles emerges. The difficulty, of course, is that the criteria employed by contending political groups may have very different frames of reference so that discussion across criteria becomes markedly conflict oriented.

The range of alternatives that achieve serious consideration is very narrow. The only options debated are those that have reached the political agenda with support from significant numbers of persons or from persons who are politically significant. The presence or absence of a conception of a crisis will often foster or retard a policy idea advancement toward a place on the national agenda. The police raid and subsequent riot at Stonewall in Greenwich Village contributed significantly to the birth of the Gay Rights movement. This does not suggest that the Gay Rights movement was stimulated by the Stonewall Inn incident in New York, only that its shape was influenced by those events. Subsequently, the acquired immune deficiency syndrome (AIDS) epidemic, too often seen as a problem of gay and bisexual men, has shaped the policy debate over gay rights and AIDS health policies.

The appeal of a policy idea to particular groups is perhaps the most critical factor in predicting which idea will receive consideration and how this will occur.

1. Ideas acceptable to well-established groups that have permanent access to the corridors of power will receive attention, even if poorly conceived. An idea that the American Medical Association likes may not be adopted, but for it not to be considered is unthinkable.

2. Ideas acceptable to groups that are neither well established nor well connected will not be considered until these groups establish their own standing. Felons in prisons might have good ideas for treatment and rehabilitation, but these ideas will go unheard if a mechanism for attention is not generated.[14]

Social workers' client groups often lack establishment credentials and access to the corridors of power. Their problems and the ideas for their correction need to be placed on the agenda of those with the formal power to act. As a case in point, the physical abuse and neglect of children now evokes significant public attention, and the idea of mandatory reporting laws as one instrument of intervention has been widely adopted. This change has not occurred without controversy. For centuries child abuse by parents, the most frequent form of abuse, was shrouded. From the founding of the Children's Bureau in 1912 until 1973 when the Mondale–Brandon Act was passed establishing limited rules for reporting suspected child abuse, the ideas supporting child protection appeared and disappeared from the political agenda. More than sixty years were required for a problem and a corresponding policy response, now seen as common sense, to find political acceptance.[15]

POLICY SELECTION

As suggested in Chapter 2, the two central elements of political choice are disagreement and power. Choice is central to the existence of every political system: **The political system exists to register political problems, to generate ideas for acting on these problems, to monitor and control the conflict over alternatives, and to record and give favor to the victor.**

Choice must begin with an agreed-upon set of rules whereby options will be put forward, they will be debated, and a solution will be chosen. In an American democracy this process is generally addressed through the building of a majority coalition of interested citizens subject to constitutional constraints to protect the right of interested minorities. That majority coalition needs to be crafted in a painstakingly careful fashion.

After an examination of the seamy side of the Congress, professionals and interest group activists, including social workers, are often frustrated by realizing that support for legislation and the shape of the compromise are created by nonsubstantive considerations. Rational problem solving takes second place to political beliefs about quid pro quo, committee appointments, leadership positions, even additional office staff and the all-important campaign contribution. These are only some of the important ingredients in the making of political choices. The focus here is not on this aspect of political pathology but on the nonpathological aspects of the policy process as a model of choice.

The opportunity for responsible political rationality in the American political system is based on the assumed presence of certain system characteristics, including the following:

1. A condition of social pluralism in which citizens are aware of their own needs and are in touch with others in similar circumstances

2. The existence of a process whereby alternatives are identified and evaluated
3. The presence and viability of diverse and competing groups seeking a majority coalition
4. A basic consensus on the rules of democratic competition and an adherence to those rules by all groups
5. Regular elections that provide citizens an opportunity to express their preferences about the substantive issues of social problems and the way in which their government responds

In general, these assumptions are more or less true although they will vary in different political environments. When a political system has these characteristics, the opportunities for both rational and democratic choice are at a maximum. When it does not, it is a defective mechanism for fair and rational collective choices. The political activist often faces a dilemma in deciding whether his or her first responsibility is to correct defects in the political system or to achieve a particular adjustment in a specific policy.

The essence of democratic elections is thought to be structured around the concept of the rational self-interested voter, but elections are often orchestrated as symphonies of image manipulation rather than realistic debates about what the voter wants. This dichotomy is illustrated in three books published in the early 1980s: John Schwarz's *America's Hidden Success: A Reassessment of Twenty Years of Public Policy,*[16] Charles Murray's *Losing Ground: American Social Policy 1950–1980,*[17] and Daniel Moynihan's *Family and Nation.*[18] These books succinctly laid out the separating issues in the welfare reform debate.

IMPLEMENTATION

Once a legislative choice is made, it is seldom self-enforcing. In the implementation phase of the policy process the focus is on the interrelated behaviors that translate a legislative decision into government action that is reasonably close to the original decision and capable of surviving in the institutional environment.[19] During the implementation phase policy actors strive to translate abstract objectives and complex procedural rules to the street-level reality where the problems are encountered.

Planning at the various levels of bureaucracy is seen as the critical aspect of successful implementation. Policies are sometimes ineffective because the policy objective and the policy instrument are incorrectly linked. That is, a policy that misspecifies a causal chain and relies incorrectly on an intervention strategy that cannot work will fail regardless of successful implementation. A policy may fail because new conditions make intervention impossible. A policy may fail because it is poorly implemented. Each policy contains an implicit hypothesis that if intervention i occurs at time t, then result r will occur, and r is compatible with the policy goal g. Clearly, policy failure can occur anywhere in this connected series. Implementation failure occurs when intervention i is not delivered on time.

There are two aspects to planning implementation—policy planning and program planning:

TABLE 3.5 Levels and Objectives of Planning/Implementation Study

	Policy Planning	Program Planning
Organization	x	
Interpretation		x

1. Policy planning is the design of a sequence of events incorporating the required task and having appropriately clear statements of objectives, performance standards, and timing requirements.
2. Program planning is the design of requirements for mobilizing resources and staff, and the accurate reporting of accomplishment of the various tasks.

There are two central elements within each form of planning:[20]

1. *Organization:* the establishment and arrangement of resources for putting a policy into effect
2. *Interpretation:* the meaningful translation of program language into feasible and consistent actions by street-level workers

If the levels of inquiry and the objectives of inquiry are placed into a conventional matrix we find that most of the academic and professional literature could be categorized as falling along the principal diagonal in Table 3.5.

The central requirements for effective policy implementation are that those who will implement the policy, in our case the street-level social workers, must know what they are required to do by the policy, and must then have the resources to do it. It is clearly impossible for the legislative body and the senior civil service to dot every *i* and cross every *t* in the design of the legislation. Successful implementation demands that the street-level worker understand the opportunities and limits of administrative discretion. Perhaps most significant is that the parameters of discretion be commonly understood by policymaker, citizen, bureaucrat, and client.

Figure 3.2 illustrates the complex process, using a Texas example, by which a policy directive from the legislature is translated, very slowly, into operation rules for the social worker at the street level of the bureaucracy.

EVALUATION

Policy evaluation is a continuous, diverse, and ubiquitous process. It occurs when two clients talk about their experience with an agency and when a multimillion dollar grant is given to a research firm to report on the impact of the program. Policy evaluation is an elastic term. The common element in its various usages is the dual notion of collecting evidence and weighing it against some explicit or implicit standard. In evaluation of policy, collecting evidence refers to the identification and discovery of the empirical relationships among the elements of the real world where the policy is carried out. Weighing the evidence refers to a judgment about the norms that are

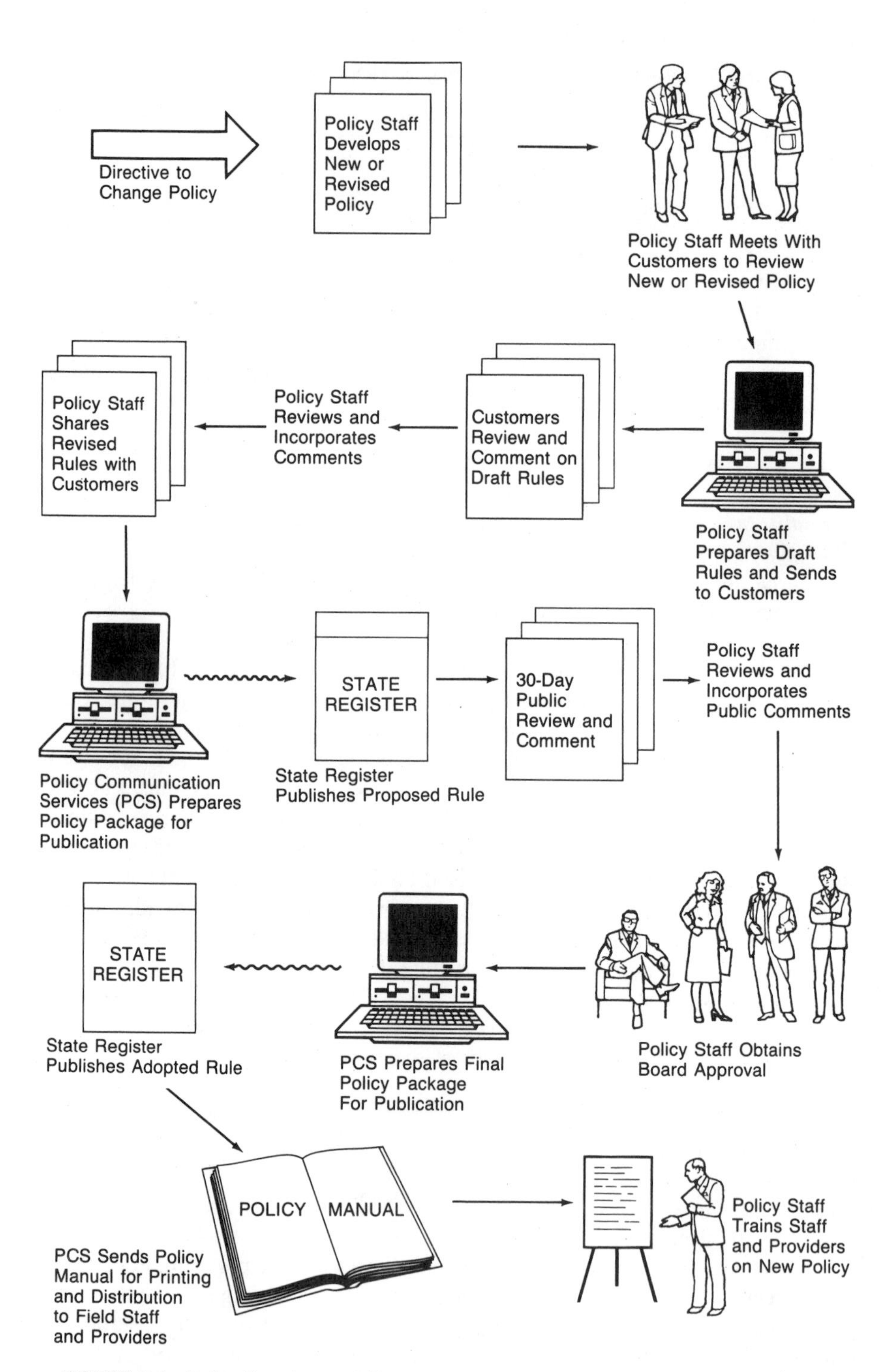

FIGURE 3.2 Policy Development Process

SOURCE: Department of Human Services, Texas, Handout for training session, 1991.

relevant for assessing what has been empirically observed. In policy evaluation, one observes and judges the actions that have been taken to close the gap between an existing state of affairs in the absence of the policy and the results that are observed as a consequence of the policy. The desirability of the policy depends on the prior condition, what has happened, and the results that are attributable to the policy intervention and how one ethically connects the effort and the consequences. For example, does capital punishment policy reduce heinous crime? Within the limitations of science various answers are given. For some the important connection is the effectiveness of capital punishment in reducing crime; for others, capital punishment is itself abhorrent and the connection is thus irrelevant.

The statement that empirical evaluations seek to provide knowledge of what happened while normative evaluations provide statements of what *ought* to have happened is accurate in a limited sense. It is a mistake, however, to think that the empirical and the normative are independent of one another. A policy designed to prepare welfare mothers for jobs is a failure if the efforts are unconnected to real-world market conditions. We can judge the policy by relating the costs of training, the savings in welfare payments, and the value to society of the jobs performed. This leaves aside an ethical question of a society's commitment to an ideal of allowing mothers the choice to be full-time mothers. By what standard do we judge an affirmative action policy? The answer requires a simultaneous consideration of what impact the policy has on hiring and what we think a hiring policy ought to be. Abortion policy provides another example of the normative and empirical interaction. The extent to which an abortion policy facilitates and makes more available the abortion option is judged by some as an indication of the policy's success; others take these same facts as reflecting the undesirability of the policy. Any extended normative analysis rests in part on empirical assumptions not fully established. Similarly, in any complex empirical analysis the very specification of variables contains both explicit and implicit normative assumptions.

From a pragmatic perspective the basic objective of policy evaluation is to determine the extent to which a policy is meeting its objectives, and if a serious policy failure is revealed, to learn what explains the failure. The welfare department will want to know whether the employment training program is working. It will also want to know if it could be made to work better. In areas where the program has gone wrong, evaluative research becomes a search for the pathology in the policy. Yet only when people know or think they know what a policy should be is the stage set for the last phase of the policy process.

POLICY ADJUSTMENT

Policies never die, they just evolve. There are two interconnected problems. One is that old policies and programs are often retrofitted to new conditions. The second is that programs often live on long after the problems for which they were created have ceased to exist. Aid to Families with Dependent Children began as a program to assist children whose fathers had died without providing for their support; it has continued to serve a very different population of children not being supported by their absent fathers. In both cases the children are in need, but the two very different populations elicit very different political environments of support and expectation.

Policy adaptation, the so-called final stage of the policy process, is not in reality a final stage at all for the simple reason that public policies are never resolved. The formal end of one policy marks the birth of a new social problem. Nonetheless, it is important to understand how the parameters of an old policy respond to a new policy, or, more frequently, to an old problem redefined in a new way.

All policies need midcourse redirection for a number of practical reasons:

1. Events change both the reality and the perception of the original problem.
2. New technologies make old responses anachronistic.
3. Institutions seek to perpetuate themselves: A department is created to do a job; later, when that job is no longer needed, a function is found so that the persons in the department can keep their jobs.

Policy changes are resisted for equally compelling reasons. Once a policy is in operation there are large political costs associated with change or redirection. Witness, for example, the problem of closing anachronistic military posts or mental hospitals. The same factors that explain why policies emerge and come to be understood gradually also explain why policies are terminated gradually. The mobilization of support for the creation of a particular policy approach continues after the original circumstance has shifted. To legislate and implement is difficult; to terminate and dismantle is at least equally difficult. The shape and structure of the old policy approach is very much a part of the reality of the new problem.

NOTES

1. Lasswell, Harold D., "The Decision Process: Seven Categories of Functional Analysis," reprinted in *Politics of Social Life,* ed. Nelson Polsby (Boston: Houghton Mifflin, 1963), p. 93.
2. David Easton, "An Approach to the Analysis of Political Systems," *World Politics* 9 (April 1957): 384.
3. Lawrene Lynn et al., *The President as Policymaker* (Philadelphia: Temple, 1983).
4. M. Kenneth Bowler, *The Nixon Guaranteed Income Proposal: Substance and Process in Policy Change* (Cambridge, MA: Ballinger, 1974).
5. John Kingdon, *Agendas Alternatives and Public Policy* (Boston: Little, Brown, 1984).
6. James Donovan, *Politics of Poverty* (Indianapolis, IN: Pegasus, 1973).
7. Brain W. Hogwood and Lewis A. Gunn, *Policy Analysis for the Real World* (Oxford, England: Oxford University Press, 1984).
8. David Truman, *The Governmental Process: Political Interests and Public Opinion* (New York: Knopf, 1951).
9. H. Wolman, "The Determinants of Program Success and Failure," *Journal of Public Policy* 1 (1981): 436.
10. Richard Neustadt and Ernest May, *Thinking in Time* (New York: Free Press, 1986).
11. Donald Dutton, *The Domestic Assault of Women* (Boston: Allyn & Bacon, 1988).
12. Y. Dror, *Public Policy Making Re-examined* (Scranton, PA: Chandler, 1968), p. 179.

13. Gordon Weil, *The Long Shot* (New York: Norton, 1973).
14. Michael Lipskey, "Protest as Political Resource," *American Political Science Review* 62 (December 1968), p. 1144ff.
15. Barbara Nelson, *Making an Issue of Child Abuse: Political Agenda Setting for Social Problems* (Chicago: University of Chicago Press, 1984); Linda Gordon, "The Frustrations of Family Violence: An Historical Critique," *Journal of Sociology and Social Work* 15 (December 1988): 139–160.
16. John Schwarz, *America's Hidden Success: A Reassessment of Twenty Years of Public Policy* (New York: Norton, 1983).
17. Charles Murray, *Losing Ground: American Social Policy 1950–1980* (New York: Basic Books, 1984).
18. Daniel Moynihan, *Family and Nation* (San Diego, CA: Harcourt & Brace 1986).
19. Walter Williams, Editorial Note, *Policy Analysis* 1 (1975): 451.
20. Daniel Mazmanian and Paul Sabatier, *Implementation and Public Policy* (Washington, DC: Urban Institute, 1983), pp. 35–41.

BIBLIOGRAPHY

Bowler, Kenneth, M. *Nixon's Guaranteed Income.* Cambridge, MA: Ballinger, 1974.
Dutton, Donald. *The Domestic Assault of Women.* Boston: Allyn & Bacon, 1988.
Easton, David. *A Framework for Political Analysis.* Englewood Cliffs, NJ: Prentice-Hall, 1965.
Jenkins, W. I. *Policy Analysis: A Political and Organizational Perspective.* London: Martin Robinson, 1978.
Jones, Charles O. *An Introduction to the Study of Public Policy.* Monterey, CA: Brooks Cole, 1984.
Smith, Hedrick. *The Power Game: How Washington Works.* New York: Random House, 1988.

CHAPTER **4**

The Political / Economic Framework

The tension between self-reliant competitive enterprise and a sense of public solidarity espoused by civic republicans has been the most important unresolved problem in American history.

Robert Bellah

Conflict over the goals and standards of welfare is one of the major defining characteristics of a society. The questions focus on whom we should help, how we should help, why we should help, and who should pay for the help. Resolving the conflicts over welfare goals and methods is the function of the political system but this resolution occurs in a larger socioeconomic context. How and when we should help the least privileged citizens are only two of the critical questions about social welfare, for decisions also need to be made about how we restructure and supplement the primary social institutions in order to serve the wider welfare interests of society. Welfare programs do more than redistribute income and/or wealth. Welfare programs are also a source of opportunity, a prime means of socialization, and a principal mechanism of social control. The Prussian general and writer on military strategy Karl von Clausewitz said of warfare that choices about warfare were too important to be left to the generals. So, too, choices about welfare are too important to be left to social workers.

Our economy is organized predominantly around the concept of a free market. Private enterprise operating in a market economy is generally considered the best vehicle to satisfy the various desires about the allocation and distribution of scarce resources. This is a general proposition, not a universal one. Even the most ardent defender of the free enterprise system wishes to make allowances for the sick, penniless, and uninsured who come to hospitals needing treatment. Should it be provided? Who should decide, and who should pay? Public and voluntary systems providing for these and other essentials lie at the heart of a society's social welfare system. As the theme of this book is understanding the political context of such social welfare choices, the book should sit on a shelf alongside a volume on the economic context of social welfare choices and another on the history of such choices.[1]

I leave it to others more qualified to provide a detailed exposition of the economics and the history of social welfare, but digress briefly from the political theme here to provide a barebones introduction to the economic context of welfare choice. Strictly speaking, it is not a digression, for the way one understands the economics of social welfare is directly related to one's fundamental political philosophy.

Within the broad structure upon which American institutions are based, a wide variety of efforts have been made and are being made to provide for those unable to provide for themselves. Other programs assist individuals, groups, and communities to attain their most satisfying level of functioning. The social welfare services are structured (1) to provide basic minimum levels of essential goods and services, (2) to offer developmental services designed to assist certain classes of persons to function more adequately, and (3) to establish and enforce rules and procedures to protect individuals and families from exploitation and self-destructive behaviors. These structured services were discussed in the first and second chapters in which public social welfare programs were shown to be created by a public process. Social welfare objectives and the social welfare system are not by any means limited to the public sector of society.

Some of these objectives are also met outside government auspices within an amorphous set of institutions called the voluntary sector. Church politics, agency politics, foundation politics, and even university politics shape our social welfare institutions. By no stretch of the imagination are the voluntary and public sectors independent of one another. The way public, market, and voluntary sectors interact, or ought to interact, constitutes the mainstream of political economy.

Three principal political philosophies can be contrasted. Political philosophy categories are oversimplifications, for within each broad political camp there is great diversity. Nonetheless, the contrasting points of view can serve as an introduction which is more helpful than it is simplistic.

In the first view, the market economy can and should divide society. Political efforts to eliminate, or even to moderate, class distinctions are doomed to failure because they attempt to contravene natural laws. In an early formulation of this approach, Malthus asserted that efforts to improve the living conditions of the working class would increase the population geometrically, while productive capacity could be increased only arithmetically. The resulting tragedy would be a worsening of the living conditions of the working class. Social reform would thus inevitably be self-defeating. Latter-day Malthusians make somewhat less drastic projections. Major works of the 1980s reflected the view that welfare did not increase suffering, but that welfare programs as structured in the 1960s were inadvertently self-defeating. The authors' argument was that the programs created a dependency because they rewarded the character flaws of those most in need and penalized the virtues that would most likely help these persons to help themselves.[2]

A second view is that welfare relationships, if unchecked, will destroy individual rights. Social welfare policies that mediate class conditions serve only to reinforce an evil and tyrannical state. In its utopian form, socialism requires a revolution in values before political institutions really change. The utopian socialist shares with the conservative a distaste for social welfare institutions. To the socialist, inequality is neither desirable nor inevitable. Inequality and its attendant suffering are, however, way stations in the march to progress. Social welfare institutions serve only to delay the evolution of the socialist state. Less draconian manifestations of the Marxist theories of doom also have a prominent place in the literature of social welfare. The argument from the left is that social welfare institutions are, at their best, a sort of benign con game. For the socialist, liberal antipoverty programs alleviate the worst excesses of capitalism and, not so incidentally, prevent the outbreak of interclass warfare. The flaw of the liberal antipoverty paradigm is that it creates the conservative illusion that with pluck, hard work, luck, and a modest boost from government, anyone can escape poverty.

Only in the liberal tradition do social welfare institutions have a valued place. The liberal shares with the conservative a belief in the inevitability of continued inequality. With the socialist, the liberal shares a belief that such inequality is distinctly undesirable. The liberal does not share the cynical view that public efforts ultimately do not help those in great need. The undesirable consequences of capitalism can be controlled by (1) fine tuning economic choice through Keynesian budgetary planning; (2) social policies that compensate for inequality and insecurity in the market through social insurance, social assistance, and progressive taxation; (3) constitutional protection of pluralistic politics to control against domination by factions; and (4) specific social welfare programs designed to reduce the probability and severity of want resulting from system failure. Specific programs like Old Age Survivors Insurance have earned good marks in reducing the rate of poverty and providing for a permanent escape from it.

Each motivation and style of welfare demands a somewhat modified paradigm or ideology. Politics, even broadly defined, is only part of the story. Historical, social, and economic variables tell their own stories. The simplified diagram of Figure 4.1 shows a minimum number of linkages that must be explored if one is to understand contemporary welfare institutions.

FIGURE 4.1 Linkages of Factors Involved in Development of Social Welfare Programs

II. Political System Variables
- A. Political Actors
- B. Political Institutions
- C. Equality of Access to Government

I. Social Environmental Variables
- A. Class Structures
- B. Family System
- C. Ethnic and Racial Bias

IV. Social Welfare System Features
- A. Minimum Standards
- B. Eligible Populations
- C. Program Structures

III. Economic Context
- A. State of Technology
- B. Natural and Capital Resources
- C. Orientation of Markets

The simplified diagram of Figure 4.1 shows the linkages one must explore in order to develop a comprehensive framework in which social welfare choices can be made. Clearly, specialization and selective orientations are required. Each orientation and each ideology highlights a different path to explaining complex welfare choices. No one orientation or ideology is inherently superior, but each adds, in its own context, to the understanding of social welfare choices.

THE ECONOMIC CONTEXT OF SOCIAL WELFARE CHOICE

At any given point a society has a fixed stock of personnel resources, natural resources, and capital goods. Decisions have to be made about how these resources are allocated to satisfy the competing individual and collective desires of the society. Only in a society in which resources exceeded desires would there be no competition over the pattern of allocation. Allocation has to do with the ways in which valuable resources of production are utilized to satisfy competing desires. A finite number of people, places, and things will be used to build cruise missiles, to cure cancer, to house the homeless, or to build louder portable stereos. With each pattern of allocation there is a distributional effect. Distribution has to do with assigning the use of the goods and services produced to particular households within the total community. If we build more missiles, these families and this section of the country will become richer; but if we spend more to cure cancer, other families and other sections of the country will fare better because of the new allocation pattern. If we produce more portable stereos, then yet another pattern of distribution will occur. Each pattern of allocation has a distinct distributional effect. Because different households and families spend their money differently, each pattern of distribution has an allocation effect. With each allocation pattern having a distributional impact and each distributional pattern having an allocation effect, there is a circularity to the economic process and the resulting flow of income to households and families. This interaction has a profound impact on the resources required and the demands placed on the social welfare system.

Virtually every textbook on introductory economics contains a discussion on the circular flow of income through a simplified pure market system. The first economist to describe the process was Francois Quesnay (1694–1774).[3] In the simplest form of the system, all goods and services are produced by firms. The goods are consumed by households. The "factors of production" are owned by households, and the firms pay households for the use of these factors. The income received by the households in the factor market is used by them in the product market to purchase the goods and services produced by the firms. Quesnay thought of the system as a closed one in which the circulation was continuous, somewhat like Harvey's contemporaneous theory on the circulation of blood.

Figure 4.2 illustrates the Quesnay model. Households purchase the goods and services of firms for a price. Firms are able to produce by paying the households for the use of the factors of production. The pattern of allocation is established in the product market and the pattern of distribution is established in the factor market.

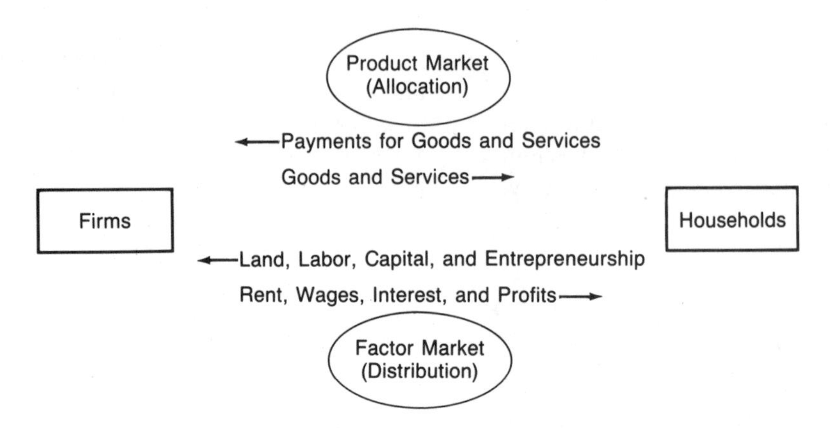

FIGURE 4.2 The Circular Flow of Income

To focus on the shape of welfare one must move beyond a pure market model. There seem to be three major processes by which basic human needs are met. One is the market system, whereby those with the ability to pay have the ability to shape allocations so that their basic desires are met. This process leaves open the problem of those who are without sufficient resources with which to obtain income or achieve opportunities. The second process, an alternative to a market-oriented structure, is a governmental intervention system that is designed to supplement the market system and to achieve specific social welfare goals. A third method is voluntary sharing. This may involve the simple act of giving alms directly or it may include a complex voluntary sector of churches, foundations, united funds, and other social agencies. Thus government institutions and private agencies are deliberately structured to alter not only the patterns of income distribution but also the kinds of goods and services produced.

For the purpose at hand, we need to add two more institutions to Quesnay's model: public welfare and voluntary welfare (see Figure 4.3). The public and private social welfare institutions are not structured to replace the market system but to supplement it and to produce patterns of allocation and distribution that are surely different and, one hopes, better.

THE DIVISION OF WELFARE RESPONSIBILITIES

The description and legitimacy of the divisions between public, private, and voluntary sectors of the economy are basic issues in the study of economics.[4] Specific welfare services, as defined earlier, may be located in a market economy, in a public enterprise, or in the voluntary sector. On one floor of a downtown office building one might find a profit-oriented firm providing job and career counseling, a social agency performing the same service, and a public agency doing the same thing. These three agencies may appear very similar. Any attempt to discuss the division of social welfare responsibilities is influenced by the fact that this division between the public, voluntary,

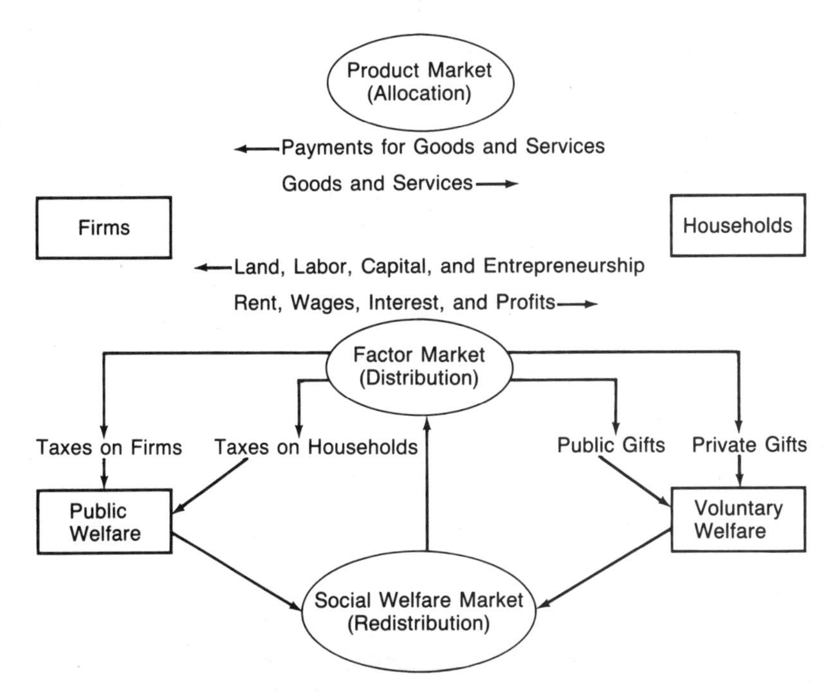

FIGURE 4.3 Welfare Institutions as Facilitators of Social Welfare Goals

and private sectors is structured as much by history and by accident as by logical design or purposeful goal.

By examining the flow of dollars through the welfare systems we can see that there is a large and relatively stable public presence. There is a smaller and somewhat less stable voluntary section. There is also a clear place for market-dominated, profit-oriented social welfare agencies. Once a society establishes voluntary agencies and public programs to deliver specific welfare services, private firms will compete to produce and/or distribute the same services. There is always a tension along the borders between sectors because of each sector's perception of its own responsibility, and the location of the borders is in flux according to current political conflicts and other circumstances.

A problem in analyzing welfare activities by economic sector is that at the street level the functions are imperceptibly merged. Saint Mary's Catholic Church rents subsidized space to Mary Ellen Burns who operates what she hopes will be a for-profit day-care center there. The fees for many of the children enrolled in the center are paid by public funds. The fees for other children are set by a sliding scale reflecting parental income. Use of the sliding scale is a condition for the rent charged for the church property. Frequently, Mary Ellen does not collect any fee because it is good for business to be charitably responsible and because she really cares for the welfare of the children. Mary Ellen's day-care center lies in all three sectors simultaneously, and it is not unique.

Table 4.1 shows the flow of income to what are ostensibly voluntary social welfare agencies.

TABLE 4.1 Agency Funding Sources, 1986

	Private	Government	Fees and Dues	Other*
Boys Clubs	66%	7%	8%	19%
Catholic Charities	21%	47%	12%	19%
Child Welfare Agency	15%	65%	6%	14%
Family Service Agency	28%	46%	17%	9%
Goodwill Industries	29%	19%	19%	33%
Jewish Community Centers	16%	7%	54%	23%
Salvation Army	57%	14%	10%	20%
Volunteers of America	13%	45%	8%	34%
YMCA, YMCA-YWCA	17%	4%	67%	12%
YWCA	29%	21%	36%	14%

*Other includes such sources of income as bequests, investment income, sale of capital goods, and sale of merchandise. The relatively high percentage of support in the "other" category for Goodwill Industries, the Salvation Army, and Volunteers of America comes from sales of donated merchandise. Source: Virginia Hodgkinson and Murray Weitzman, *Dimensions of the Independent Sector* (Washington, DC: Independent Sector, 1986), p. 21.

SOURCE: Howard J. Karger and David Stoesz, *American Social Welfare Policy: A Structural Approach* (White Plains, NY: Longman, 1990), p. 117

One sees that the divisions are highly artificial. Some voluntary agencies receive the bulk of their income from fees, much like a private firm, while others are very dependent on public payments, much like a governmental bureau. Because the division of responsibilities is difficult to see in such a case does not mean that it does not exist. The shape of the divisions is important to the type and quality of all social welfare activities. In this chapter we will discuss some of the ways each sector meets its various social welfare responsibilities in a society.

SOCIAL WELFARE STRATEGIES FOR GOVERNMENTS

Robert Lampman has suggested that there are four essential public strategies for the reduction of poverty.[5] These four strategies may be used to focus on a more general discussion of what governments do to meet social welfare objectives as defined in the first chapter.

The first and most significant social welfare policy focuses on making the market economy work. A second attempts to adapt and modify the system of the market to the special needs of the distinct population groups. The third policy form involves changing the clients and adapting them to the demands of the market system. The fourth focuses on relieving the distress that occurs with the incomplete success of the first three.

Make the Market System Work for Those in Special Need

Speaking of welfare and the market economy John F. Kennedy used a famous metaphor, "The rising tide lifts all boats." Many economists argue that a well-structured and efficient economy, even one that permits inequality, will eventually eliminate want and allow individual consumers to purchase the service program they need for themselves. Economic history shows clearly that real economic growth, without regard to distribution, is an effective antipoverty strategy. From its outset, American governments have played a strong role in shaping the capacities of our private markets. In Europe since the mid-nineteenth century and in this country since the New Deal, the economic responsibility of governments to be both stimulator and regulator has been supplemented with the expectation that government will care for those who, for one reason or another, are not served by the economy. Governments have sought to offset the ravages of business cycles and in many other ways to use public power so that the economy will be productive and stable.

Over the course of the twentieth century the rate of poverty, measured as the proportion of households unable to purchase with their cash income a minimum market basket of goods and services, closely tracks the performance of the economy. The association is a strong one that reasserts itself with many measures of poverty and indicators of economic growth. In Figures 4.4 and 4.5, the official nonelderly poverty rate is plotted along the vertical axis; a measure of economic performance indicated by the median wage divided by the poverty line is plotted on the horizontal axis. The latter measure shows how strong the impact of the economic system is on the purchasing power of median income households. The figures show a marked coincidence between the two observations.

The evidence of real economic growth and effective antipoverty policy is strong, though there is disturbing evidence since the mid-seventies that the economic impact of the healthy economy on poverty is less strong now. That is, as our economy improved its impact was very great, but over time the impact has been weaker. The reasons for this new divergence are not entirely clear and in any case cannot be quickly or easily defined. Those who have studied the relationship between economic growth and the patterns of income distribution among households appear to agree on only one thing: Economic growth is now a less sensitive instrument for the eradication of poverty.[6]

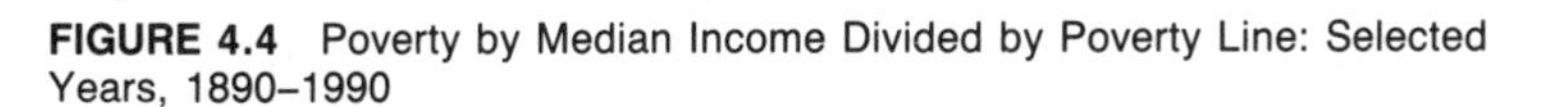

FIGURE 4.4 Poverty by Median Income Divided by Poverty Line: Selected Years, 1890–1990

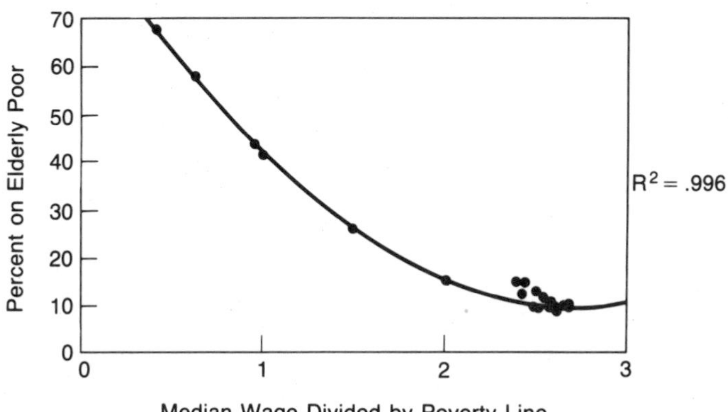

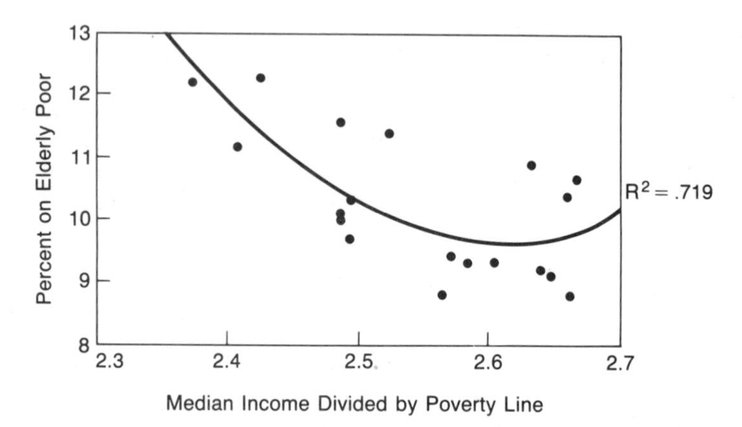

FIGURE 4.5 Poverty by Median Income Divided by Poverty Line: 1970–1990

SOURCE: Author's calcuations from data in *Economic Report of the President, 1990* (Washington, DC: U.S. Government Printing Office, 1990).

Nonetheless, a stable and growing economy provides not only a natural way to escape poverty and want but also the resources for other necessary social welfare actions. Alice Rivlin makes the point well:

> In a growing economy public choices are less agonizing and divisive. It is possible to modernize the armed forces; keep the nation's infrastructure in repair; provide for the elderly, the sick and the needy; improve education and other public services; and still have private incomes that rise after taxes. Public choices are never easy, but they generate far more conflict in a declining or stagnating economy.[7]

Adapting the System to the Needs of Special Population Groups

A healthy and vibrant economy is not enough, particularly if that health and vibrancy is dependent on exploitation, or if exploitation is a direct by-product of the way an economy is structured. It is meaningful, though perhaps less useful in practice, to distinguish between economies based on exploitation and economies for which exploitation is a by-product. Clearly, the opportunities for policy correction differ dramatically in the two circumstances. The abolition of slavery is the most dramatic correction of the first sort. In the second instance the U.S. courts and legislatures are constantly modifying permissible practices that bear directly on the opportunities of those most vulnerable to exploitation in our society. Minimum wage, hour, and safety regulations are among the most obvious ways in which the economy is deliberately restructured to meet the special needs of people at risk and/or in special need. Laws that require the removal of artificial physical barriers for the handicapped are another illustration.

The political history of these matters has been characterized by a gradual emergence of ever-greater federal responsibilities to regulate and limit economic activity in order to protect special populations. Though gradual over the long term, the actual shifts in public regulation of the market has been one of fits and starts, with swings of responsibility from local to state to federal governments. In public opinion polls from 1978 to 1982 there was a dramatic increase in the number of persons believing that the federal government had become too powerful. This was the theme of the Reagan administration. In 1989, a new shift became clear in these polls: sixty-two percent reported that they now wanted a more *active* government.[8] There is very little doubt that the demand to use public institutions, such as regulatory and redistributive strategies, to alter welfare patterns will remain a volatile topic.

Adapting the Clients to the System

From the 1890s' "friendly visitors" approach to today's sophisticated models of case management, there has been a tension between the desire to provide rehabilitative services and the desire to modify the social patterns of persons in need. In part this is a manifestation of the conflicts over the assimilation and the preservation of distinct subcultures. The poor have always been exhorted to practice thrift, temperance, prudence, and self-discipline. The implication is that the absence of these traits explains their objective plights. A different emphasis has introduced a broad range of service from literacy programs to personal therapy. This approach has required the extension of special services in some cases and modification of services in others to address the distinctive needs of certain populations. This type of assistance is sometimes seen as a form of cultural imperialism and sometimes as merely aid in socialization for those with special needs.

The third broad strategy for helping the subordinate populations is to change those aspects of their life-style which the majority see as contributing to their special social needs. This strategy has two overlapping modes. One is to instigate life-style changes by imposing negative sanctions for certain forms of behavior. The second is to provide those in need with special training and rehabilitation services to help them function more effectively to meet their own needs in an open economy.

The way a society acts (or fails to act) to alter an undesirable social practice often reveals as much about the conceptions of the problem by those contending for power as it does about the problem itself. The facts about teen pregnancy illustrate one particularly sensitive case in point. In 1988, over 350,000 single-parent teen families were begun. Virtually no one sees this social fact as a desirable condition. Nearly three-quarters of these teen mothers had themselves begun life as children of teen parents; more than half were still in homes partially dependent on welfare benefits.[9] It would appear almost axiomatic that better birth control information could help slow the rate of teen pregnancies; at least it is difficult to see how birth control information could make matters worse. Yet the introduction of reproductive hygiene as part of welfare benefits is nonetheless opposed by curious coalitions of the fundamentalist right and low-income community power groups.

In the popular press the debate between changing life-styles and changing economic capacities captures a lot of space. William Julius Wilson in *The Truly Disadvantaged* notes that the argument about life-style approach to those in need is not, at root, a debate between conservatives and liberals. Nor is it a debate about the role of racism in our society. Liberals have sometimes argued that the appearance of a convergence between race, ethnic membership, and the plight of America's social underclass is a function of the broader social problems of racism, discrimination, and social class subordination. Thus, they emphasize progressive social programs to open the opportunity structure to all. Conservatives, in contrast, have traditionally stressed some distinct ethnic values as superior to others. Thus, when reference is made to community programs, it is in the context of the adverse effects of various public programs on group behavior and incentives within particular groups. Wilson suggests that the debate between conservative and/or liberal paradigms ill serve those most in need. He asserts that the best solution does not lie in imposing a single paradigm but in a more open dialogue among people with different premises in order to raise new questions and to stimulate new policy research on how best to help.[10]

The work of Wilson and others shows that the design of social programs must reflect social, cultural, and personal factors. Liberals are beginning to learn that there is, in fact, an underclass. They have also learned that some social programs while helpful to the majority of those in special need, may sometimes be harmful to particular subgroups. Conservatives are beginning to learn that the underclass was not created by the welfare system, despite the presence of deceptive statistical correlations.

Relieving Distress

When the strategies for strengthening the economy, adapting the economy to those in need, and/or adapting those in need to the structure of the economy do not work or work imperfectly, other forms of help must be found. Relief payments, social insurance payments, and in-kind benefits are seen as a fourth policy to help. Here the idea is not to change the problems but to minimize the distress that the problems would otherwise cause.

During the period from 1964 to 1989 the concept of cash assistance was a policy idea in the ferment of transition. The idea of a guaranteed income became the focus of many proposals intended to transform fundamentally the shape of American welfare. With the exception of Lyndon Johnson, each president was associated with a major reform of the relief system. Nixon's Family Assistance Plan was submitted and passed the House twice. Ford readied his Income Security Plan for submission after his reelection, which never came. Jimmy Carter's Program for Better Jobs and Income caused a political stir but failed to receive congressional endorsement. Ronald Reagan sought to change, or rather, exchange, federal and state roles in his "welfare swap." All these proposals had a common feature, which was to use taxes and welfare payments as an integrated system of income redistribution. The degree to which these redistributional programs would have replaced other welfare programs varied widely among the programs.

The direct income support system that these programs would have in part replaced includes those that range from the local program of general assistance to the comprehensive national social insurance program. During President Ronald Reagan's terms the emphasis of reform shifted from helping the poor directly to reducing welfare costs so that investment income could be freed to stimulate the economy. A series of reforms were enacted that cumulatively produced a reduction in real costs of welfare benefits.[11] The liberal indictment of the Reagan policy shift did not lead to a return to higher social spending but to a shift in program focus. The new law, passed in the late fall of 1988 and just now being implemented by the states, places a new emphasis on work reform rules, enhanced child support, and strengthened social services. The public strategy of changing the work habits of the poor is directly linked to the provision of welfare benefits.[12] It is too early at this writing in the summer of 1991 to make a judgment on the new program's impact.

THE INTERACTION OF PUBLIC AND VOLUNTARY STRUCTURES

President Bush made clear in his campaign and in the first two years of his presidency that he saw a greater role to be played by the voluntary sector. A government's acceptance of the responsibility to provide adaptation services or to guarantee basic necessities does not imply that the service or benefit needs to be produced and distributed by government. Although governments can and often do act as providers and distributors, this is not the only way of implementing their social welfare policy. At one extreme the governments could stand aside and allow private firms to produce and sell social services. At the other end of this continuum, the government could produce and distribute its own benefits. In between, a wide variety of options is open to public decision makers. Through its tax breaks and regulative policies, government may encourage private firms and the voluntary sector to accept and execute specific programs. In fact, there is a wide range of public actions that facilitate the availability and affordability of social services. Some of these ways are listed below:

1. *Government as provider with subsidized and nonsubsidized user charges:* The price charged may be used to provide partial financing and/or a means to ration the service. The charge may reflect the full cost to government or the government may provide the service at less than full cost to some selected population groups.

   Hospitals may, for example, "overcharge" (that is, charge more than the real costs of providing the service) in order to finance other services. Normal obstetric services may be overcharged so that the hospital will have sufficient funds to operate a comprehensive neonatal problem program. The story of charging policies in public agencies, particularly agencies providing the essential social services, is a fit topic for intensive investigation with regard to any particular service strategy.[13]
2. *State as competitor:* The state may provide the service at full or subsidized price but is in the market to be a market leader in terms of price and quality. It acts not so much to provide the service as to set an exemplary standard against which private firms are forced to compete. Mental health services and many other rehabilitative services fit into this category.
3. *State as mandator of services:* An idea that appears to be gaining much appeal is for the government to require firms to provide certain basic social and health services to their employees. These services may be health insurance, day care, or even nutrition and general health education. The firms may indeed be able

to provide such services more efficiently than governments but the appeal does not lie there. Rather, it lies with the perception that such services are without cost to the taxpayer, since it could be made to appear to the public that the costs are passed on to business.

4. *State as provider of last resort:* This scenario is the stereotypical social welfare situation in which the goods and services are readily available in the open competitive market, but for reasons of discrimination and inadequate incomes, some households have no realistic capacity to use the market mechanism to satisfy their need for these goods or services. Goods or service provided in this way are often "rationed" by the use of various stigmatic devices and eligibility rules to keep other potential consumers out of this closed market.

THE VOLUNTARY SECTOR

Voluntary modes of helping preceded modern governments and government programs have never fully replaced them, nor are they likely to do so. As shown earlier, one of the ways governments act to provide services is to engage both profit-oriented and nonprofit agencies. The so-called voluntary sector of our economy is organized and chartered privately but it has a public function. Neither the economic model of the private firm nor the public finance constructs of the public economic sector catch the essence of the voluntary sector's operations. It exists in an ill-defined buffer zone between the public and the private sectors. Although the historical and administrative developments are significant to an understanding of any particular voluntary agency, the point that needs to be explored is that there are politics in private agencies that operate in a manner that is structurally but not conceptually different from public agency conflicts. Every private agency has a need to secure a reliable source of resources, to obtain a form of legitimacy for its intervention into society, and to marshal the necessary skills to act and coordinate the actions of its donors, administrative staff, professional staff, and clients. These are all essentially political tasks.[14]

There are many reasons for a nonpublic agency. A voluntary organization may be created to pursue a public social welfare end because the providers distrust government or because a particular group desires to exercise greater control than they could in the public sector. The best way to understand why we have voluntary agencies performing public functions is to examine what they do. One soon recognizes that though they are called voluntary, or nonprofit, what really unites these agencies is that they are controlled by nongovernmental bodies. The so-called voluntary agencies are really alternative governmental agencies. This does not mean they are organized against government, but that they are organized to influence government, to supplement government, to use public funds, and to exercise controls not obtainable in the public sector.

Public, private, and nonprofit hospitals, for example, compete against one another and often perform essentially similar services for their community. The services can be readily observed. The purpose behind the organizational auspices is not so easily seen, but it is not inconsequential for public policy understanding. Voluntary agencies are sometimes thought to exist as the result of a perceived failure of the private market structures or public agencies to meet the needs of clientele groups. This explanation treats voluntary social welfare structures in a negative and restrictive way. The voluntary agency plays a special role in our three-sectored social service economy. It is bounded on one side by profit-oriented providers and on the other by politics. Economics as a discipline has developed a comprehensive set of paradigms to explain the behavior of the for-profit providers. Political science as a discipline has done the same to explain the structure and operation of public programs. There is no comprehensive paradigm to explain how voluntary agencies operate and survive. In the absence of such a paradigm, the voluntary sector has been discussed in normative and descriptive terms, resulting in either too little analysis or overglorification.[15]

A policy perspective requires that we focus attention on how the three sectors cooperate or fail to cooperate. We need normative examinations of each sector's strengths and weaknesses and we need empirical evidence so that we can better design integrated patterns to produce a comprehensive set of welfare services for society as a whole. Public social welfare policy is shaped by the collective of what private voluntary agencies do or fail to do and voluntary practice is shaped by the collective of what public agencies do.[16] The impacts of privatization of public options and the public politicalization of private agency practice need to be made a part of all social welfare policy debates.[17]

THE CORPORATE SECTOR

In the literature of social welfare the impact of the corporation on American welfare is normally treated in a negative manner with accusations, both founded and unfounded, of corporate insensitivity to the plight of the poor, to women, and to minorities. Most observers now agree that the record of the corporation is mixed. For the bulk of American history, the private sector employer has been one of the mainstays of American welfare. Whatever its motivation, the American corporate practice of retirement benefits has changed the shape of the welfare of American elderly. The corporation is generally judged to be less effective in supplementing health care and day care for the children of its workers. Service programs in the area of mental health and addiction programs draw mixed reviews. The corporate decision-making process about welfare programs for its employees and the larger community requires a separate text. Here it is only noted that what the corporation does and fails to do must be a fundamental part of the study of a society's social welfare needs.[18]

NOTES

1. The following make up a conveniently focused set of companion volumes: Andrew W. Dobelstein, *Politics, Economics and Public Welfare* (Englewood Cliffs, NJ: Prentice-Hall, 1986); Michael Katz, *In the Shadow of the Poor House: A Social History of Welfare in America* (New York: Basic Books, 1986).
2. Charles Murray, *Losing Ground: American Social Policy 1950–1980* (New York: Basic Books, 1984).

3. Marguerite Kuczynski and Ronald R. Meek, *Quesnay's Tableau Economique [1758]* (London: Macmillan, 1972).
4. Robert Haveman, *Public Expenditures and Policy Analysis* (Chicago: Markham Publishing Co., 1970).
5. Robert J. Lampman, "The Anti-Poverty Program in Historical Perspective," lecture presented to the UCLA Faculty Seminar on Poverty, 25 February 1965.
6. For a more complete discussion of this issue see Sheldon Danziger and Daniel Weinberg, *Fighting Poverty: What Works and What Doesn't* (Cambridge, MA: Harvard University Press, 1986); and David T. Elwood, *Poor Support: Poverty in the American Family* (New York: Basic Books, 1988).
7. Alice Rivlin, *Economic Choices, 1984* (Washington, DC: Brookings Institution, 1984), p. 2.
8. Louis Harris, "A Vote for an Activist Government," *New York Times,* 9 November 1989, p. 25.
9. "Poor Mothers, Poorer Babies," *New York Times,* 9 November 1989, p. 25.
10. William J. Wilson, *The Truly Disadvantaged* (Chicago: University of Chicago Press, 1987), p. 5.
11. Children's Defense Fund, *A Children's Defense Budget* (Washington, DC: Children's Defense Fund, 1986), p. 145.
12. American Public Welfare Association, *Conference Agreement on Welfare Reform* (Washington, DC: American Public Welfare Association, 28 September 1988); Committee on Ways and Means, U.S. Congress, *Background Material and Data on Programs within the Jurisdiction of the Committee on Ways and Means* (Washington, DC: U.S. Government Printing Office, 15 March 1989), p. 590ff.
13. K. Judge and J. Matthews, *Charging for Social Care* (London: Allen & Unwin, 1980).
14. Burton Gummer, *The Politics of Social Administration* (Englewood Cliffs, NJ: Prentice-Hall, 1990).
15. A balanced set of perspective commentaries is found in Brian O'Connell, *American Voluntary Spirit: A Book of Readings* (New York: The Foundation Center, 1983).
16. Harrison Welford and Jane Gallagher, *The Role of the Non-Profit Human Service Organization* (Washington, DC: National Association of Voluntary Health and Social Welfare Organizations, 1987).
17. Michael Brown, ed., *Remaking of the Welfare State* (Philadelphia: Temple University Press, 1988), pp. 232–252.
18. David Stoesz, "Privatization: Reforming the Welfare State," *Journal of Sociology and Social Welfare* 14 (Summer 1987): 3–19.

BIBLIOGRAPHY

American Public Welfare Association. *Conference Agreement on Welfare Reform.* Washington, DC: American Public Welfare Association, 28 September 1988.

Bellah, Robert. *Habits of the Heart: Individualism and Commitment in American Life.* Berkeley, CA: University of California Press, 1985.

Children's Defense Fund. *A Children's Defense Budget.* Washington, DC: Children's Defense Fund, 1986.

Committee on Ways and Means, U.S. Congress. *Background Material and Data on Programs within the Jurisdiction of the Committee on Ways and Means.* Washington, DC: U.S. Government Printing Office, 15 March 1989.

Dobelstein, Andrew W. *Politics, Economics and Public Welfare.* Englewood Cliffs, NJ: Prentice-Hall, 1986.

Gummer, Burton. *The Politics of Social Administration.* Englewood Cliffs, NJ: Prentice-Hall, 1990.
Harris, Louis. "A Vote for an Activist Government." *New York Times,* 9 November 1989.
Judge, K., and J. Matthews. *Charging for Social Care.* London: Allen & Unwin, 1980.
Karger, Howard J., and David Stoesz. *American Social Welfare Policy: A Structural Approach.* White Plains, NY: Longman, 1990.
Katz, Michael. *In the Shadow of the Poor House: A Social History of Welfare in America.* New York: Basic Books, 1986.
Kuczynski, Marguerite and Ronald R. Meek. *Quesnay's Tableau Economique [1784].* London: Macmillan, 1972.
Lampman, Robert J. "The Anti-Poverty Program in Historical Perspective." Lecture presented to the UCLA Faculty Seminar on Poverty, 25 February 1965.
"Poor Mothers, Poorer Babies." *New York Times,* 9 November 1989.
Rivlin, Alice. *Economic Choices, 1984.* Washington, DC: Brookings Institution, 1984.
Wilson, William J. *The Truly Disadvantaged.* Chicago: University of Chicago Press, 1987.

PART **2**

Social Work Roles in the Political Process

Part One dealt extensively with the complexity of social welfare choices. Without a structure for analysis, the student is easily overwhelmed by the multiplicity of factors impinging on such choices. Part Two is intended to provide the student with the opportunity to look, in sequence, at a series of interrelated questions of both substance and process. Its purpose is to establish an intellectual structure for a systematic examination of social problems and of public responses to those problems.

The third chapter of Part One provided a sort of catalog of functional activities in the policy process and demonstrated the cyclical nature of policy choices. Part Two will focus on the social worker's opportunities and responsibilities in four functional stages of choice in the policy process: perception and presentation; formulation and selection; implementation; and evaluation.

CHAPTER **5**

Perception and Presentation of Social Problems

A plausible but incomplete definition of the problem can be more dangerous than a wrong definition. . . . An excellent solution to an apparent problem will not work in practice if it is a solution to a problem that does not exist in fact.

A. W. Steiss and G. A. Daneke

Social psychologists have demonstrated that when a dramatic event is acted out before a class and the students are asked to describe what they saw, the descriptions vary widely. These variations in the descriptions are not random. Neither are they a function of where the students sat in the classroom. Rather, they vary as a consequence of prior social experience, social class, race, and ethnic association, all of which are systematically linked to what we "see." Social events and the delineation of some social events as public problems are a function of social affinities and social conditioning. The definition of a social problem must take into account these social constructions of reality. Not all citizens "see" the same problem. Some even assert that there is no such thing as an objective social reality. Clearly, the very act of problem definition is a political act.

A primary cause of political disagreement is the range of significantly different perceptions of social problems held by various groups in a society. The resolution of political disagreements is ultimately made by public officials, elected or appointed, whose positions are in part a product of the officials' competitive struggle to obtain and retain office.[1] The political system is more than a mechanism for resolving social differences; it is also a mechanism for defining a social problem and selecting the sets of social problems to be addressed by governments and voluntary social agencies.

Anthony Downs in *Economic Theory of Democracy*[2] sets forth a "rational theory of democracy" in which all voters are well informed and act in their rational self-interest. His definition of self-interest includes an expressed desire to be altruistic.

In Downs's axiomatic system citizen groups establish clear priorities and preferences regarding public problems. When all of these preferences are known, officials (and political parties) select a pattern of response that they believe will garner the greatest support for their bids to seek or retain public office. Downs's use of economic modeling was developed from earlier work that focused on the behavior of firms in the marketplace. Retail outlets tend to locate close to one another; where there is a McDonald's so also is there a Burger King. The apparent purpose is to establish outlets so that neither company will gain a location advantage. Political parties follow the same practice. Each party seeks to locate itself where it believes it has gained an advantage and/or blocked the advantage of opposing parties. Voters, being rational, will select the party that best represents their views. The political campaign is a marketplace of ideas in which the voter's preference is the coin of the realm.

For the purpose of illustration let us assume that there is an infinite range of options ranking left to right from the most liberal to the most conservative (see Figure 5.1). A further assumption is that the numbers of voters favoring the various options roughly approximates the traditional bell-shaped curve. In a two-party system both the party of the left and the party of the right would position themselves as near the center of the distribution as historical circumstance would allow. To do otherwise would be to cede locational advantage to the opposition. When issue preference has this unimodal distribution, the two parties appear to be very similar, and those who hold more extreme positions in either direction complain that they have no real choice. Because the two parties hold highly similar positions, it makes little difference which party wins the election.

A number of things are obvious about Downs's assumptions. Voters are seldom well informed, they do not establish clear priorities, nor do they always express a clear desire to be altruistic. Although politicians do take positions with regard to what they think the voters want, politicians do not think of all voters as equal. Political parties in general and individual politicians in particular also have interests other than winning elections. Further, neither voters nor politicians nor party officials are always rational actors. Democratic presidential candidates and Republican congressional candidates seem to be forever locating themselves along some unknown line that reflects something other than a calculus of voter sentiments. This fact helps to explain the dominance of Republican presidential candidates and Democratic congressional

FIGURE 5.1 Downs's Model of Party Competition

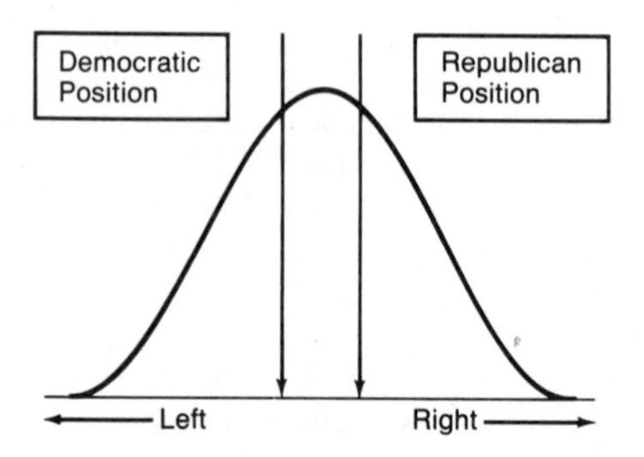

candidates in elections since the late 1960s. With the declining significance of American political parties, individual candidates rather than a party system designate positions to be taken. The result is that positions adopted and presented to the voters appear to be more random than systematic, have a shorter history, and often appear to be guided by public opinion polls.

Both parties and candidates seek to lead or manipulate (depending on one's level of cynicism) the voter. Thus a great deal of campaign time is spent trying to inform or sway public opinion. Candidates and those in political office clearly attempt to persuade voters into accepting one particular view of social reality. Those in office or seeking office also respond to what they think voters want. The relevant question is, does the issue define the candidate or does the candidate have a conscious agenda by which he or she defines the issues? In American politics both occur. Our concern here is how social welfare issues are presented to officials and candidates for officialdom and how these persons respond.

PERCEPTION AND PRESENTATION OF A PROBLEM AS A POLITICAL PROBLEM

Social problems follow an orderly path. The stages are awareness, policy determination, and reform. In the first, some cherished values are understood to be at risk. The policy determination stage occurs when a problem is transformed from a social problem into a political problem. Three central requirements must be met if a problem in the society is to become a political problem.

First, there needs to be a belief that the problem is one that the government can affect. Second, a significant number of citizens must feel sufficiently committed to press different solutions onto government(s). The third requirement is that there must be some institutional arrangements within governmental structures that allow the particular perceptions of an issue to be presented and debated.

CENTRAL PROBLEM DEFINITION: PERCEPTION

Not all things that bother citizens are defined as political problems. Individuals define problems for themselves and devise ways to articulate these problems to others. The interest of the social worker is often focused on the question of why some persons suffer apparent political abuse without visible response from the political system. This problem was discussed earlier in the presentation of the formal neo-elitist model in Chapter 2. Our attention here is on the initial encounter, or nonencounter, between the citizen with a complaint and the political system. For a problem to be perceived as political it must be viewed as originating from some political action or be considered amenable to some action by the government that would alleviate the problem. When there is a perception that some issues are simply not within the legitimate purview of government, this bias deflects the problem away from the public political system. The problem might be deflected into the voluntary sector of the welfare system because of a belief that certain problems are better handled by formal agencies outside of government. It might be deflected to the informal networks of society where problems are resolved by informal interactions without either public or formal agency involvement. Often the problem is deflected into limbo where it lies unresolved.

The bias that generates the deflection might occur because the problem is perceived not to have public substance. Students might be worried that their grades will not be good enough to win entrance to medical school. It is unlikely that they would think a law should be passed requiring the faculty to give them higher grades or admit them over others with higher grades. Readers might also believe that race, gender, or ethnicity are factors involved in the likelihood of medical school admission. In the latter case public discussion might follow. At the very least, an effort might be made to consider the entrance decisions as they relate to these three factors. The elements that cause individuals to see their personal considerations as topics for public decision making are quite complex.

Often the first question for the social worker is how current or potential clients perceive the problems they encounter. This approach focuses attention on the factors that encourage or discourage clients from bringing their problems to the attention of public officials or responsible voluntary agency workers. We are speaking here of something more profound than apathy or a reluctance to seek public help. Rather, it is in the sociological and psychological processes that cause individuals to perceive their problems as part of the political system. In one view, the individual fails to respond to the personal problem as a social one and fails to act within a political system. The neo-elitist model discussed earlier shows how the political system can establish deliberate roadblocks to bringing the problem to public attention when in fact the problem is one of social bias rather than individual fault. Much of the advocacy literature, particularly that concerned with the problems of women and minorities, operates from this assumption of bias. Although much of the literature is written this way, it is not always the case. Thus it is important to start the study of a social problem's political response (or lack of response) by seeking the best explanation of why the problem is included, or excluded, from the agenda of ordinary politics.

A definition of the discomforting issue in political terms does not automatically suggest a clear political response. Few would deny that the homeless condition is a significant social problem demanding action by government and social agencies. Yet it is clear that no two observers seeing a homeless person on the street "see" the same thing. The problem starts with the same ambiguity that characterized the descriptions provided by students in the experiments mentioned at the start of this chapter. How society should act is a value issue, depending on one's view about social obligations. How governments and agencies should act is also a practical issue, depending on one's understanding of the dynamics of this social condition and the effectiveness of alternative public interventions. How society will act is also a political issue, depending on the ways in which the society is organized to make collective choices. Issues are shaped in terms of what we want, the normative or value issue; what we think will best work, the practical issue; and our best guesses about what is obtainable, the issue of political feasibility.

It is clear that normative, technical, and political feasibility questions are not separate from one another. Schattschneider put it correctly when he said, "Antagonists can rarely agree on what the issues are because power is involved in the definition.

He who determines what politics is about runs the country, because the definition of alternatives is the choice of conflicts, and the choice of conflicts allocates power."[3] Gaye Tuchman also makes the same point from a slightly different perspective. She writes, "When the intentions of [variously] situated actors conflict, some have at their disposal more resources than others do to impose their definitions of the situation. Some social actors thus have a greater ability to create, impose and reproduce social meanings—to construct social reality."[4] The public agenda process impacts not only *what we think about events* but also *what events we think about.* The specific focus here is on a conventionalized statement that shapes the central principles of the problem and a nascent suggestion of remedial strategy to correct the condition.

The homeless are a diverse population who share the common characteristic of having no claim on a place of shelter. The central characteristic of policy definition is the articulated or unarticulated belief about the causal path of the problem and how that path is connected to corrective options available to society. With regard to the homeless, we could imagine citizens and their political spokespersons describing and defining the events of the homeless in the following ways:

1. The homeless problem results from the decline in real wages and opportunity for the least-skilled workers at the same time that escalation of rent property and interest costs make affordable housing an impossibility for these persons and their families.
2. The homeless problem is but one manifestation of the simultaneous closing of state mental hospital facilities and the failure to provide a coordinated system of community mental health facilities.
3. Homeless people are not a problem to themselves. They prefer to live that way and are a problem only to others who would prefer not to see them or come into contact with them.
4. The homeless are a symptom of an incomplete and inadequate welfare system that is unable to deal with problems of the alcoholic, the drug addict, and the irresponsible but potentially employable individual.

A comprehensive perspective might suggest that responding to the homeless requires a strategy that is focused on the housing market, community mental health, drug addiction policy, the psychology of the homeless, and a focus on total welfare reform. These formulations are not incompatible with one another. All of them may be true or only some of them may be relevant for today's homeless populations. But most citizens see one of them as the single most appropriate "reality" about the social condition we call "homelessness."

Because public officials have limited resources they cannot do all things at once. Thus the definitions of the problem tend to compete with one another. In social science the effort is often to find ways in which various views of a social condition can complement one another in the search for a better explanation. In the political system, each formulation contains the seeds of problem resolution and each option also alters the distribution of power within the political system. The political conflicts focus on the debates over which option offers the best solution. Beliefs about the problem compete with rather than complement one another.

ACTORS IN THE DEFINITION PROCESS

With regard to most social problems we can normally expect that more than one group will suggest a response to that problem and that these suggestions will change over time. The participants in the process will vary from one social problem to the next. It is possible, however, to make some generalization about the character of the groups involved. Some social problems touch a great number of citizens and are widely discussed in the media. Others touch only a few citizens and information of even the most elemental sort will be hard for the ordinary citizen to come by. The styles of definition and presentation vary accordingly. The content of some social problems evokes intense emotional response while other problems are seen as more technical in character.

The cast of actors in each policy debate will shift from one situation to the next. In major federal legislation the following is a minimal list of the major players:

1. The central bureaucracy of the president; that is, the Office of Management and Budget, the Council of Economic Advisors, and the many formal and informal groups upon whom the incumbent president relies
2. The bureaus of government, which have or will have operative responsibilities for the policy, if and when it is adopted
3. The leadership of Congress
4. The relevant congressional committee members and their staffs
5. Interested private citizens, including, but not limited to
   a. potential beneficiaries—the client group to whom a policy is directed
   b. the entrepreneurs and professional providers of those services
   c. academic specialists in the substantive area
   d. good citizen organizations that reflect various altruistic motives present in society

Because the print and electronic media report the actions of these individuals and groups to the public and to other players in the game, their role as the central communicators of relevant information makes the media, collectively, a primary actor in the process.

THE PLACE OF INDIVIDUAL AND SOCIAL RATIONALITY

Once a problem has been defined, the next step is to evaluate alternative corrective actions. Western conceptions of rationality are structured around the individual decision maker and the maximization of the individual's welfare. When there is competition between sets of beliefs and values of citizens, there is a necessity for some form of either rational or power-based accommodation. It is generally recognized that there can be a rational conflict between an individual's welfare and the social welfare.

Two metaphors are frequently used in the college classroom to illustrate the character of conflict between the two forms of rationality. In "The Prisoner's Dilemma," two accomplices in crime are arrested and held in separate cells. The prosecutor does not have enough evidence to convict either one of the major crime without a confession, but he does have enough to convict each on a minor crime without a confession. The prosecutor tells each prisoner that if he does not get a confession he will try both on the minor crime which carries a certain one-year sentence. If both confess to the serious crime he will recommend a lesser sentence for both. However, if one confesses and the other does not, he will recommend probation for the one confessing and throw the book at the other. The situation for the prisoners is as shown in Figure 5.2.

In the matrix in Figure 5.2, the social optimum, from the perspective of the two prisoners, is for both to stonewall. If they were in communication and trusted one another, this is what they would surely do. But put yourself in the position of prisoner A. When there is no possibility of communication between the prisoners and each has greatest fear of the ten-year sentence, prisoner A would see that he or she gains most by confessing since he or she cannot guess what prisoner B will do. If A confesses and B stonewalls, A goes free, but if A stonewalls while B confesses, A loses ten years. The twist, of course, is that the mirror image situation exists for prisoner B. Thus, if each pursues a narrow rational path of pure self-interest, the result is a double confession and five years for each. This is a socially suboptimal solution from both prisoners' perspectives. The critical point the metaphor makes is that individual rationality may be on a collision course with social rationality.

Some environmentalists propose an alternative framework, "The Parable of the Commons," to show the lack of a parallel between individual and social rationality. In this metaphor, first presented by Gilbert Hardin,[5] a collection of farmers shares a common pasture but each sells individually. For each farmer the benefit of placing one additional animal on the commons is the full value of that animal when sold, yet for each farmer the cost is only in proportion to the number of farmers sharing the commons. As each farmer shares only a portion of the marginal costs and each enjoys the full marginal benefit, each farmer is under pressure to put more animals to pasture. Eventually, of course, the commons is overgrazed and everyone loses. The

FIGURE 5.2 The Prisoners' Dilemma

		Prisoner B	
		Stonewalls	Confesses
Prisoner A	Stonewalls	1 Year Each	10 Years for A 0 Years for B
	Confesses	0 Years for A 10 Years for B	5 Years Each

metaphor suggests that short-term, small individual benefits are likely to result in long-term, major social costs. For each individual the personal costs involved in a clean car exhaust system are large in comparison to the marginal impact of his or her car's exhaust on the community. Presumably, for the community the social benefits of requiring exhaust control is larger than the aggregate of individual costs. Public action is thus required.

The public interest requires a form of reasoning that places social costs and social benefits above individual costs and individual benefits. Making the translation is easier to recommend than to accomplish. There are several critical problems associated with being rational in policy formulation. The very act of being rational is time-consuming. Problems placed for study face three dangers: (1) Social conditions may be transformed drastically by the time the recommendation is ready so that the rational recommendation is no longer relevant; (2) as the parable of the commons suggests, the canons of the social good run counter to the canons of individual or primary group self-interest; and (3) the political appeal of alternative solutions is in no way equal to all it impacts upon.

INDIVIDUAL AND SOCIAL DIMENSIONS OF THE PROBLEM

Most problems have social and individual elements; they are neither entirely exogenous nor entirely endogenous. Nonetheless, the inability to understand the general locus of the problem generates a profound problem for the political system and for the individual. Consider the formulation as it is structured in Figure 5.3.

In the type I error the client may press a claim on the government that is truly a matter of individual responsibility. The client thus deflects his energy and capacity from his or her problem onto a "false" social political condition. In the type II error the individual wrongly assumes personal responsibility for faults that lie within the system. Both errors are harmful to the individual and to society.[6]

FIGURE 5.3 Perceptions of Individual as Social Dimensions of a Problem

		Perception of Problem	
		A Public Problem	A Private Problem
Reality of Problem	A Public Problem	No Error	Type II Error
	A Private Problem	Type I Error	No Error

The "real" nature of any problem is always an unknown as it is a function of time, place, and ideology. As an illustration of this problem, the term *underclass* has been avoided by many social theorists and ridiculed by others because the label itself might encourage a tendency to blame those most affected as causing their own problems. The difficulty in understanding the issues of the interaction between individual responsibility and public programming might yield a type II error. This mistake might have the unintended effect of actually generating the very conditions that programs are structured to correct. On the one hand, there is the tendency to see almost all social problems in individualistic terms (a type I error). On the other hand is the denial of social responsibility when such responsibility exists. With either error there is the danger of closing the search for more effective responses. It is facile to suggest that type II errors are dramatically more numerous when this assertion is used to underestimate the consequences of type I errors. Arguments that have associated ghetto-specific behavior with ingrained cultural characteristics often ignore the interplay among public programs that reinforce individual irresponsibility.[7]

Problem definition requires a very careful reconstruction of the underlying circumstances associated with the situation under investigation. Among the homeless, for example, policies that effectively respond to the condition of those in need because of mental illness might be counterproductive for those trapped by a problem of affordable homes. Among AFDC recipients there appear to be two very distinct populations: those who are experiencing an acute economic condition, and those with chronic social problems. To define the problem properly often requires a movement contrary to the political desire, that is, lumping dissimilar populations together because they share one political circumstance. The difficulties associated with the definition and perception of the problem quickly become entangled with its political presentation.

STYLES OF PROBLEM PRESENTATION

A problem that is perceived and defined in political terms must also be presented in political terms. The political system as an entity functions to ward off new problems. Overcoming this inertia requires an understanding of the historic circumstance that brings the newly perceived problem to the political agenda.

Few problems are new under the sun. How the problem has been dealt with recently and why a new formulation is now being sought are issues that must be addressed. It is important to show why past formulations have been seen as wanting and what new dimensions to the current problem now require policy adjustments. While it is clear that decision makers need to be informed about the history of the problem, the focus is not on formal historical explanations, but rather on an understanding of the historical context of the issue to be presented. Providing this information is the responsibility of the people, agencies, organizations, and interest groups that have a stake in the outcome of the social policy debate.

At a minimum, the following questions need to be addressed:

1. Why are the problems *now* on the political agenda? Certainly there were homeless people before the current efforts focused a public debate about what

should be done for them. Has the issue come to the agenda through the efforts of a spirited activist, such as Mitch Snyder? Has a journalistic event such as the publication of Jonathan Kozol's book *Rachel and Her Children*[8] and the television movie of the same name focused attention on an old but nagging problem? The explanation of *why now* often provides insights into the range of new options that are likely to be considered.

2. What are the precedents for the ideas and values that appear to be shaping this policy debate? The stream of ideas and values of a policy debate are a fundamental dynamic of the debate.
3. Who is now defining the problem and are they different from definers of the immediate past? Who are the participating stakeholders and who are the non-participating stakeholders? The policy investigator needs to take note not only of the likely winners and losers in a policy shift but also of whether they are aware of their positions. Recently, the relatively affluent aged saw themselves as losers in a Medicaid policy shift. They were unmoved by actuarial investigations that identified them as the real winners in the dollars and cents columns and fought successfully to reverse the action. How these individuals perceived the costs and benefits was far more important than the reality of the costs and benefits. As phrased by Robert Merton, "If men define situations as real, they are real in their consequence."[9]

ANALOGOUS SEARCH

It is important for problem presenters to understand how this social problem is both similar and different from comparable problems as they have been encountered and addressed by other governments in other states or in other nations. Too often the analogue is used as an instrument to persuade rather than to identify realistic options. Depending on how one views the proper public role in day care, one uses the Swedish public system or the French privatized system as the basis for analogue. Analogues are often used to advocate a particular position rather than to construct a policy-useful definition of the parameters of the problem.

Although analogue can be misused in political debate, it is often an effective tool in policy formulation. The first task in using analogue well in policy formulation is to note the similarities and differences between the problems. It is particularly important to distinguish these in regard to three aspects of any policy formulation: (1) what is known about the problem, (2) what the unknowns are that make the policy definition difficult, and (3) what the guiding presumptions are that shape the analogue and make it relevant to the new condition.[10]

CONCLUSIONS

Examining the ways policy problems are defined and presented shows that making policy is both an intellectual activity and an institutional process. The decisions that shape public social policy and guide agency practices are influenced by individual and group perceptions, definition, and presentation of what constitutes the problem. The decision of how to act is actually the outcome of the complex interactions of a number of such judgments. The presentation of the problem that prevails circumscribes the options that will be considered and the stakeholders who will be involved. To the extent that realistic dimensions of the problem are not effectively presented, or that images of the problem are not closely connected to objective considerations that dominate discussion, the remainder of the policy process is distorted.[11]

The social worker shaping a definition with a client must do the following:

1. As clinician/behavior changer, the social worker needs to help the client to understand both the social problems and the client's own behavior and options. Care needs to be exercised so that personal problems are not made political, nor political problems personal.
2. As consultant/educator, the social worker needs to help the client assess options in terms of their economic constraints and political feasibility.
3. As researcher/evaluator, the social worker needs to show the client and political community the purely technical aspects of the problem.

While no one social worker can be expected to perform all these functions, they must all be effectively accomplished if the social policy options are to be defined with attention to the technical aspects of the problem, issues of political feasibility, and issues of economic limitations, while remaining in accordance with the prevailing social norms. The definition and redefinition of a social policy issue is central to the political processes of negotiation, conflict, and compromise surrounding social policy choice. In the "win at all costs" view of public elections, the essence of political leadership is the formulation of a social problem so that a winning political coalition can be mobilized behind a particular response. In a "candidate as servant of clients" view of public policy, the essence of effective leadership is the formulation of technical and political constraints so that the goals and aspirations of the client groups are best served. In a third view, political problem solving is seen as an extension of technical problem solving in which the alternate "best solutions" are specified according to the values that they maximize with a mature recognition of the institutional constraints that restrain the range of choices. These three views need not be in conflict with one another. Politics is a process by which conflicts are to be managed, but politics must also allow for the effective presentation of competing values.

NOTES

1. Edward Banfield, "The Use and Limitations of Comprehensive Planning in Massachusetts," cited in Robert Linebery, *American Public Policy* (New York: Harper & Row, 1977), p. 10.
2. Anthony Downs, *Economic Theory of Democracy* (New York: Harper & Row, 1967).
3. E. E. Schattschneider, *The Semisovereign People* (New York: Holt, Rinehart & Winston, 1961), p. 68.
4. Gaye Tuchman, *Making News: A Study in the Construction of Social Reality* (New York: Free Press, 1978). This is also covered in Lynda Peterson, "Manifest Destiny and the Media:

The Hawaiian Revolution of 1893 as Local Occurrence and National Event" (Master's thesis, University of Texas at Austin, 1985), p. 11.
5. Gilbert Hardin, "Tragedy of the Commons," *Science* 162 (13 December 1968): 1243–1248.
6. The reader will see the similarity of this situation and the more familiar problem of hypothesis testing.
7. William J. Wilson, *The Truly Disadvantaged* (Chicago: University of Chicago Press, 1987), p. 14.
8. Jonathan Kozol, *Rachel and Her Children* (New York: Crown Publishing, 1988).
9. Robert K. Merton, "The Self-Fulfilling Prophecy" in *The Pleasures of Sociology,* ed. Lewis A. Coser (New York: New American Library, 1980), p. 29.
10. Richard E. Neustadt and Ernest R. May, *Thinking in Time* (New York: Free Press, 1986).
11. Thomas Schelling, *The Strategy of Conflict* (Cambridge, MA: Harvard University Press, 1960).

BIBLIOGRAPHY

Banfield, Edward. "The Use and Limitations of Comprehensive Planning in Massachusetts." Cited in Robert Linebery. *American Public Policy.* New York: Harper & Row, 1977.
Downs, Anthony. *Economic Theory of Democracy.* New York: Harper & Row, 1967.
Hardin, Gilbert. "Tragedy of the Commons." *Science* 162 (13 December 1968): 1243–1248.
Neustadt, Richard E., and Ernest R. May. *Thinking in Time.* New York: Free Press, 1986.
Peterson, Lynda, "Manifest Destiny and the Media: The Hawaiian Revolution of 1893 as Local Occurrence and National Event." Master's Thesis, University of Texas at Austin, 1985.
Schattscheider, E. E. *The Semisovereign People.* New York: Holt, Rinehart & Winston, 1961.
Schelling, Thomas. *The Strategy of Conflict.* Cambridge, MA: Harvard University Press, 1960.
Steiss, A. W., and G. A. Daneke. *Performance Administration.* Lexington, MA: Lexington Books, 1980.
Tuchman, Gaye. *Making News: A Study in the Construction of Social Reality.* New York: Free Press, 1978.
Wilson, William J. *The Truly Disadvantaged.* Chicago: University of Chicago Press, 1987.

CHAPTER 6

Policy Formulation and Selection

Leaders in a political system try to ensure that whatever governmental means are used to deal with conflict, the decisions arrived at are widely accepted not solely from fear of violence, punishment, or coercion but also from a belief that it is morally right and proper to do so.

Robert A. Dahl

The last chapter examined the diverse origins of beliefs about what government should and should not do about social problems. The chapter also looked at how these ideas were presented within the political system. The focus of attention was on those circumstances that must be met for a policy idea to be placed on the political agenda. The perception of a need for collective action and the capacity to bring this perception to the attention of political leaders were seen as the first requisites for serious policy debate. The focus now shifts to the process of selection. The political process whereby one course of action is selected among the options offered has at least two manifestations, both central to the selection of a particular policy.

The patterns of political disengagement, disagreement, conflict, coalition, and political decision making have different manifestations in each political debate. Ripley and Franklin have demonstrated that various classes of policy debates in the legislature have distinct political styles. This is shown in Table 6.1. Lowi's formulation of domestic policy debate types makes a case for distinct patterns of engagement and agreement within the legislative process.[1]

There are, moreover, distinct phases of the process between the point of political division around distinct ideas and the point of implementation of a new policy. In this chapter attention is directed to these two central stages of policy selection: (1) policy formulation, which refers to those actions that occur as general policy ideas and are translated into specific proposals for public endorsement; and (2) policy legitimation, the processes associated with the selection and sanctioning of specific formulations.

Formal action by legislation is only the most visible way in which particular policies are legitimized. Legitimization may also occur through the system of

TABLE 6.1 Characteristics of Different Policy Types

Domestic Policy Type	Main Feature	Primary Actors	Relationship among Actors	Stability of Relationship	Main Decision Makers	Visibility of Decision
Distributive	Short-run, disaggregated decisions; no losers	Congressional subcommittees and committees; executive bureaus; small interest groups	Logrolling	Stable	Congressional subcommittee or committee	Very low
Regulatory	Application of a general rule; some win, some lose	Full House and Senate; executive agencies; special interest groups (e.g., trade associations)	Competition; bargaining	Unstable	Congress	Moderate
Redistributive	Long-run reallocation of resources among classes; winners and losers clearly defined	President and his appointees; committees and/or Congress; "big" interest groups (e.g., AFL-CIO and U.S. Chamber of Commerce) "liberals and conservatives"	Ideological and class conflict	Stable	Executive	High

SOURCE: Adapted from Randall B. Ripley and Grace Franklin. *Congress, The Bureaucracy and Public Policy* (Homewood, IL: Dorsey, 1976), p. 17.

administrative rule making, which is explored in Chapter 8, and in the court system, which is not reviewed in this text. Legislative authorization legitimates some governmental action. Before those actions can actually occur there must also be an appropriation through the budget process. The legitimization model employed here implies a sequenced series of discrete legislative events with inputs, outputs, and outcomes. As suggested in Chapter 3, this model is based on David Easton's generalized system.[2] In this chapter the effort, for analytic purposes, is to isolate the events in the context of the formulation and selection in the legislative phases of the general process. These events are reviewed in light of specific social worker roles in this part of the policy process.

POLICY CHOICE: FORMULATION

A fundamental political reality is that policymakers are not faced with a given problem but rather with many conceptions of the same problem and many views of the opportunities for intervention. In the previous chapter we recounted the many sources of policy ideas. Attention is now directed to the process of developing such general ideas into proposals for specific public actions. This process is known as policy formulation.

Policy formulation refers to development of the specifics. This is the first of many levels of detailed specifications for how governments should act. The formulation process is similar to but also unlike social planning. The latter is a specific professional task accomplished by individual professionals,[3] while policy formulation is a process involving many actors and institutions.[4] Social policy ideas are general statements of a linkage between a public problem and a social problem. Formulation demands the translation of these broad ideas into specific proposals. Suppose, for example, long-term and persistent unemployment is seen as associated with worker skills rather than with general economic conditions or defects in the labor market system. The general policy idea is that corrective actions in response to the problems of chronic unemployment require programs dealing with a worker's skill levels. The individuals who champion this idea must develop a specific action strategy for a public program to upgrade skills. A Job Corps concept, for example, is one strategy that provides education and training to the hard-core unemployed. Detailing how a Job Corps will function, who it will recruit, how it will select among applicants, the specific forms of training to be provided, and where the centers will be located are all politically sensitive issues that often set off a series of political conflicts. The side issues of detailing may well become more important than the grand issues. A belief in a broad general consensus is often revealed to be empty when the attempt is made to specify the details of the consensus.

Tracing the process of formulation is often difficult. Many times the participants themselves do not recall the sequencing of events that contributed to a policy idea's being packaged in a specific way. Formulation rarely results from a single event; it is much more likely to be accomplished by a group interacting frequently with rival groups. Lawrence Lind's case study of President Carter's failed welfare reform effort is a useful example of the interactions between policy problem experts, academics, and professional administrators on the one side, and the political operators, congressmen, and their staffs on the other.[5]

To understand formulation, one may approach it from either a retrospective or a prospective frame of reference. Retrospectively, one is concerned with recounting the most accurate story of how *that* policy idea was packaged in a particular way. Prospectively, the concern is with how one might formulate a policy idea to ensure the greatest chances of adoption. A retrospective approach should inform a prospective approach. As suggested, the process is iterative and formulation takes place with the aim of legislative selection. The perceived demands of legislative selection structure the process of formulation. Both prospective and retrospective viewpoints require that attention be paid to (1) who the stakeholders and participants are in the formulation process, and (2) what the styles are that they use. Policy formulation concentrates attention on the central belief systems and political styles the various participants bring into the political bargaining process that precedes formal legislative debate.

STAKEHOLDERS AND PARTICIPANTS IN FORMULATION

Many persons inside and outside government are involved in the formulation process. Douglas Cater once suggested the notion of an iron triangle whereby policy is formulated by a close-knit interaction of (1) representatives of one or more interest groups; (2) executive branch representatives, such as assistant secretaries and undersecretaries and their deputies; and (3) congressional subcommittee staffers. Cater noted that the persons in this triad are not fixed in position; this year's undersecretary may be next year's interest group spokesman; last year's congressional staffer may be this year's assistant secretary. The policy formulation drama is like a play with a fixed cast of characters produced by a repertory company of actors who are continually exchanging roles. Cater argued that these units, which he designated *subgovernments,* actually formulate policy options. The intense and long-standing personal interactions among a small number of persons with shifting responsibilities fundamentally shape the nature of the options that will be seriously addressed.[6]

John Gardiner, founder of *Common Cause,* testified before Congress on the operation and the stability of small sets of fixed decision making:

> As everyone in this room knows but few outside Washington understand, questions of public policy . . . are often decided by a trinity consisting of (1) representatives of an outside body, (2) middle level bureaucrats, and (3) selected members of Congress, particularly those concerned with appropriations. In a given field, these people may have collaborated for years. They have a durable alliance that cranks out legislation and appropriations on behalf of their special interests. Participants in such durable alliances do not want the department secretaries strengthened. The outside special interests are particularly resistant to such change. It took them years to dig their particular tunnel into the public vault, and they don't want the vaults moved.[7]

Identifying those involved in policy formulation is of fundamental importance. Cater's triad suggests the dominant presence of interest group representatives, along with legislative and executive branch personnel. Most students would suggest that a list of who is involved in formulation cannot be so general because circumstances of involvement vary from one issue to the next. Understanding the process of formulation demands a knowledge of who is involved, but it also requires knowledge of who is not involved when there is substantive reason to expect that they would be involved.

In the formulation of major and substantive social policies that require legislative endorsement at the federal level, participation of the following groups is expected: (1) the central bureaucracy of the president, the Office of Management and Budget, the Council of Economic Advisors, and the many formal and informal groups upon whom incumbent presidents rely; (2) the bureau of government which has or will have operative responsibilities for the policy if and when it is adopted; (3) the leadership of Congress; (4) the relevant subcommittees and their staffs; and (5) interested private citizens including but not limited to (a) potential beneficiaries, that is, the client group to whom a policy is directed; (b) the professional providers of those benefits; (c) academic specialists in the substantive area; and (6) the media.

Policy innovations that are formally presented to Congress will reflect negotiations, compromises, and the coalition of most of these centers of endorsement. What is unique about social welfare policy is the question of who speaks for whom. If a banking law were up for consideration various kinds of financial institutions would hire their own experts to represent them and to act on their behalf in the formulation process. It is often but not always the case that in a social welfare debate the client group most affected will not have its own hired expert. It is unlikely that a member of Cater's triad will even have a personal acquaintance with a recipient. Social workers will often find themselves in the ambiguous role of being the spokesman for both providers and recipients.

As an illustration of this point, it is instructive to compare child support legislation with old age pensions. A number of groups present themselves as speaking for the dependent children who are the law's intended beneficiaries. The custodial parent (typically mothers), the absent parent (typically fathers), lawyers, social workers, and others will likely come before the relevant congressional subcommittees to present formulations and endorsements that are always couched in terms of what is in the best interest of the children. By way of contrast, when policy changes in this country's old age pension system are under consideration, groups of aged persons speak for themselves and hire and direct their own lobby. The shape of the options presented to subcommittees in child support and old age income security reflect very clearly the views of the participants in the policy formulation process.[8] Congress will not select from a full range of options but will consider only those options that have been effectively formulated and presented for consideration. The skill and expertise with which the policy idea is formulated fundamentally shapes the realistic options before Congress.

The central point for our purpose is to understand policy formulation in terms of both political feasibility and technical rationality. Ultimately, *policy success* results from the formulation process that produces technically rational plans that are politically feasible.

The technical rationality of a formulation is defined in terms of the effectiveness and efficiency of a policy intervention; that is, there is a clear and logically connected relationship between the policy intervention and the desired outcome. It is also important that there be realistic estimates of the potential costs and benefits of all options.

The political feasibility of a formulation refers to the capacity of a formulated policy to attract a majority consensus. We all know of many policies that are technically efficient but politically unfeasible because they contain features unacceptable to a sufficient number of citizens who have the capacity to block the passage of the policies. Particularly important in this regard is the necessity of paying attention to budgeting decisions. Authorization legislation is only part of the battle; it provides public legitimacy for government to act. Permission to spend for that purpose comes only with the appropriations act, which is ordinarily endorsed in separate legislative actions. A political battle at the early stage essentially has four outcomes, shown in Figure 6.1.

A retrospective examination of the origins of policy formulation should reveal the following:

1. The process of including and excluding groups in the formulation stage fundamentally shapes the structure of the policy debate and the resulting formulations presented to the legislature.
2. Conflicts are present within the substantive intent(s) of the policy goals. Those involved in the formulation often do not have clear priorities or goals. Personal ambitions, cross-cutting loyalties, and many other factors influence the options presented.
3. Options and proposals are tainted with a sense of distrust and lack of respect between political decision makers and program experts. The experts dismiss the decision makers as crassly self-centered and the former dismiss the latter as hopelessly naive and unable to see beyond their own field of expertise.

The insight to be gained from the retrospective inquiry into formulation is often the best predictor of policy success or the lack of it.

FIGURE 6.1 Policy Formulation Matrix Outcomes

Feasibility Potential of Political and Benefits Estimations: Close capacity to win majority consensus		Technical Rationality: Close fit between intervention and desired response with realistic costs: High	Low
	High	Policy Success	Program Failure
	Low	Political Failure	Political and Policy Failure

POLICY CHOICE: LEGISLATION

For a policy formulation to clear Congress there are a half dozen times in each chamber when a majority coalition has to be achieved: (1) a favorable report by subcommittee to full committee; (2) a favorable report by committee to the leadership of Congress; (3) docket placement for a vote by full House or Senate; (4) a favorable vote on the floor; (5) a favorable vote for a compromise plan between House and Senate versions; and (6) a final favorable vote in each chamber. The multiple coalitions required place a considerable demand on policy advocates as well as policy analysts. Our government was deliberately designed to make legislation difficult. This was one of the founding fathers' ways of keeping power in the hands of the people. The factors that might make a particular formulation attractive in a needed coalition may be a burden in a second coalition.

The principal means of legitimizing a policy is through legislative action, which requires the creation of successive working majorities. To achieve this end a policy must seek to mobilize support in terms of both the definition of the problem and the best means available for action. The maximization of the one may mean the subordination of the other. Mobilization occurs or fails to occur as a consequence of the interactions among interest groups, political parties, individual legislative leaders, and the media around a specific issue. In order to mobilize support for an action by government, important distinctions among apparently similar problems are made to appear less significant than they really are. The rhetoric required to mobilize support too often becomes the rhetoric that impedes effective compromise.

Faced with multiple demands that are often contradictory, the political system fails to provide all citizens with a sense of legitimacy in the process of choice. What is fair, right, and reasonable to one citizen may not be so for a second citizen. A further complication is that in most close political conflicts each group sees its opponent group as having the unfair advantage. Participants' faith in the fairness of the process of choice is important to the way the formulations are received. Legitimacy can be achieved in two ways. One is the process of interest group mediation; the second involves maximization of net social benefits.

In Robert Reich's description of interest group mediation, legislative leaders and political parties are not oriented toward the substance of policy; they are interested in the process of mediation and compromise. Reich provides a statement of the public manager's responsibility.

> The job of the public manager, according to this vision, was to accommodate—to the extent possible—the various demands placed on government by the competing groups. The public manager was a referee, an intermediary, a skillful practitioner of negotiations and compromise. He was to be accessible to all organized interests while making no independent judgement of the merits of their claims. Since, in this view, the public interest was simply the amalgamation and reconciliation of these claims, the manager succeeded to the extent that the competing groups were placated.[9]

Giandomenico Majone provides his version of the public manager's responsibility as an alternative paradigm:

> To achieve an optimal allocation the policymaker must specify the objective that is sought, lay out alternatives that can accomplish the objective, evaluate the costs and benefits of each alternative, and choose the course of action that maximizes net benefits. An instrumental conception of rationality underlies this maximizing approach to policy analysis; rationality consists of choosing the best means to a given end.[10]

To use a football analogy, the first view makes the legislator the referee, the second makes him or her the offensive coach calling in plays from the outside. The publicly elected legislators see themselves in both roles—as mediators and evaluators of the "best single policy." Only rarely are they aware of the conflicts between the two demands they face.

Congress is the principal legislative body in the United States. It is also the last bastion of amateurism in an increasingly technocratic society. Once rather loosely organized by a flexible system of party domination and a seniority system, it is now seen as the residence of 435 independent political entrepreneurs.[11] With the decline of party control, concurrent with the explosion in the information demands placed on political decision makers, many observers question whether a paradigm of either mediator or evaluator can work. To make itself work, or at least to make it appear as if it works, Congress places a great deal of emphasis on procedural legitimation. The legislative history of fundamental welfare reform has repeatedly been traced to the inability of advocates to produce the critically required coalitions in Congress. The jobs of the policy analyst and the floor leader are to structure the presentation at each point in the legislative process in ways that appear to be both technically "correct" and politically feasible.

Appealing to the actual merits of the proposed legislation is only one way to build the requisite coalition. The strategies of constructing coalitions require appeals to party loyalty, appeals to specialized considerations of each congressman's district, and the use of legislative logrolling. Coalitions are seldom built around a single piece of legislation. Congressman X favors bill A but is indifferent to B and hostile to C. Congressman Y favors bill B, is indifferent to C, and hostile to A. Congressman Z favors C, is indifferent to A, and hostile to B. A complex system of bidding for the indifferent vote goes on. Should Congressman X trade with Z to pass his favorite bill A or should he side with Y to defeat his feared bill C? In either case, Congress overlegislates or underlegislates, which is precisely what citizens complain about.

When citizens see their elected officials yielding to appeals to party loyalty, narrow district considerations, and actions of special interest groups who "buy" the vote, they do not form a favorable impression of Congress or congressmen. The problem is how to express a set of social preferences in a series of single votes. The reality is that it cannot be done. The emergence of the negative political ad as a principal mechanism of campaigning compounds the problem. A frequent comment of members of Congress as they line up to cast a recorded vote is "Watch out for what the opposition can do with a thirty-second ad on this vote."[12]

TABLE 6.2 Presumed Intentions of Advocate and Analyst in Preparing a Policy Statement

Content of Policy Research Statement	Advocate	Analyst
Key Policy Issues	State in symbolic terms	State in substantive terms
Goal of Statement on Stakeholders	Influence them	Inform them
Legislative History	Biased to activate supporters, neutralize opponents and win converts	Explanatory so that stakeholders make a more informed decision
Range of Options Presented	Selective	Encyclopedic

CONTENT OF POLICY STATEMENT

Presenting a policy proposal to a member of the legislative branch of government requires the presenter to have more than a substantive knowledge of the topic and a normative commitment to a particular set of values. If it is to be usable and effective, the statement must address the overall political realities that make its adoption difficult. Of particular importance is that it address the influence and intentions of those who advocate an alternative response.

The legislative choice phase of the position paper needs to address (1) the identification of key policy issues as they are seen on the floor, (2) the identification of the principal stakeholders in the political dispute, (3) the identification of the range of options presented, and (4) the prior legislative history of the issue.

To inform and influence the legislator, the policy statement typically requires a mixture of the advocate's desire for a specific law and the analyst's insight into the complexity of the problem. Table 6.2 describes the roles played by each in producing a statement with the necessary mix.

KEY POLICY ISSUES

Too often the groups seeking to formulate a policy statement assume that the key issues are clear; frequently they are not. By key issues we refer to the perceptions that define the problem and, as we have seen, few problems can be objectively defined. The context of a debate defines its key issues while the key issues in turn define the context of the debate. Many problems fester in society because we cannot agree on a mutually acceptable definition of the key issues. In the world of politics, the key issues are those that the principals in the debate say they are, not those identified in a seminar room. In 1990, the debate over public funding of day care was shaped by beliefs about the propriety of using public funds in connection with church-operated day-care centers. Thus the key issue became the question of church/state relationships rather than substantive issues of family and state responsibilities in a society in which most mothers work outside the home.

Because the identification of key issues is a difficult and never wholly objective task, we need to examine three sources to help us learn how the participants in the policy-making process define these issues. The first of these sources is the written record introduced as testimony before committees and in other hearings, documents and memoranda presented to congressional committees and in other forums. Transcripts of public debates by activists in essentially neutral forums, such as serious television talk shows and the opinion-editorial pages of major newspapers, should also be examined.

Media accounts of the debates, events, and actions related to the legislative discussion provide a second source of information on key issues. Written participant/observer accounts of the same critical events are a less common but effective supplement to media reports.

The third source of insight into the key issues is direct interviews with the stakeholders and participants themselves. Interviewing those most active in the debate, particularly while the debate is in progress, is difficult. The keys to the policy are also instruments of negotiation; thus there may be a difference between what participants *say* the critical key problem is and what they *believe* the critical key problem is. Those who are in the trenches doing the work of transforming ideas into actions do not represent the broad panoply of beliefs about a topic, but their beliefs and values both shape and are shaped by the ongoing political debate.

No one source, be it primary records, media and observer accounts, or participant interviews, is intrinsically more valid and/or more reliable than any other. Each source of policy information is biased in its own way. The advantages and disadvantages of each are covered in a useful commentary on the construction of case studies by Harry Eckstein.[13]

KEY LEGISLATIVE PLAYERS

The dimensions of the political debate are shaped by those who take part and those who choose not to take part. For the study of a particular issue, one starts with the media's identification of the actors in a political dispute. To this list others are added as the first-round nominees are interviewed and the primary and secondary written records are examined. The identification of participants and stakeholders is not the same thing. Participants are uncovered as one watches the policy drama unfold, and in the manner of the Japanese play *Rashomon,* their biases are uncovered as the drama progresses. Some participants will try to hide their involvement while others will dramatize and inflate theirs. Good investigative skills and a relentless search for collaborative evidence are required to track and know the degree to which various individuals are involved and the extent of their investment in the resolution of the debate.

Identifying stakeholders is not so much a matter of collecting empirical evidence as it is evaluating the logical implications of the manifest and latent consequences of the policy under consideration.

RANGE OF OPTIONS AND THE VALUES THEY MAXIMIZE

In any policy study one finds a Gordian knot of values, beliefs, perceptions, and strategies. Participants in an issue typically define the issue in ways that specify a solution or pick a solution and find a problem to fit. Maggiotto and Bowman examined legislators and their beliefs about air pollution.[14] Two camps emerged: those concerned first with economic costs and those concerned first with environmental hazards. The first group resisted governmental regulation while the second saw governmental regulation as the first imperative. It is clear that with zero production there would be zero pollution. Similarly, there would also be no jobs. The political question is the degree to which the environment will be sacrificed for jobs. With a child safety issue one may ask how many children will be placed at risk in order to preserve the sanctity of the family from governmental regulation.

Any problem is on the political agenda because at this point a politically acceptable trade-off has not been determined. There are those among us who would have U.S. military forces reenter Vietnam even now. These individuals, however, are politically insignificant at this time and the issue is not on the political agenda. Not long ago those who favored public restriction of abortion on demand felt that their political cause was hopeless, but in recent years their position has gained strength. Understanding the dimensions of any political debate requires one to grasp the interrelation of the various structures, beliefs, and institutional factors that propel or retard the proposition that a particular position is politically feasible.

PRIOR LEGISLATIVE HISTORY

Few legislative issues are new to the political scene. An interesting aspect of position papers on both sides of most questions is that both sets of advocates would have their readers believe that their value propositions are the more long-standing and prevailing ones.[15] The legislative history of any issue is presented to provide an informative and influential historical perspective to the dimensions of the present debate. The author of the history may wish his story to serve as a strategic guide to advocates on one or the other side, as an instrument of persuasion, or as a professional commentary on the personal and institutional forces involved in this form of policy debate.

The specific items to be included in a legislative history will vary from topic to topic, depending principally on the author's intent. There are, however, a few basic questions which are common to most legislative histories:

1. What were the specific forces and events that placed this legislative initiative on the calendar at this time?
2. What are the manifest and latent intents of each legislative proposal?
3. Which constituent groups and which legislators in what legislative positions will play a significant role in the disposition of this legislative debate?
4. How are consensual majorities to be created or dissolved in the views of the major players on each side of the legislative aisle?

These are the traditional "who, what, and how" questions of legislative dispute resolution. The principal source of details about what happened and when to previous legislative efforts is found in the *U.S. Code Congressional and Administrative News* (USCCAN). This publication is considered an accurate source of content of current and recent law. It is much more objective than the pamphlets and other publications of participants in the debate. It is indexed by subject and available online, which means it is accessible in both print and electronic forms. USCCAN provides a brief summary of congressional actions that led to the present law. It offers a section-by-section summary of the law itself and details of the actions of committees and subcommittees. It also provides a reference to the House or Senate hearings and to reports issued during the legislative debate.

For legislation in progress the principal source is the *CCH Congressional Index.* This publication provides an indexed source of current efforts to change the laws. Published weekly, it provides a list of bills and resolutions introduced as well as information on companion bills and committee actions. Companion bills are created when nearly identical legislation is introduced into each house separately. Another useful source is the *Congressional Quarterly Weekly Report* (CQ), published weekly by Congressional Quarterly, Incorporated. It is a summary of the weekly activity of Congress. An indexed and online quarterly and annual version is available in the government documents sections of most major libraries. CQ, USCCAN and *Congressional Index,* used in conjunction with major media coverage in the *New York Times* and the *Washington Post,* are major sources of what has happened and who the major players have been.

CONCLUSIONS

Legislative authorization is the core of the policy cycle. Understanding what has happened and what can happen is crucial to influencing the process and its outcomes. At the same time legislation should conform to the demands of the logical conditions for rationality and the normative conditions for democratic rule. Often these demands are in conflict with one another. The normative conditions of democratic rule appear arbitrary when real-world conditions systematically prevent some citizens from full participation in the legislative process. Realistic political constraint is as important as technical substance; one cannot be sacrificed for the other. The intent of developing a useful legislative statement is to understand the constraints, both technical and political, involved in the pursuit of social welfare policy.

NOTES

1. T. A. Lowi, "Four Systems of Policy, Politics and Choice," *Public Administration Review* 32 (1972).
2. David Easton, *A Systems Analysis of Political Life* (New York: Wiley, 1965).
3. Herbert J. Gans, "Regional and Urban Planning," in *Encyclopedia of Social Science,* vol. 12, eds. Neil Gilbert and Harry Specht (New York: Macmillan, 1968), p. 129.

4. Charles O. Jones, *An Introduction to the Study of Public Policy* (Monterey, CA: Brooks Cole, 1984), p. 77.
5. Lawrence Lind, *The President as Policymaker* (Philadelphia, PA: Temple, 1983).
6. Douglas Cater, *Power in Washington* (New York: Random House, 1964).
7. Shafritz, *Dorsey Dictionary of American Governments and Politics* (Chicago: Dorsey, 1988), pp. 148–149.
8. Joseph Heffernan, "New Zealand's Liable Parent Contribution Scheme" (Honolulu, HI: East West Center, March 1986).
9. Robert B. Reich, "Policy Making in a Democracy," in *The Power of Public Ideas,* ed. Robert B. Reich (Cambridge, MA: Ballinger, 1988), p. 129.
10. Giandomenico Majone, "Policy Analysis and Public Deliberation," in *The Power of Public Ideas,* ed. Robert B. Reich (Cambridge, MA: Ballinger, 1988), p. 157.
11. Hedrick Smith, *The Power Game: How Washington Works* (New York: Random House, 1988).
12. "Campaigns and the Congressman's Vote," *New York Times,* 18–22 March 1990.
13. Harry Eckstein, "Case Study and Theory in Political Science," in *Strategies of Inquiry,* eds. Fred Greenstein and Nelson Polsby (Reading, MA: Addison-Wesley, 1975), pp. 79–132.
14. M. A. Maggiotto and A. Bowman, "Policy Orientations and Environmental Legislation," *Environment and Behavior* 14, no. 2 (1982): 155–170.
15. Kristin Luker, *Abortion and the Politics of Motherhood* (Berkeley: University of California Press, 1984), chap. 2.

BIBLIOGRAPHY

Broder, David. *The Party's Over: The Failure of Politics in America.* New York: Harper & Row, 1972.

Dahl, Robert A. *Modern Political Analysis.* Englewood Cliffs, NJ: Prentice-Hall, 1976.

Easton, David. *A Systems Analysis of Political Life.* New York: Wiley, 1965.

Eckstein, Harry. "Case Study and Theory in Political Science." In *Strategies of Inquiry,* eds. Fred Greenstein and Nelson Polsby. Reading, MA: Addison-Wesley, 1975.

Gans, Herbert J. "Regional and Urban Planning." In *Encyclopedia of Social Science,* vol. 12. New York: Macmillan, 1968.

Luker, Kristin. *Abortion and the Politics of Motherhood.* Berkeley: University of California Press, 1984.

Maggiotto, M. A., and A. Bowman. "Policy Orientations and Environmental Legislation." *Environment and Behavior* 14, no. 2 (1982): 155–170.

Majone, Giandomenico. "Policy Analysis and Public Deliberation." In *The Power of Public Ideas,* ed. Robert B. Reich. Cambridge, MA: Ballinger, 1988.

Reich, Robert B. "Policy Making in a Democracy." In *The Power of Public Ideas,* ed. Robert B. Reich. Cambridge, MA: Ballinger, 1988.

Starling, Grover. *The Politics and Economics of Public Policy: An Introductory Analysis with Cases.* Homewood, IL: Dorsey Press, 1979.

CHAPTER 7

Implementation

There are in all governmental systems two primary or ultimate functions of government, viz. the expression of the will of the state and the execution of that will.
Frank J. Godnow

The focus of this chapter is on the implementation perspective of social workers who are required to play various parts in the social policy process. Implementation is the activity of actually carrying out the basic policy decision that has been specified in statute. It begins with the law itself and continues until the objectives of the law have been achieved or until the program is abandoned, terminated, or transformed by a new law. The traditional thought is that the policy is made by legislative actions and that administrators simply follow the guidelines set forth in statute. This perception neglects the view of policy as a continuous and iterative process. In the "civics ideal" a law clearly identifies the problem to be acted upon, stipulates with precision the objectives to be pursued, and authorizes specific procedures with which to accomplish these objectives. In most cases this view does not reflect the reality of the administrative world.

Implementation is a particularly elusive concept; it is not the same thing as impact. A program may be fully implemented yet effect few of its intended impacts, or it may have unintended impacts that cancel the expected benefits of the program. However well intended, the expected impacts may not have been logically connected to the means specified in the law. A number of states introduced legislation that required high school athletes to maintain a C average as a condition of interscholastic athletic eligibility. According to committee testimony given when the laws were under consideration, the intent was to motivate high school youth, particularly minority youth, to place more emphasis on their academic pursuits. Early research indicates that the program was implemented as intended. The widespread predictions that strategies would be found to evade the law did not materialize. The evidence on the presumed impact on academic achievement is more problematic. One thing was clear: The number of

		Consequence	
		Favorable	**Unfavorable**
Impact	Law Implemented as Intended	+ +	+ −
	Law Perverted by Implementation Phases	− +	− −

FIGURE 7.1 Impacts and Consequences of Implementation Stream

male minority students who left high school before graduation increased after the program was implemented, and many gave as their reason ineligibility for high school athletics. Another difficulty is that a law may be fully implemented and have its stated impact but that impact may be abhorrent. A case in point is that of anti-Semitic laws in Nazi Germany. Because a law may have intended as well as unintended consequences (see Figure 7.1) and either consequence must be normatively judged, measures of policy impact need to be clearly specified.

In this chapter our intent is to look at implementation as it relates to social work practice and thus to focus on three subphases of implementation: interpretation, organization, and adaptation. Before doing this it is useful to review briefly the basic literature of implementation from political science studies. These forms of inquiry include but are not limited to (1) the general analytic and descriptive literature, further subdivided into that reflecting the management perspective and that which focuses on administrative behavior; (2) case studies of the implementation process; and (3) the normative literature.

GENERAL DESCRIPTIVE AND ANALYTIC LITERATURE

The first body of literature is the descriptive and analytic literature designed to provide a theory of implementation behavior within public organizations.[1] As Clarence Stone has demonstrated, two conflicting paradigms have guided the study of implementation.[2] In contemporary investigation both paradigms are incorporated. In one, the classical paradigm of management predominates and implementation is treated as a technical problem where principals of managerial control and administrative efficiency dominate the discussions. This focus can be traced back to Woodrow Wilson's famous book, *Congressional Government,*[3] which built a wall between the study of politics and the study of administration. The second and more recent paradigm is derived from political sociology and finds administrative behavior and political behavior to be part of an iterative process. Both streams of literature have been adapted to the social work environment.[4]

PERSPECTIVE FROM THE SCHOOLS OF MANAGEMENT

Traditionally the first literature stream has been organized around specific tasks associated with the administrative process. In 1937, Luther Gulick coined an acronym, POSDCORB, in order to provide a descriptive framework for the administrative functions of the public manager.[5] The acronym stands for the following administrative tasks: planning, organizing, staffing, directing, coordinating, reporting, and budgeting.

To understand the process of policy implementation one needs to examine how each of these administrative tasks is conducted vis-à-vis the policy under investigation.

> *Planning*—How have the broad outlines of the tasks been identified and linked to the agency's resource requirements?
>
> *Organizing*—What is the formal structure of agency authority established for the performance of the needed tasks?
>
> *Staffing*—How are the personnel activities, recruitment, training, staff retention, and so forth adjusted so that people in the jobs are qualified to perform their tasks?
>
> *Directing*—What are the procedures for providing clear general and specific guidelines to staff as they perform their assigned functions?
>
> *Coordinating*—How have the various interrelated tasks been brought together so that the enterprise works?
>
> *Reporting*—What mechanisms are in place so that those who are in the line report their accomplishments (and failures) to their immediate supervisors?
>
> *Budgeting*—What are the specific tasks of fiscal planning, accounting, and control of funds within the implementing agency?

Any effort to understand the implementation of a policy requires integration of the findings and insight into the disparate administrative functions required to achieve effective implementation. Collectively these data provide a reasonable overview of what occurs and explains the way the factors interact to assure or impede successful implementation. The analytical literature tends to focus on the "pathology of implementation"; that is, the literature gives emphasis to the potential obstacles to program implementation. "Waste! Overlap! Duplication! Red Tape!" are some of the words often heard in the cacophony of voices raised in criticism of public performance. The professional analytic literature attempts neither to decry nor to deny public organization failure. It seeks to provide an understanding of past social policy failure and to use that understanding to improve future performance.

Despite its manifest expression of interest in dealing with administration as a whole, most of the early descriptive literature became what Bertram Gross called "the architectonics" of formal organizations.[6] The early literature became the subject of abuse and ridicule. The principles of administrative behavior were denounced as empty proverbs "not unlike those used by a Ubangi medicine man to discuss disease."[7]

PERSPECTIVE FROM POLITICAL SOCIOLOGY

The second paradigm focuses on the actual behavior of participants in the administrative process. This paradigm begins with the assumption that there are clear limits to what can be accomplished by the manipulation of structures and procedures. At base, human behavior and attitudes must be influenced if policies are to be implemented. Two factors dominate the behavior of individuals in organizations. One is their resistance to change. The second is their desire to find satisfying rather than optimal solutions.[8] As information is never perfect and timely and all of the available alternatives are not listed and considered because of costs and time constraints, the process stops when a satisfactory means, as contrasted to an optimal means, of achieving a desired end is presented. The search is for something that looks like it will work rather than for the very best possible solution.

In recent years the focus has shifted again to the notion that the alternatives in an organization are seldom as stark as acceptance or resistance, nor solutions as clear as optimal or satisfying. We can generalize knowledge about the behavior of those implementing the policies and note the sources of resistance to change and the procedures adopted by management to counter this tendency. We can observe the limits of the search for the best way to put programs into effect by recognizing both the ideal of a technically efficient management of public programs and the pragmatic reality.

CASE STUDIES OF IMPLEMENTATION

In the case study approach, evaluation of the implementation process of particular laws focuses on those factors that affect the achievement of specific statutory objectives. Donald Van Meter and Carl Van Horn provide a summary of many such efforts and establish their own systems model that identifies seven critical factors to explain the success or failure of implementation efforts. These are the following:

1. The precision of policy standards and sufficient resources to meet the standard
2. Support for (and opposition to) the policy in its immediate political environment
3. Economic and social conditions
4. Structural characteristics of the implementing agency
5. Communication standards within the implementing agency
6. Policy dispositions of implementing officials
7. Incentive of target populations to comply with policy decisions[9]

Sophisticated observers recognize that not all the variables are of equal relevance in each case. They do provide a set of clues as to what to look for in the pursuit of a useful explanation of how a law was translated into practice. The general tendency in the literature of political science is to explain successful implementation by negative example. Thus in their classic study of the administrative implementation of economic development programs in the 1970s Pressman and Wildavsky point to factors that hampered administration: (1) incompatibility of goals between the implementing

TABLE 7.1 The 48 Contiguous States' AFDC Benefit Schedules and States' Speed of Compliance

	Slow States	Fast States	Other States	All States
Mean Benefit	$417	$266	$284	$296
N	6	13	331	51*

P < .01 *Includes Washington, D.C.
SOURCE: J. Heffernan, "Implementing the Omnibus Reconciliation Act of 1981," paper presented at a conference of the Association of Policy Analysts and Policy Administrators, Minneapolis, November 1983.

agency and funding authorities, (2) distinct differences in priorities between the implementing agency and funding authorities, (3) prestige and other power conflicts between agencies that were expected to cooperate, and (4) procedural impediments that prevented timely cooperation.[10]

The overriding conclusion of the various studies of administration is that a clear connection between stated legislative intent and formal action is a function of the number of agencies involved, the number of actors involved, and the degree of discretion that is required at the street level.[11] As one example of this, in 1981 the Reagan administration maneuvered Congress into passing legislation that restricted AFDC eligibility. The states were required to alter their administrative rules to comply with new federal regulations. States demonstrated their compliance by placing new requirements into their own procedures at very different rates. Thirteen states were in compliance within sixty days; six states were not in compliance as late as eighteen months later. A survey of the speed of compliance showed a clear association between the speed with which states adopted the more restrictive procedure and their past level of generosity (see Table 7.1).

THE NORMATIVE LITERATURE

There is no single unifying metaphor that permeates the implementation literature unless it is E. E. Schattschneider's metaphor of politics as a gigantic and neverending game of power, but a curious game in which the cheers and boos of the spectators have an impact on the score.[12] As a game of power is played out first in Congress then in the halls of the bureaucracy, we need some standard of accomplishment by which we can judge the action.

One specific set of normative standards that is particularly useful in our context is that the process be judged by one of three imperatives: (1) respect for the legal intent of the instrument, (2) the civil servants' concern for rationality, and (3) the general expectation that the actions be in accordance with a consensus between the implementing agency and its immediate external political environment.

Clearly, implementation is something that is more easily described than judged. The establishment of any standard of implementation reveals as much about the evaluator as it does about the evaluation process. We now shift our attention to the social workers' roles in the overall process of implementation.

A PROCESS ORIENTATION

The central intention of this chapter is to explicate the process of implementation and to examine the multiple products or stages of implementation. Each subphase of the implementation phase produces a particular observable product. This observable product becomes the new independent variable, the next subphase of the implementation game. The social worker, when he or she is conducting an investigation of a particular policy, will want to know what the products of the implementation process are and will want also to understand the process of each subphase. These are shown in Figure 7.2.

Passage of a law is the obvious starting point. The law is then given detailed qualification in the form of an administrative rule, which in a national case is a specific formal statement found in the *Federal Register*. Between laws and rules lies a process of *interpretation*. The administrative rule in its turn requires the establishment or modification of a particular agency structure to create formal standard operating procedures (SOPs) to enforce the rule or deliver the services and benefits of the law as interpreted by the administrative rule. The transformation from rule to agency SOP is the process of *organization and planning*. Formal agency practice has to be put into place by a worker in the field. This involves a process of *adaptation*. It is by the actual pattern of service delivery that the client receives a benefit or is asked or forced to comply with a rule. This function is interpreted in a unique setting that Michael Lipski calls the street-level bureaucracy.[13] To complete the process citizen reaction gives rise to *policy evaluation*, resulting in a desire to maintain, transform, or abolish the law. The steps of implementation appear in Table 7.2 showing how each element, beginning as an independent variable, is transformed through the applicable process into a dependent variable.

FIGURE 7.2 Products and Processes of the Implementation Subphases

Product: The Law as Passed by Congress

Process: Interpretation

Product: The Administrative Rule as Entered in the *Federal Register*

Process: Organization and Planning

Product: Formal Agency Structure and Procedures

Process: Adaptation

Product: Specific Actions Taken with Regard to Specific Clients

TABLE 7.2 Policy Steps of Implementation as Independent and Dependent Variables

Phase	Start	Process	End Product
	Independent Variable		***Dependent Variable***
One	Law	*Interpretation*	Administrative Rule
Two	Administrative Rule	*Organization & Planning*	Formal Agency Structure & Procedures
Three	Formal Agency	*Adaptation*	Street-level Action
Four	Street-level Action	*Evaluation*	Demand for New Law

INTERPRETING LAWS

Few laws have self-evident intents. The social worker's first task when evaluating a law is to understand how the law has been interpreted; the second task is to investigate that interpretation process. The first requirement of consistent implementation is that the administrators know what they are supposed to do. Implementation directives need clarity throughout the chain of command. Within the federal government, interpretation is formalized with an entry of the law into the *Federal Register.* Agencies differ in the sequencing of their activities as an administrative rule is prepared for entry into the *Register.* Most often a two-stage process occurs in which a proposed regulation is written, followed by a period of time for comment by interested parties. The amount of time and the methods for soliciting public comment are spelled out in the proposed administrative rule. After this period has passed and modifications are accepted, the administrative rule acquires the force of law. Statutes generally contain language such as, ". . . according to regulations that the Secretary shall provide." This wording means that the cabinet secretary will sign regulations that have been developed at the subcabinet level. The first task is to isolate the rule itself.

Rules that have been formulated for particular laws are listed in the *Code of Federal Regulations* which has a print index and is available online (*online* means that the index is available on an electronic disk as well as in print form). When an investigator must examine many laws, electronic retrieval makes the search for the rules associated with a specific law much quicker and easier.

The investigator should begin the search for the appropriate administrative rule by consulting *The Federal Register: What It Is and How to Use It: A Guide for the User of the Federal Register—Code of Federal Regulations System.*[14] From this work he or she will proceed to the *Code of Federal Regulations*[15] itself. This basic primary source publishes the general and permanent orders of the president, the executive departments, and other federal agencies. It is organized into fifty titles that represent broad subject areas. Proposed rulings and regulations are published daily, except Sundays and Mondays, in the *Federal Register.*[16]

Obtaining the needed information is made easier by using the *CIS Federal Register Index* and the *CIS Federal Register Abstracts.*[17] As their names imply, these two volumes are an index and abstracting service that has been provided commercially since the mid-1980s. Most public document units of major libraries have available electronic online searches that can greatly facilitate an investigator's task.

Gaining access to the details of a regulation is essential to understanding implementation. The process of obtaining corresponding state regulations clearly varies from state to state. To understand these procedures the student should consult *Information Sources of Political Science.*[18] Using any or all of these sources is tricky and the student would do well to ask for help at the reference desk of the public documents section of a university library, a state documents library, or a law library. The basic tenet known to all professional social workers—that they are most helpful to clients when they ask well-focused questions—applies here. Before consulting the professional librarian the student is advised to read the initial chapter of *Congressional Publications and Proceedings.*[19]

UNDERSTANDING INTERPRETATION

The library search for the administrative rule informs the investigator about what happened but may well leave him or her bemused as to how it happened. The administrative rule confers specific benefits on and extracts specific costs from the stakeholders in the policy process. During the legislative phase there was a premium on generality of language. Every time a phrase was stated precisely a shaky legislative coalition was threatened. In the interpretive phase the premium is on *specificity.* Those who interpret the law from an administrative perspective have very different demands placed on them from the demands on those who write the law.

It is important to understand that these actors in the interpretive phase are not the same as the actors in the legislative phase. An important aspect of the implementation phase is that the actors receive considerably less media attention. Studying the results of the interpretive process often produces surprising findings. The rules, as entered into the *Federal Register,* are often only distant cousins of the law as shaped in the legislative phase. In the recent housing scandal at Housing and Urban Development during the Reagan administration everything that was done, so far as we now know, was perfectly legal and in strict accordance with administrative rules. The problem was that those who wrote the rules were also the same persons who distributed vast benefits to developers for the construction of low-cost homes. Secretary Samuel Pierce and his associates were charged with using ambiguity and designing loopholes in the federal regulations to benefit intermediaries rather than the low-income recipients intended to be aided by the housing legislation. One need not focus only on laws that have been selfishly interpreted to encounter examples of this kind of manipulation of interpretation. Many vague laws have been creatively interpreted to provide more benefits to people in need.

The critical point of the investigation is to supplement formal interpretation with a comprehension of the process that resulted in the interpretation. The general research rules for the preparation of good ethnographic/administrative investigations are explored in later chapters. By its nature a study of an administrative rule is a single-cell study. The critical questions of the interpretive phase are these:

1. Who were the individual actors and what organizations were represented in the development of the proposed rules?
2. What efforts were made to expand or constrict this list of participants?
3. What are the expressed motivations of the various actors and what are their latent motivations as far as can be determined by the evidence?
4. What do we know about the styles of operation of each set of actors and how did the various styles interact in this case?

Because implementation itself is such a fuzzy concept and because interpretation in particular occurs under shrouded circumstances, one cannot expect too much from understanding how a rule was made. Those who know the most have little incentive to share their secret. The investigators must remember they are operating on the fringes of social science research methodology. The purpose is to find satisfying practical understanding rather than optimal theoretical understanding. Thus goal-oriented adaptation, compromise, and improvisation are essential in the production of useful results in this context.

ORGANIZATION AND PLANNING

The administrative rule identifies a product or service that is the responsibility of some specific public agency. To plan for the delivery of that product or service is the aim of implementation planning. However, public agencies have a life and vitality of their own that dominate the planning process. A retail outlet sells a product but the purpose of the retail outlet is not the sale but the profit for the owners of the firm. The outlet serves many other purposes, such as providing employment to its workers and a service to its clients; if it is a bookstore or some other cultural outlet, it may alter the culture of its community. Nonetheless, its primary purpose is clear: to make a profit for its owners. If it fails at that it ceases to exist. The retail planner has an unambiguous standard; the public planner faces a more complex set of goals.

Administrative planners may or may not have played an active role in the development of the administrative rule. Some rules are in accordance with the long traditions of an agency and are not controversial within the agency or the public at large. Others are new and definitely controversial. In almost all cases the budget authority is too small for the authorized task. The implementation planners must take all these factors into consideration as they develop a specific structure and set of operating procedures by which the rule will be put into practice.

All governmental agencies face the task of establishing the credibility of their decision-making process, incorporating widely different views of what they are expected to do and establishing at least a "permissive consensus" for their strategies of implementation. Ideally, a "supportive consensus" is the goal of implementation planners. Certainly the planners seek a structure and procedure that does not generate hostility from the community that is to be served.

Locating a mode of practice for the agency requires knowing and confronting community values (see Figure 7.3). If there is a single unimodal public consensus, the agency seeks to locate its practice in the center of that consensus. If the consensus

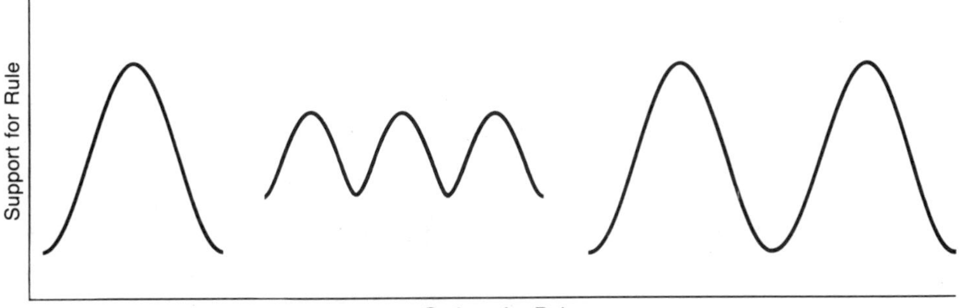

FIGURE 7.3 Public Support for Agency Plans

breaks down and the agency has a set of interested public groups, each with widely distinct views as to how it should act, then the problem is more difficult. In the case where there are two interested but highly diverse publics competing, implementation planning becomes the most difficult.

There is rarely one best agency plan, but most plans are developed with a focus on four critical and interacting factors:

1. Resources Available—This refers not only to the budget itself but also to the availability of the resources within the agency and community.
2. Duration—The amount of planning is dependent in part on the real time available. Clearly, one does not start planning for a natural disaster after hearing it predicted on the daily newscast.
3. Technical Complexity—This factor addresses how technically and politically complex the rule is to be.
4. Amount of Frontline-level Discretion Required—The clearly expressed public wish is that all clients with similar circumstances be treated the same and clients with different problems be treated differently. The rules of operation should be sufficiently precise to cover the first and sufficiently flexible to allow for the second.

With the administrative rule in place organizations must develop staffs, budgets, structures, and sets of standard operating procedures to respond to the unique problem of a particular client for whom the general policy was developed. When a client walks into the agency, the agency must follow a pattern. Certain forms are filled out, certain personnel will interview the client and verify the information provided, and specific published rules will be used to determine the client's eligibility for the service or benefit. Knowing the implementation plan means knowing just how all these things transpire.

UNDERSTANDING IMPLEMENTATION PLANNING

To plan for the delivery of a social service one must understand the vast network of choices that have to be made. In the absence of a profit motive the resolution of ambiguity often falls on the planner. A specific social agency with a newly acquired responsibility or a new agency being created to implement an administrative rule must have a staff, a procedure, and a set of clients to be served. The implementation plan must consider a whole series of assessments, shown in Figure 7.4. The technical rational perspective assumes that the planning process can be judged by the optimal fit between the rule and the procedure. This view, however, is too limiting. At least ten adjustments need to be made, as shown in Figure 7.4. A rule outlining a procedure must fit client expectation and circumstance as well as agency and staff needs.

Each choice has an impact on every other choice so that the plan must be made without a dominating mandate. The implementation plan looks sequentially at the best fit between each set of demands. As an illustration, if one were to look at the relationship between staff and procedure the specific focus would, at a minimum, be on (1) determining staffing requirements established by the procedure; (2) determining the abilities, knowledge, and skills essential for the performance of each procedure; and (3) setting staff assignments so that staff are neither underutilized nor expected to perform at a level beyond their abilities. This illustration assumes that procedure dictates staff, but sometimes the reality is that procedures have to be altered because the staff is fixed.

Implementation choices do not reflect the preference of any one group or individual but are the consequence of compromise, coalition, and competition. The plan for implementation must reflect rather than deny this reality. The investigator seeking to understand the choices made to implement a social program will need to focus attention on specific decisions. The explanatory power of an implementation model is determined by its ability to show the dynamic interaction among distinct players, each of whom is examining a different part of the same play.[20]

Policy is always in process. Its immediate impact is felt by a citizen when his or her case is acted on uniquely. This immediacy of impact leads some writers to suggest that "real" social welfare policy is determined by how caseworkers, eligibility workers, receptionists, and others respond to particular clients.[21] Granted, all aspects of the policy process are important, but some aspects are more easily observable than others. Traditional political science literature has tended to denigrate the importance of decision making in policy at the bottom of the organizational ladder.[22] At the other side of the controversy, some of the sociological literature of organization tends to

FIGURE 7.4 Choices of the Social Agency Planner

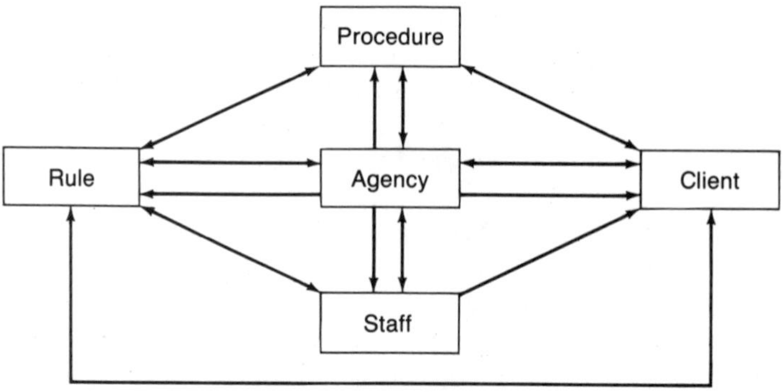

Procedure

Rule Agency Client

Staff

focus too exclusively on this level of bureaucratic behavior.[23] Just as the formal law establishes constraints on how the administrative rule is written, so too the agency's operation manuals constrain the worker in the field. Yet the worker in the field is not an automaton acting without emotion or failing to engage the emotions of the clients.

It is our belief that policy cannot be understood without a focus on how the street-level worker operates. Borrowing from Michael Lipski, the street-level worker is defined as the bureaucrat (1) whose primary job responsibility is to be in direct contact with clients, and (2) who is governed in these contacts by the rules of the agency but is also judged by the manner in which he or she exercises on-the-spot discretion. One component of street-level discretion is that which is formally established in the rules and regulations of the agency. Perhaps a more important component is the general demeanor of the social worker toward the client.

The investigator must understand both formal discretion and street-level discretion to comprehend the policy fully. Four variables appear to be critical from an organizational perspective for understanding the fit between "policy objective" and street-level worker response: (1) the adequacy of the resources for the task assigned (to what extent is the street-level worker expected to perform bureaucratic triage?), (2) the level of physical and psychological threats to the worker posed by the client contact environment, (3) the level of ambiguity in the expectations of job performance as specified by both formal and informal agency norms, and (4) the significance of the worker's discretion (in both senses) on the well-being and life circumstances of the client. Four additional worker characteristics seem to be significant. These are (1) the educational level of the worker relevant to the job requirements, (2) the certainty of professional ethical standards, (3) the degree of perceived conflict between bureaucratic expectations and expected compliance to professional ethical standards, and (4) the "burnout" phenomenon as it expresses itself in worker–client contact.

None of these variables is easily quantifiable even by direct observation. In order to understand street-level policy formation the focus of attention has to be on how these tensions are resolved by the workers. Basically the question to ask is how job and professional expectations are redefined by the street-level worker so as to minimize cognitive dissonance. The street-level bureaucrat can ease the tension by redefining the client's needs. This approach may take the extreme forms of absolving clients from any responsibility for their client status or blaming clients for their client status. There are, of course many intermediate positions. It is not the task of this chapter to define a precise research strategy for examining street-level policy formation. Rather, we have indicated some of the critical variables that need to be considered by the investigator of street-level policy-making behavior. These are outlined in skeletal form in Figure 7.5.

CONCLUSIONS

During the implementation phase a new group of political actors moves toward center stage. The central point is that the policy is not fully shaped by what Theodore Lowi called the "rule of law"[24] nor controlled by what Michael Lipsky described as street-level behavior. Because professional social workers spend most of their time

Organizational Independent Variables	
Resources Threats	Ambiguity Client Significance
Street-level Dependent Variables	
Job Redefinition Strategies	Client Redefinition Strategies
Worker Independent Variables	
Education Professional Standards	Perceived Conflicts Burnout Levels

FIGURE 7.5 Organizational and Worker Variables as They Impact on the Street-level Definition of Job Performance

interpreting the law, planning and organizing for the delivery system of the law, and finally, interacting directly with clients, these areas have been the focus of this chapter. The product at this point is still unfinished. How clients believe they are treated by the policy and how taxpayers believe they ought to be treated become the stuff of a new debate as the policy's impact is examined.

NOTES

1. J. March and H. Simon, *Organizations* (New York: Wiley, 1958); see also Peter Blau, *Bureaucracy in Modern Society* (New York: Random House, 1956).
2. Clarence Stone, "The Implementation of Social Programs: Two Perspectives," *Journal of Social Issues* 36 (1980).
3. Woodrow Wilson, *Congressional Government* (Boston: Houghton Mifflin, 1913).
4. Bruce Gates, *Social Program Administration: The Implementation of Social Policy* (Englewood Cliffs, NJ: Prentice-Hall, 1980); Burton Gummer, *The Politics of Social Administration* (Englewood Cliffs, NJ: Prentice-Hall, 1990).
5. Luther Gulick and Luther Urwick, "Notes on a Theory of Organization," in *Papers on Scientific Management* (New York: Institute of Public Administration, Columbia University, 1937).
6. Bertram Gross, *The Managing of Organizations: The Administrative Struggle* (New York: Free Press, 1964), p. 145.
7. Herbert Simon quoted in Gross, *The Managing of Organizations,* p. 182.
8. Herbert Simon, *Administrative Behavior* (New York: Free Press, 1945); J. March and Herbert Simon, *Organization* (New York: Wiley, 1959); see also Peter Blau, *Bureaucracy in Modern Society* (New York: Random House, 1956).
9. D. Mazmanian and P. Sabatier, *Effective Policy Implementation* (Lexington, MA: Lexington Books, 1981), chap. 1.
10. Jeffrey L. Pressman and Aaron B. Wildavsky, *Implementation: How Great Expectations in Washington Are Dashed in Oakland* (Berkeley: University of California Press, 1973).
11. Ira Sharkansky, *Public Administration: Agencies, Policies and Politics* (San Francisco: W. H. Freeman, 1982), chap. 11.
12. Hedrick Smith, *The Power Game: How Washington Works* (New York: Random House, 1988), p. 82.
13. M. Lipski, "Toward a Theory of Street Level Bureaucracy," in *Theoretical Perspectives on Urban Politics,* eds. M. Lipski and W. Hawley (Englewood Cliffs, NJ: Prentice-Hall, 1976).

14. U.S. Office of the Federal Register, *The Federal Register: What it Is and How to Use it: A Guide for the User of the Federal Register—Code of Federal Regulations System* (Washington, DC: U.S. Government Printing Office, 1977).
15. U.S. Office of the Federal Register, *Code of Federal Regulations* (Washington, DC: National Archives and Record Service, 1938–1991).
16. U.S. Office of the Federal Register, *Federal Register* (Washington, DC: National Archives and Record Service, 1984–1991).
17. Congressional Information Service, *CIS Federal Register Index* (Bethesda, MD: Congressional Information Service, 1984–1991); Congressional Information Service, *CIS Federal Register Abstract* (Bethesda, MD: Congressional Information Service, 1984–1991).
18. Frederick Holler, *Information Sources of Political Science* (Santa Barbara, CA: ABC-CLIO, 1986).
19. Jerrold Zwirl, *Congressional Publications and Proceedings* (Englewood, CO: Libraries Unlimited, 1988).
20. G. Allison, "Conceptual Models and the Cuban Missile Crisis," *American Political Science Review* 63 (1969): 689–718.
21. B. Guy Peters, *American Public Policy: Process and Performance* (New York: Franklin Watts, 1982), chap. 5.
22. Peters, *American Public Policy.*
23. Peter M. Blau, *Bureaucracy in Modern Society* (New York: Random House, 1956).
24. T. Lowi, *The End of Liberalism* (New York: Norton, 1979).

BIBLIOGRAPHY

Allison, G. "Conceptual Models and the Cuban Missile Crisis." *American Political Science Review* 63 (1969): 689–718.

Congressional Information Service. *CIS Federal Register Abstract.* Bethesda, MD: Congressional Information Service, 1984–1991.

Congressional Information Service. *CIS Federal Register Index.* Bethesda, MD: Congressional Information Service, 1984–1991.

Gates, Bruce. *Social Program Administration: The Implementation of Social Policy.* Englewood Cliffs, NJ: Prentice-Hall, 1980.

Gross, Bertram. *The Managing of Organizations: The Administrative Struggle.* New York: Free Press, 1964.

Gulick, Luther, and Luther Urwick. "Notes on a Theory of Organization." In *Papers on Scientific Management.* Institute of Public Administration, Columbia University, 1937.

Gummer, Burton. *The Politics of Social Administration.* Englewood Cliffs, NJ: Prentice-Hall, 1990.

Heffernan, J. "Implementing the Omnibus Reconciliation Act of 1981." Paper presented at a conference of the Association of Policy Analysts and Policy Administrators, Minneapolis, November 1983.

Holler, Frederick. *Information Sources of Political Science.* Santa Barbara, CA: ABC-CLIO, 1986.

Lipski, M. "Toward a Theory of Street-level Bureaucracy." In *Theoretical Perspectives on Urban Politics,* eds. M. Lipski and W. Hawley. Englewood Cliffs, NJ: Prentice-Hall, 1976.

March, J., and Herbert Simon. *Organizations.* New York: Wiley, 1958.

Mazmanian, D., and P. Sabatier. *Effective Policy Implementation.* Lexington, MA: Lexington Books, 1981.

Peters, Guy. *American Public Policy: Process and Performance.* New York: Franklin Watts, 1982.
Pressman, Jeffrey L., and Aaron B. Wildavsky. *Implementation: How Great Expectations in Washington Are Dashed in Oakland.* Berkeley: University of California Press, 1973.
Sharkansky, Ira. *Public Administration: Agencies, Policies and Politics.* San Francisco, CA: W. H. Freeman, 1982.
Simon, H. *Administrative Behavior.* New York: Free Press, 1945.
Smith, Hedrick. *The Power Game: How Washington Works.* New York: Random House, 1988.
U.S. Office of the Federal Register. Washington, DC: National Archives and Record Service, 1938–1991.
Wilson, Woodrow. *Congressional Government.* Boston: Houghton Mifflin, 1913.
Zwirl, Jerrold. *Congressional Publications and Proceedings.* Englewood, CO: Libraries Unlimited, 1988.

CHAPTER **8**

Policy Evaluation

There is no unambiguous datum constituting policy and waiting to be discovered in the world. A policy may usefully be considered as a course of action or inaction and such course needs to be perceived and identified.

H. Hugh Heclo

We know now that the events that occur at each stage of the policy process are not random occurrences. The events are shaped by the formal and informal behavioral norms that are part of those institutions and are further shaped by the historical circumstances and value considerations that originally propelled the issue onto the agenda. These events, circumstances, and values may be thought of as the independent variables. As has been shown, the process itself molds the events that determine the policy. The process is iterative but generally flows in a circular path, as was shown in Chapter 2. Studies that seek to explain how a particular policy came into being treat the policy under investigation as the dependent variable. The effort is to use the previously mentioned independent variable in the creation of a parsimonious explanation of the policy itself. In this chapter the process is somewhat reversed: the analyst seeks to view the policy as the independent variable and to illustrate and explain the consequences observed and/or expected from the policy. The three basic forms are decision analysis, impact analysis, and program evaluation.

DECISION ANALYSIS

It is axiomatic in the empirical social sciences that one cannot investigate an event that has not yet happened. Public officials might reasonably expect, however, that social workers could inform them in advance of the consequences that might be expected to occur. Decisional analysis takes many forms and all employ empirical data. Since they are concerned with the anticipation of the effects of a policy that has not been implemented, however, the investigators must employ techniques based on simulation. Formal models of choices are specified, and empirical data are collected and fed into computers, which project expected consequences given a variety of assumptions. The projections, of course, can be no better than the formal models, the data, and the assumptions. The use of simulation procedures has been greatly enhanced by developments in survey research, which are now able to supply a more valid data base, and advances in artificial intelligence data processing.

Macrosimulation of policy impacts is at least as old as the Keynesian revolution but microsimulation is still in the developing stages. Its earliest use in welfare policy can be traced to the work of Nelson McClung and Gail Wilenski, staff members of the President's Commission on Income Maintenance (1968–1970). McClung and Wilenski were able to project cost estimates on income maintenance reform packages but the range of their estimations was large. Nonetheless, this pioneering work did establish the visability of simulations for estimating specific consequences, such as which demographic groups would be more likely to withdraw from the labor force if welfare policy were shaped differently.[1]

A variant of simulation analysis occurs when the policy is attempted in miniature under circumstances that allow for inference to a larger society. This analysis is known as policy experimentation. The attempt is to replicate the condition of a social policy using real-world observations. The technology for this technique is well advanced, although serious problems of the ethics of the mode of inquiry need to be addressed anew in each case. A social policy experiment is always subject to the strictures of human subjects' review procedures. Here the requirement is that the benefits of the investigation are larger than the risks and that the subjects themselves participate with informed consent. These conditions are often difficult to meet, with the result that our intellectual capacity to estimate policy consequence is larger than our empirical capacity to verify such impacts. It is nonetheless possible to arrange experimental design for policy analysis. The results of such social policy experiments have had a profound impact on the design of policy for topics as diverse as home health care for geriatric patients and the mode of governmental payments for out-of-home infant day care.[2]

IMPACT ANALYSIS

Policy impact investigations are designed to measure and report the full range of consequences observed when various policies have in fact been in place. Quasi-experimental models are frequently employed in the simultaneous examination of impacts in real-world conditions in agencies and communities where the policy is in place, and where essentially similar conditions are replicated in another agency or community where the policy is not present. The purpose of a policy is to alter or preserve certain social conditions and the goal of impact analysis is to suggest the importance of the policy in achieving this aim.

Policy impact studies are a special form of applied policy research that seeks to measure the degree of success that might be reasonably attributed to a policy intervention. Impact analysis consists of five parts, each demanding a distinct method of research:

1. Identifying normative considerations
2. Determining the program's manifest and latent objectives
3. Establishing outcome measures that are related to the objectives
4. Understanding the program impact as opposed to other factors
5. Assessing the economic context

Identifying Normative Considerations

The focus of attention in this phase is to address the values problem as program evaluation. We have reached the state of affairs when policy evaluations are prepared by both sides in any political controversy. The condition is analogous to both the defense and the prosecution producing their own psychiatrist. This state of affairs produces cynicism on the part of those who read the policy evaluations and presents a formidable problem to those who produce them. Almost by definition, controversy in public policy is concerned with the conflicts in social values. Any analysis that does not confront the value conflicts will be of minimal use to the public official in the field who must take such value conflict into consideration. Traditionally, policy analysts have addressed the problem of values in one of two ways.

The first is to be candidly *value committed.* This approach requires the investigator to state at the outset the value to be maximized and to present evidence in support of that position. This position maintains that all analysis is, at root, an argument for a particular set of values. Since the value bias is always present, it is best to admit it openly.

A second alternative is to be *value critical.* This approach does not ignore values, nor does it take them as a given. In this approach the value problem is central to the analysis.[3] The value-critical approach relies heavily on methods adopted from empirical social theory. All the significant theoretically related and empirically confirmable consequences of a policy are noted. Thus policy A is said to reduce poverty by 2 percent but has the associated condition of reducing work incentives by 1.5 percent. Another example might be that a proarrest strategy in domestic disputes will save Y number of abused spouses from subsequent beatings, but that a crisis intervention approach will avoid X number of "avoidable family splits." We would clearly prefer a policy that would be the best at both goals but normally this is just not possible. With the precision of empirical projection it is then up to the policymakers to select the policy of their own choice. Empirical projections linked to a sound theory allow for a selection with a higher level of knowledge about the real costs and real benefits that are associated with the choice. This alternative has been roundly condemned as being semantically elusive. Terms such as *avoidable family splits* are given operational dimensions and definitions only remotely linked to the concept that the term evokes. In this way it does not ignore value issues but it may hide them, often from the analyst himself.

In a now famous essay be Lawrence Tribe, "Policy Sciences: Analysis or Ideology," the issue was put into a different perspective.[4] Tribe argues that each methodology of analysis is based on its epistemological assumptions; all analytic approaches look at the world in fixed ways. He suggests that the selection of a methodology of analysis ordains the resulting evaluation. It is not that analysts are necessarily personally biased but that analytic methodologies are. Tribe's distinctions make clear the problem. *All the methodologies of analysis have the potential for suggesting what issues are significant and what facts need to be examined, but no analytic technique can substitute for political judgments.* Investigators beginning any evaluation need to be aware of its limited potential for policy resolution and of its potential contribution to a more rational level of discourse. Students who wish to explore this problem further should read Fischer and Forester's excellent collection of essays on the topic, *Confronting Values in Policy Analysis.*[5]

Determining Program Objectives

It is clear that programs have multiple and sometimes conflicting objectives. Adding to the confusion social program objectives are often stated in vague and general terms that create difficulty in discerning what is really intended. High-sounding phrases such as "strengthening family life" or "encouraging self-sufficiency" are used when the program's real intent is to encourage people to stay married even if the quality of the relationship is destructive, or to stay employed even if their jobs have low wages, poor working conditions, and little or no opportunity for advancement, or to finish an occupationally oriented training program not linked to probable employment. That is, the successful attainment of one goal may render other far more significant goals impossible. Goals are sometimes incompatible. For instance, some people believe that only those best prepared should be admitted to the universities. Others believe that all social classes should have equal opportunity for admission. To the extent that various inequalities in society provide some classes with a greater chance of better preparation for university entrance, university admission policy based on the preparation standards would violate the normative equal opportunity standard.

An examination of the materials in the *Federal Register* and the agency operation manual will give strong clues to the program's objectives. Seldom are objectives stated with the clarity, specificity, and measurability a researcher might desire. One does not find objectives stated in terms of, say, reducing the incidence of juvenile delinquency in the tenth ward by 15 percent, though that might well be the real intent.

To learn a program's objectives, an investigator must examine the written record of the statute itself as it has been interpreted in the *Federal Register.* He or she must also examine the agency's own printed documents. These written records need to be supplemented with direct interviews with participants in the delivery system at various levels of the organizational hierarchy. The investigator will also want to garner the reactions of members of the target population and the perceptions of the objectives held by the original legislative sponsors. These printed and oral sources will lead not to the discovery of a single objective but to a variety of objectives. Understanding this system of objectives, policy evaluators can then focus on one or more of the supporting subobjectives.

Within the service agency itself one finds that objectives are specified along a hierarchical dimension in relation to organizational units responsible for the service delivery. There should be a logical connection so that the objectives at the subordinate level are prerequisites for the objectives of the next superordinate level. Social program objectives are then seen as a chain of events consisting of means-ends relationships and program evaluation can be an examination and validation of these relationships. For example, in an employment training program prospective clients are screened for their employment training needs. If the screening fails to separate literate and preliterate populations and this factor is ignored in the training program, the almost certain failure of the training will be related to the lack of a realistic connection between the selection process and the training programs. A social program ideal is programs structured so that there is a harmonic movement up and down the scale of the organizational delivery system.

There are distinct stakeholders who have distinct views about what the program ought to do. Should all of the applicants be screened and placed in a training program even if the estimation of eventual placement is low, or should clients be screened, perhaps even creamed, so that only those most likely to find jobs are allocated a training slot? A clear statement of program objectives from the various perspectives is a prerequisite to a comprehensive policy impact statement.

Establishing Outcome Measures

Policy evaluations have as their intent the systematic and empirical investigation of the consequences of a policy on its target populations in terms of the goals that were intended.[6] It is important to distinguish among the various consequences that result from a policy's being put into place. The policy outputs are the measure of the public investment in the problem; thus we measure the *per capita expenditure* on welfare in a particular jurisdiction. This is not the same thing as policy impact. Policy impacts do not measure the activity of government but the changes in the environment that are a consequence of that activity. As policies almost always have spillover impacts on other populations, these consequences also need to be measured. Finally, the consequence might be considered as either substantive or symbolic. The multiple impacts of a policy can be sketched as in Table 8.1.

In the world as we know it, it is difficult to isolate symbolic and substantive impact or to distinguish target and spillover population. Table 8.1 alerts us where to look for the impacts. Each of these impacts, A through D, is capable of being measured, albeit often imperfectly. The difficulty of measuring results from a number of factors:

1. The impact sought may have a time frame much longer than the time frame of the policy evaluation.
2. The data that measure the impact may be difficult and/or prohibitively expensive to obtain.
3. The data that are available may present serious problems of reliability and validity.
4. The more symbolic impacts, while of undeniable significance, may present serious problems of quantification.

TABLE 8.1 Policy Impacts on Target Population and Spillover Impacts

	Impact on Target Populations	Spillover Impact on Other Populations
Substantive	Net Cost or Benefit of A	Net Cost or Benefit of B
Symbolic	Net Cost or Benefit of C	Net Cost or Benefit of D

While no problem of measurement is easy to deal with, all can be addressed to some extent. The principles of scaling and measurement in most basic research texts will provide the student with useful insights into how to measure policy impacts. For policy impacts that are not amenable to direct observation, the investigator may wish to consider some proxy measure. Unlike the physical sciences where measurement is often mechanical, and unlike the basic social sciences in which the useful dependent variables are selected deliberately for their measurability, in policy science the critical concept is often difficult even to observe, and difficult to measure when it is observed. The important thing to remember and to note is how the measuring instruments interject a bias into the determination of a program's success or lack of it. The indicators should be as close as possible to an undistorted reflection of the concept; where distortion is inevitable, its implication for the evaluation should be prominently noted.

Understanding the Impact of the Policy Itself

Policy evaluation has a limited goal: to verify the impact of the policy and to specify the conditions under which the policy is effective. Reporting that a favorable outcome occurred after a program was put into place or that something very bad occurred while a policy was in place is insufficient. The task of evaluative research is also to show that the observed consequence has a theoretically and empirically demostratable relation to the policy. The social work literature is filled with examples of dubious statistical connections between a public policy and its supposed consequence.

In a classic paper Paul Lazarsfeld established the basic elements that one must consider before inferring policy success or failure from an observed correlation—that is, to suggest that the policy produces the observed consequence.[7] The first of these is the *spurious connection.* One can observe that the number of fire engines at a fire and the amount of damage from the blaze are correlated. It is illogical, however, to infer that fire engines cause damage. The most realistic assumption is that the size of the fire influences the extent of the damage and the number of engines dispatched.

The second element involving a policy operates only through *intervening variables.* Federal incentives to increase or decrease local welfare spending are accomplished only by an impact on state officials. The impact that is intended is difficult to measure because of the indirect path of the intervention. The local governments may want to respond positively to the federal incentive but are frustrated by state inaction. Often the intervening variable is not as obvious or as easily observable as in this illustration.

Federal Incentive ——→ State Response ——→ Local Spending

The third element arises when the policy is a *conditional variable.* For example, if only high school graduates are accepted for a training program the impact of that training program alone on subsequent employment cannot be clearly determined. Care in examination procedures must be employed to show whether the policy variable and not the conditional variable explains the observed policy response.

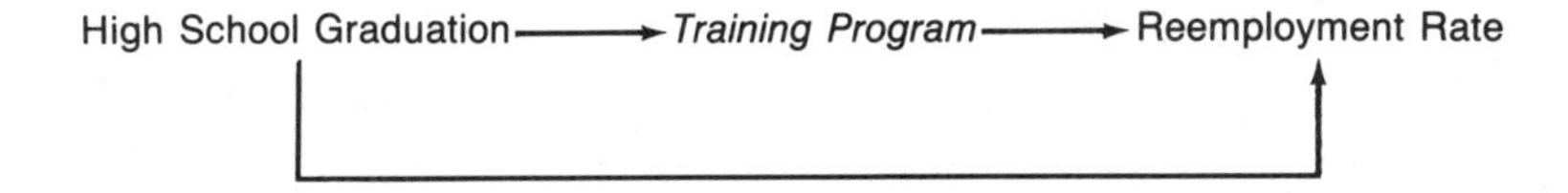

The purpose of policy evaluation is to determine the magnitude of the impact of the policy. In social science the search is for an explanation of the chain of causation. This is what is meant by causal analysis. Nothing can be the ultimate cause of something else if it, in its turn, has a cause. But ultimate causes cannot be the object of policy intervention precisely because, being ultimate, they cannot be changed. A distinction needs to be made between proximate cause in a path of causality and those factors open to policy change. Native intelligence, parents' aspirations, and peer expectations fundamentally shape a student's school performance. Educators have only a very limited capacity to influence these more fundamental variables. Given these variables, for example a policy of using parents instead of paraprofessionals as school teacher aides can influence the general level of school performance. As another example, crime is a function of many variables, but given those, the decision to use car or foot patrols has been shown to lower the crime rate.

Policymakers often express a desire for a policy that gets to the cause rather than the symptom. But the world is not that simple. Is the source of the cocaine problem the crop in the field in Colombia or the demand on the street in the United States? Perspective of cause structures the debate. Cause and effect becomes a two-way street. The policy evaluation has a limited goal: to verify the impact of the policy and to specify the conditions under which the policy is effective.

Assessing Economic Context

Program impact studies tend to focus on highly specific aspects of a program rather than the broader policy issues. The basic objective of program evaluation is to determine whether a program is achieving its objectives in an efficient manner. The most frequent form of program evaluation is the use of some variant of benefit-cost analysis. This technique uses a set of procedures to identify the payoff from the program, to quantify that payoff, and to translate that quantification into dollar terms. The real cost of the program is evaluated the same way. The dollar-estimated benefits are related systematically to the dollar-estimated costs. Programs then can be judged in terms of the following:

1. The ratio of benefits to cost
2. The rate of return of the invested dollars
3. The program that produces the largest return
4. The program that produces a given effect for the minimum investment

Although somewhat similar, these outcome measures are not identical. A program that produces a $5 billion benefit for a $1 billion cost has a cost-benefit ratio of 5:0; its rate of return is 500 percent. However, a $5 billion result on a $1 billion cost that takes twenty years is not a good investment because time is required to produce the results and programs must be evaluated by their "rate of return." The general rule is to reject any program that has a cost-benefit ratio of less than one and, more restrictively, to reject any program that has a rate of return less than the "prevailing discount rate." Benefit-cost analysis is a beguiling but highly complex mode of investigation. The intricate techniques of cost-benefit analysis typically require a full semester course in most graduate schools and, unfortunately, no shortcut can be provided here.

The difficulties are not only the technical ones of collecting the data and selecting the most appropriate mode of calculation. What ought to be counted as a benefit or a cost and how it should be estimated is as much a philosophical question as it is a technical one. Those preparing to use cost-benefit studies should become familiar with this complex and demanding literature.[8]

CONCLUSIONS

Policy evaluation by definition has explicit political overtones. It is designed to yield insights about the ability of particular social actions to influence particular social conditions. Such activity is intended to affect the outcomes of government policy and the allocation of resources. Because power is unevenly divided, because the conflict of values is the central ingredient of politics, and because there is a natural uncertainty surrounding any intervention, strategy policy evaluation is a many-sided phenomenon. Evaluation research is used in combination with the other techniques of policy analysis. More so than other forms of inquiry into policy, policy analysis and particular program evaluation pose a difficult problem associated with the demands of research and the demands of the sponsoring institutions. The social worker cannot avoid these circumstances, but he or she can be aware of them. The choices between value commitment and value neutrality, and the choices between being an advocate for a cause and a neutral provider of information, are never easy or even clear.

NOTES

1. Robert Haveman, *Poverty Policy and Policy Research* (Madison: University of Wisconsin Press, 1987), chap. 11.
2. Haveman, *Poverty Policy,* chap. 8.
3. Marty Rein, *Social Science and Public Policy* (New York: Penguin, 1976).
4. *Philosophy and Public Affairs* (Fall 1972): 66–110.
5. Frank Fischer and John Forester, *Confronting Values in Policy Analysis* (Newbury Park, CA: Sage, 1987).
6. D. Nachmias, *Public Policy Evaluations* (New York: St. Martin's Press, 1979), p. 4.
7. Paul Lazarsfeld, "Evidence and Influence in Social Research," *Daedalus* 87 (1958): 99–130.
8. Carol Weiss, "Ideology, Interests and Information: The Basis of Policy Positions," in *Ethics, the Social Sciences, and Policy Analysis,* eds. Daniel Callahan and Bruce Jennings (New York: Plenum Press, 1983), pp. 213–248.

BIBLIOGRAPHY

Haveman, Robert. *Poverty Policy and Policy Research.* Madison: University of Wisconsin Press, 1987.

Heclo, H. Hugh. "Review Article: Policy Analysis." *British Journal of Political Science* 2 (1972): 84–92.

Rein, Marty. *Social Science and Public Policy.* New York: Penguin, 1976.

PART **3**

Research Strategies in Policy Studies

In the first eight chapters of this text we reviewed the stages in the policy process in the context of the social worker's roles in each stage. At least two insights emerge from that review. The first is that policy choice is not a discrete event but emerges as a consequence of many choices. The second is that there are multiple motives within the coalitions that are formed at each stage of the policy process. This book was written to help advanced undergraduate and graduate students understand the various social worker roles in the policy process. The subject matter of Part Three is the design of policy research statements structured to facilitate social workers' tasks at each stage of the policy process as they work with others engaged in resolving social problems with better social policies. We assume the availability of timely and relevant knowledge and the presence of open-minded policymakers, two conditions not always present. Even when the conditions are present, the task of developing and presenting a policy research paper is almost always daunting. In Part Three we examine the distinctive demands faced by the social worker, social investigator, or social scientist as he or she prepares such documents with specific reference to the development of a policy-relevant history of the policy issues, the collection of qualitative information, the appropriate quantitative analysis, and the presentation of the research in a useful way.

CHAPTER **9**

Conceptualization of a Policy Research Statement

Substantive experts often engage in the social policy process as if it were a rational process based on a fixed empirical deductive research orientation. Advocates for particular groups often engage in the policy process as if they were actors in a morality play; they act as if policy choice is a conflict between good and evil. Legislators and senior administrative officers tend to see the policy process in yet a third way. Their task is to find a politically acceptable compromise rather than a technically correct or morally right response.

When policy is viewed as process, as we think it should be, and when this process is evaluated from alternative roles that must be played, it is clear that there is no single template that can serve as a model for a policy research statement. The political pragmatists and the substantive experts often view the same problem in very different lights even when they have a shared value base. Office holders and senior administrative officials often see their roles in the political process as the care and perpetuation of the negotiation system itself, the generation as well as the maintenance of a faith in the decision-making process.[1] For the substantive expert, the rationality of a decision is judged by the technical quality of the fit between means and ends. For the advocates of particular causes, the quality of choice is determined by the specific ends sought.

In a sense all views are correct. Effective policy choice require that (1) the social problem is objectively understood in terms of an objective social reality as it is, rather than as an expression of what one would like it to be; (2) the value priorities implicit in the various corrective strategies are fully understood by all the participants in the decision process; and (3) the process of decision making is in accord with constitutional constraints and the current norms for public choice so that harmony and faith in the political system are maintained. Nonetheless, the policy study requirements as seen by expert, advocate, and decision maker are distinct from each other.

Political decisions are reached in a series of disjointed activities. These problems are complex conditions driven by competing value systems. Further, they often require decisions before all the facts are known. In response to this condition, policy researchers are often asked to provide successive approximations of "good" answers. Each approximation depends on the experiences and awareness that have been accumulated earlier. Because the policy process is continuous and iterative, decisions are never final. The policy study requirements are distinct for each stage of the policy process. As previously suggested, they are also distinctive in terms of their substantive intent. Thus there is not one policy statement, but many. Insight into this complexity is shown in Table 9.1.

Table 9.1 locates policy studies in terms of substantive intent and stage in the policy process. The reality is that the process is iterative rather than sequential and real-world actors often have mixed substantive intents; thus any particular policy study may contain a distinct mixture of the features indicated.

To clarify the options involved, we can set forth the following distinctions surrounding substantive intent:

Expert model

1. Definition of problem in objective terms
2. Specification of trends that are applicable
3. Delineation of alternative actions that impact trends
4. Examination of each alternative's cost and benefits

Advocate model

1. Definition of problem in terms of the values sought
2. Specification of criteria for the evaluation of alternatives
3. Selective presentation of the evidence

Political model

1. Indication of choices that are seen as available
2. Investigation of support for each choice
3. Exploration of opportunities for compromise

Given the complexity of the process and the multiple purposes that policy research statements are expected to serve, there is considerable room for disagreement about

TABLE 9.1 Potential Number of Policy Statements by Substantive Intent and Place in the Policy Process

	Substantive Intent		
Stage in Policy Process	***Expert***	***Advocate***	***Public Official***
Problem Definition	1	2	3
Policy Formulation	4	5	6
Policy Selection	7	8	9
Implementation	10	11	12
Evaluation	13	14	15
Policy Adjustment	16	17	18

what constitutes sound policy research. According to Ann Majchrzak, "Policy research is defined as the process of conducting research on or analysis of a fundamental social problem in order to provide policymakers with pragmatic, action-oriented recommendations for alleviation of the problem."[2] For Robert Mayer, policy research is "empirical research undertaken to verify propositions about some aspect of the means-ends relationship in policy-making."[3]

Mayer sees policy investigations as moving through nine rationally related parts. The policy research must make definitive statements with regard to each part as follows:

1. The place of the research process as one of the effective instruments in the resolution of the policy problem
2. The history of the policy problem
3. The conceptual framework of the policy problem
4. The objective of the policy study
5. The populations involved in the choice and the populations affected by the policy under consideration
6. The data to be collected
7. The procedures of data collection
8. The modes of data analysis
9. The administration and the presentation of the policy research findings[4]

Policy occurs as a process, and any particular policy study is structured to provide policymakers with timely and relevant information. It is thus the case that the investigation needs to be structured for the particular stage in the process where the decision maker finds him- or herself. The requirements of a policy research study may also vary according to the substantive perspectives of the investigator and his or her client. Because of these factors there is no single boilerplate format that could become a checklist for a policy research study.

POLICY RESEARCH CHARACTERISTICS

Despite these constraints there are some distinct characteristics of a policy investigation that distinguish it from other forms of social investigation. In Ann Majchrzak's characterization a policy research statement is an effort by the professional to inform the client about the nature of the problems and the options available, along with the economic and political risks associated with each option. In her view the principal characteristics of policy research are that it is (1) value explicit, (2) future oriented, and (3) pragmatic.[5]

Value Explicit Research

Policy research is distinctive in that its goal is neither scientific discovery nor the justification of an ethical system. Thus neither the value neutrality of the social scientist nor the value commitment of the social activist is appropriate. The avowed intent of policy research is the improvement of policy-making. Its most persistent aim is to recommend modes of analysis which, if consistently employed, would result in a policy decision in which the facts are as clear as circumstance allows and the values being pursued are as explicit as possible. Policy analysis is not simply a doctrine of economic rationality whereby the most efficient means of achieving stipulated ends are specified. The goals of a policy are seldom presented in clear, unambiguous terms, nor does useful analysis seek to persuade the policymaker toward one set of values. A policy does, however, rest on some conception of desirable public purpose. It is the responsibility of the policy investigator to make that conception of public purpose as clear as possible.

It is sometimes suggested that empirical analysis seeks to inform the policymaker about the world as it is, normative analysis seeks to inform the policymaker about the world as it could be, and policy analysis provides a full atlas of maps showing how to proceed from the first view to the second. This description is perhaps as clear as any characterization can be. Nonetheless, it diverts attention from the basic observation that few policy research papers rely independently on one form of analysis.

Future-Oriented Research

Policy research is focused on the future. Its ultimate function is to provide a series of projections of what is likely to occur under a variety of explicit assumptions. Because of its future orientation, policy investigations contain a historical perspective that suggests important trends that need to be watched. The aphorism that military history teaches the generals how to win the last war contains a fundamental assumption about future-oriented investigations; our fears of what can go wrong are typically based on our understanding of what has gone wrong. This perception is illustrated with two books on very different approaches to the poverty problem. Charles Murray's *Losing Ground* advocates a lessening of government support. His prescription is based on a belief that poverty has increased at the very time social spending on poverty has ballooned. It is his belief that the programs of assistance have encouraged the very behavior the assistance programs were designed to change.[6] Michael Harrington's *The New American Poverty* recommends directly opposite action because Harrington sees the spending balloon as a myth. He sees the problem of rising poverty as caused by government inaction.[7] Useful policy analysis requires that investigators set forth their own projections of the future tied to a clear statement of their own readings of the recent past.

Pragmatic Research

Policy research involves manipulable variables rather than explanatory variables. Social problems are a function of many things only a few of which can be altered by decisions made by responsible political actors. Causal analysis attempts to find the most significant independent variables that "cause" a social problem to have its current shape. Obviously nothing can cause something else if it is itself caused by yet another more significant variable. In that case it becomes an intervening variable. Even if something could be identified as the ultimate cause, that ultimate cause could not be changed by an active policy because, being ultimate, it cannot be changed. Beliefs about the cause of a problem structure beliefs about what to do. For example, conservatives and liberals both want to end dependency on government handouts but differ as to how to accomplish this end. Welfare researchers know that youth joblessness is connected to welfare status. Not only are youth from higher-income homes more likely to have part-time jobs than youth from welfare homes; even when total income is a constant for all other family members, youth from welfare homes are less likely to work than youth from nonwelfare homes.[8] The empirical connection is clear: Being in a welfare home means a youth is less likely to seek or hold a part-time job. Explanations for this phenomenon range from beliefs about discriminatory hiring by employers to the lack of motivation among welfare recipients. Assuming a cause often means assuming a policy strategy: Are we to focus on job discrimination or low motivation among welfare youth? Because human action is ultimately derived from a complex of human volitions (tastes, attitudes, beliefs, etc.), all such factors probably contribute to the low labor force participation by welfare youth. However, since government has at its disposal only a limited set of policy instruments, the policy investigations often appear to compete with one another. The scientist might conclude that job discrimination and low work motivation play interactive roles in the creation of low employment rates among welfare youth. When there is a conflict over scarce political resources there is often a debate over "the best" explanation. Though most investigators see the two explanations as interactive streams of causation, the policy debate often appears to be a war between experts hired by competing advocates for each approach.

Elements of a Policy Statement

The need to be value explicit, future oriented, and pragmatic places an incredible number of demands on a clear policy statement. Nonetheless, each policy statement contains some irreducible elements, shown in Table 9.2:

TABLE 9.2 Elements of Policy Research Statement

I. Substantive Statement of the Social Problem
   1. Current social condition
   2. Estimate of the current trends

II. Policy Context
   1. Identification of key policy issues
   2. Identification of key players

III. Specification of Policy Constraints
   1. History to this point
   2. Design of feasible alternative actions

IV. Political Strategy
   1. Estimation of sources of political support and of political opposition

THE IDENTIFICATION OF A SOCIAL PROBLEM IN A POLICY STUDY

Current Condition

Some conditions we now consider social problems were not viewed this way in earlier times, and some conditions previously considered social problems are acceptable without question today. A social problem becomes a political problem when a perceived condition is incompatible with the values of a significant number of people (or a number of significant people) who are in agreement that some public action would be meaningful and desirable. There is a close correlation between the formal agenda of governments, as reflected in congressional hearings or speeches on the topic inserted into the *Congressional Record,* and the media play, as reflected in references in sources such as the *New York Times Index.* Media attention both promotes and reflects public interest in an issue. In some cases media reflect the formal units of government that are paying attention, while in others the very phenomenon of media attention is sufficient to provoke policy proposals within formal government.[9]

This morning's newspaper reports a variety of social conditions that most readers of this text would regard as political problems. The same social conditions do not always lead to the same political problem. Thirty-seven million Americans have no health insurance. To hospital administrators this condition means that hospital rates have to be increased to cover the cost of "donated care" to the uninsured. The increased rates raise the cost of health insurance to employers who provide coverage. There is both social and moral concern about how those uninsured are cared for. Peter Liabassi, senior vice-president for Traveler's Corporation, finds a unique problem in the condition. Because of the large number of uninsured, "the federal government may move to adopt some foolish, ill-advised, ill-concerned national health insurance strategy."[10] The objective condition of the uninsured, through the curious paths of politics, led to a coalition of the Chamber of Commerce, the American Medical Association, the Children's Defense Fund, the American Hospital Association, and the Blue Cross/Blue Shield Association to press for a significant expansion of Medicaid. When fully operative in 1995, the program will provide public insurance to 9.2 million uninsured children. The partners in the coalition were responding to the same social condition but very different political problems.

Trends

In politics, as in life, most problems get worse if we ignore them. Some problems require no intervention as the seeds of solution lie in the dynamics of the problem itself. From two very different perspectives, William Julius Wilson and Charles Murray have examined the relationship between social trends and the policy interventions used to affect them.[11] A policy investigator must look at the relevant trends in order to estimate the consequences of various actions as well as the consequences of inaction.

One of the many confounding factors in the development of a policy response to the problem of AIDS is the variation in the period of latency.[12] In another example, Lisbeth Schorr's influential book, *Within Our Reach,* makes the point that simply correcting a vision problem of a preschooler will improve the life chances of the child growing up in a single-parent home. The policy action that provides the vision correction may not be the most significant variable, but it is one significant variable in changing the life chances of the child. The problem as Schorr sees it is not *beating* the odds but *changing* the odds.[13] An important aspect of a policy study is to inform the policymaker about the trends related to the problem. Projections about the future of the problem can err in the direction of misplaced complacency or in the direction of overly dramatic projections of horrendous consequences. The projections should reflect the expected outcomes from inaction as well as the expected outcomes from all feasible alternatives for policy action.

POLICY CONTEXT

Key Policy Issues

In order to suggest policy interventions and to understand the dimensions of a policy debate one must first understand what is at issue. A clear statement of the problem and its trends goes a long way in formulating the context of the policy issues. In reality, the participants in the debate define the issue as the process goes on. The definition and redefinition of the issues are central to the process of debate and negotiation that takes place. In this view the key skill of leadership lies in defining the issue so that a winning coalition can be mobilized in support of it. The major difficulty in formulating the central issue is to overcome the misleading notions that are interjected for political advantage. If we define the abortion issue in terms of freedom of choice and the rights of privacy, then we come down on one side of the policy debate. If, on the other hand, we define the issue in terms of the protection of life (and define life to include the fetus), then we come down on the other side of the debate. Insofar as it is lexicographically possible, the policy research statement should attempt to frame the issue in terms of the *real* debate rather than the propaganda of the antagonists in the debate.

Key Policy Players

Who the participants are in a debate dictates the shape of the issue, the process of the debate, and its outcome. The key to political success lies in motivating one's own supporters and neutralizing potential opponents. The parties involved or potentially involved in any policy issue have many other obligations and interests. Mobilization of support is mostly a matter of expanding the number of persons involved in the debate. Before mobilization one needs to have at least a descriptive understanding of who is involved and what causes some persons to become intensely interested and committed. A policy research paper must pay attention to the stakeholders and participants in the debate. These two groups are not identical populations. After the issue is specified the investigator must determine who has been a participant, gleaned from the policy history to be discussed later; who will almost certainly become a participant, gleaned from a clear knowledge of the policy process; and who the uninvolved stakeholders are, deduced from a clear statement of the problem and a knowledge of its political history. It is also important to understand why some parties who might reasonably have been expected to participate have not participated. Understanding how the debate is likely to go forward requires insight into the levels of participation and involvement that can be expected as well as the openness of stakeholders to new options. It is not only the reality of the costs and benefits of a social policy but also the beliefs about those costs and benefits held by significant participants that will shape the course of the policy debate.

SPECIFICATION OF POLICY CONSTRAINTS

Typically, the policy investigator will not have to develop a new policy history since, at some level at least, it is usually already available in the literature. The procedures for uncovering the political and administrative history of past policy are covered in the history chapter of this book.

The policy statement is not limited to an expression of rationality that specifies how to move from the current condition toward some well-specified alternative. Yet the policy research statement should provide a precise description of these instruments with clear citations so that the readers of the policy statement can examine the full document should they so choose.

It is neither possible nor particularly meaningful to develop an indicator of net social costs across all groupings of participants and stakeholders. What is possible and meaningful is to develop a summation of the expected tangible benefits and the expected symbolic benefits, as well as symbolic and tangible costs. These costs and benefits are frequently not measurable in dollar amounts. Nonetheless, it is important to decision makers that they have an awareness of how participants and stakeholders perceive what they think they will gain and what they think they will lose if a particular policy is adopted and implemented.

POLITICAL STRATEGY

It is difficult to know what is politically feasible before the political battle has been fought. In fact, not knowing that you can't beat city hall often becomes a formidable political weapon. Some observers have suggested that had Rosa Parks been more politically sophisticated she would never have sat down in the front part of the bus in Montgomery, starting one of the most significant political movements of this century.

No policy statement is complete without some estimation of what role the policy debate will play. What is the need to mobilize those who are already involved and to sensitize the significant stakeholders who are unaware of their involvement? Is the problem one of broad dissemination of general information or one of specialized education of a small number of central political players? A map of the decisional process indicating where each decision will be made is useful in developing a complete campaign for committing political resources. This mapping should also include estimations showing where opposition to the preferred policy is most likely to appear.

CONCLUSIONS

With regard to estimating the instrumental rationality of the policy and the political complication that will occur in the process of adoption, it would help if our foresight were as good as our hindsight. It never is. Eveline Burns, commenting on the role of knowledge in the social policy process, wrote, "When contemplating the policies that have been applied in the past and considering those which might be applied in the future, it is impossible not to be impressed and depressed by the extent to which policy decisions are made and perpetuated on the basis of beliefs about facts rather than tested knowledge."[14] The number of retrospective books illustrating that failed social policy has been formulated on the basis of illusions is sizable. Projective policies encounter the problem of both bad luck and bad policy planning. Backpackers ought not to leave a trailhead without an awareness of the difficulties to be encountered and the resources available in the pack to overcome them. They might arrive at a "dry creek" and find it a raging torrent. That would be bad luck and they would have to retrace their steps. If they arrived and found the water passable with a rope and they had brought the rope, that would be good planning. Starting out with the hope that the creek would be dry would be bad planning that might not necessarily yield bad results, for the creek might indeed be dry. Allegorically speaking, you cannot control your luck but you can control your planning and that is precisely what a policy strategy statement is all about.

NOTES

1. John Brandl, *Policy Evaluation and the Work of the Legislator* (San Francisco: Jossey-Bass, 1980).
2. Ann Majchrzak, *Methods for Policy Research* (Beverly Hills, CA: Sage, 1987), p. 12.
3. Robert Mayer and Ernest Greenwood, *The Design of Social Policy Research* (Englewood Cliffs, NJ: Prentice-Hall, 1980), p. 42.
4. Mayer and Greenwood, p. 9.
5. Ann Majchrzak, *Methods for Policy Research.*
6. Charles A. Murray, *Losing Ground: American Social Policy, 1950–1980* (New York: Basic Books, 1984).
7. Michael Harrington, *New American Poverty* (New York: Penguin, 1985).
8. Richard B. Freeman and Harry J. Holzer, eds., *The Black Youth Unemployment Crisis* (Chicago: University of Chicago Press, 1986).
9. Fay Lomax Cook and Wesley Skogan, "Evaluating the Changing Definition of a Policy Issue in Congress," in *Public Policy and Social Institutions,* ed. Harrell Rodgers (Greenwich, CT: JAI Press, 1984).
10. *New York Times,* 4 November 1990, p. 14, col. 3.
11. Charles Murray, *Losing Ground: American Social Policy, 1950–80* (New York: Basic Books, 1984); William Julius Wilson, *The Truly Disadvantaged* (Chicago: University of Chicago Press, 1987).
12. Michael Tanner, *The Politics of Health: A State Response to the AIDS Crisis* (Lexington, KY: American Legislative Exchange Council, 1987).
13. Lisbeth Schorr, *Within Our Reach* (New York: Doubleday, 1988).

14. Cited in David Rochefort, *American Social Welfare Policy* (Boulder, CO: Westview Press, 1986), p. 147.

BIBLIOGRAPHY

Brandl, John. "Policy Evaluation and the Work of the Legislator," in *New Directions for Program Evaluation.* San Francisco: Jossey-Bass, 1980.

Freeman, Richard B., and Harry J. Holzer, eds. *The Black Youth Unemployment Crisis.* Chicago: University of Chicago Press, 1986.

Majchrzak, Ann. *Methods for Policy Research.* Beverly Hills, CA: Sage, 1987.

Mayer, Robert and Ernest Greenwood. *The Design of Social Policy Research.* Englewood Cliffs, NJ: Prentice-Hall, 1980.

CHAPTER 10

Histories of Policy

Our concern is now with the contribution historical sensitivity can make to our understanding of how social problems are defined and how social policies are developed. The chapter is entitled "Histories of Policy" rather than "History of Policy" because there is never one history of any policy. Nye Bevin, a former British Foreign Minister, was fond of saying in the midst of a political negotiation, "This is my history of the problem, now you tell me what is yours." Bevin's comment provides two insights. First, perceptions of the origins of a social problem are the fundamental determinants of conceptions of social solutions. Second, the social history is only a part of the more general social construction of reality in which the ideology of the observer provides both insights and blind spots. Further, all histories are written from a particular vantage point. The vantage point provides a perspective and is a source of valuable insight, but it also obscures vision. The combination of ideological conceptions and facts made visible through a vantage point means that each observer's knowledge of events contains both exact and erroneous knowledge. Only an omniscient being could have perfect knowledge of the events as they really happen. A Job Corps participant, a social worker, a teacher, and an administrator would all have different "real" stories of how the same program was put into place.

Precisely because objective history is impossible, historical sensitivity is essential. It is also essential if one is to understand the way in which particular social problems have been defined, alternative policies identified, specific programs selected, and programs implemented as well as the consequences of that implementation. The purpose of policy history is to reveal patterns of belief that shape our insight into how policy interventions develop in response to social problems.

THE USES OF HISTORICAL PERSPECTIVES

It is commonplace to suggest that historical appreciation of a social problem is necessary to the development of an effective social policy. Beyond this admonition lie some very diverse assumptions about how social policies actually emerge and why a knowledge of their history is useful. For the sake of simplicity these assumptions can be placed in two opposing categories. One is the case study approach, which views policy as grounded in time and place—a specific response to a specific problem. The study of biography, historical contexts, and timelines is required to comprehend the choices made. In this view significant events are explained by the verisimilitude of details that constitute microscopically constructed case studies. The alternative approach is a functional perspective, which has many manifestations. In each, policy development is seen as the inevitable product of certain basic economic/political forces. In one view, the modes of production shape all choices; in a second, policies are designed to perpetuate the power of those already in control; in yet another there is evidence of a grand law of progression to some ill-defined greater good. In each functional perspective the individuals in the policy development are merely actors who are actually being controlled offstage. Policy history statements generally incorporate both functional and individual perspectives. Richard Spano refers to the statement of historical development as the construction of a comprehensive statement of the historical context.[1] Bevin's statement reminds us that the assertion of comprehensiveness is often an effort to structure the past in such a way that we can shape the future as we want it to be.

GRAND FUNCTIONAL PERSPECTIVES

Not far below the surface in any functional perspective of social welfare policy development lie some rather dogmatic assumptions about property rights, individual rights, and the capacity of a society to correct for the inequality of its institutions. Below are three simplified views of welfare history and the role of government in the economy.

In the first view there is a fundamental belief that the market economy can and should divide society. Political efforts to eliminate or even moderate class distinctions and their attendant suffering are doomed to failure because they attempt to contravene natural laws of the social order. An early proponent of this approach was Malthus, who opposed the poor laws and other welfare inventions on the basis of hard reason and moral considerations as he saw them, rather than selfish indifference.[2] He believed that social programs would result in an increased population that would outstrip productive capacity, thus further lowering the living standards of the working class. Latter day Malthusians are still present in many policy debates.

A second view holds that the concept of *natural social* laws is a contradiction in terms because property relationships are inherently unnatural and are created by the state. These property relations create inequality and will, unchecked, destroy individual rights. In such a society, social welfare policies that moderate class conditions serve only to reinforce an "evil and tyrannical" state. The holders of this view share with the Malthusians a distaste for social welfare institutions, but the distaste is based on the fear that the laws will at some minimum level meet the needs of the least-privileged citizens. They are, thus, seen as a way in which the "real" march to social equality is delayed. Social welfare institutions are a patch on the torn fabric of capitalism and, as such, are a poor substitute for genuine social change. Social welfare institutions serve only to delay the evolution of the social welfare society.[3]

In this view, normally equated with the Marxist perspective on social welfare, social welfare agencies in a capitalistic society are seen as instruments of oppression. In many Marxist-oriented historical inquiries the purpose is to show how powerful elitists have used the appearance of benevolent programs to mask a comprehensive control of the working classes.[4]

It is only in the liberal tradition, the third view, that social welfare institutions have a valued place. The liberals share with the conservatives a belief in the inevitability of continued inequality. With the Marxists they share a belief that such inequality is distinctly undesirable. Unlike the Marxists they believe that the dysfunctions resulting from inequality in capitalism can be controlled by specific actions:

1. Fine tuning of the economy through the use of budgetary planning, monetary policy, and fiscal control designed to moderate the shifts between inflations and deep recessions
2. Social programs to compensate for inequality and insecurity attendant in a market economy that function through systems of social insurance, social assistance, and progressive taxation
3. Constitutional protection of minority rights to control against domination by economic factors
4. Specific social welfare programs designed to respond to the unequal occurrence of poverty among some social groups and to moderate the severity of the economy, resulting from the inherent limits of capitalist reforms. These social programs combat poverty, but not only monetary poverty. They are designed to combat also poverty of opportunity, communal poverty, and poverty of relationships, which may be a product of the market economy.

In the liberal paradigm, social welfare programs play a central role in the maintenance of the democratic state. They minimize the social dysfunctions that accompany a competitive market economy.

In each of the three functionalist perspectives—Marxist, Malthusian, and liberal—the further suggestion is made that social welfare policy choices are not a consequence of their unique historical context but are framed by basic structural/functional forces. The conflict over social programs can best be seen as a kind of Hegelian story of thesis and antithesis as social programs evolve and are, occasionally, frustrated. In the liberal view of history there is a slow but steady progress toward social equality but there are also inevitable setbacks. Recent social welfare political history is seen as a continuation of this theme. From roughly 1960 to the mid-1970s, there was a period of rapid expansion of public social programs with the result that the incidence and severity of poverty in America was dramatically reduced.[5] Nonetheless, from the mid-1970s to the present we have witnessed a gradual disengagement based on a belief that activist social welfare programs are inefficient and self-defeating.[6]

An overview of the various viewpoints is made by looking at some of the relevant statistics. The overall poverty rate is not a perfect measure of a social welfare system's responsiveness, but it is a rather good indicator of what does occur in a complex political economy. As a type of shorthand, we rate the progress of the economy and its social programs by the number of persons who, after taxes and welfare payments, have income below the official poverty line (Figure 10.1).

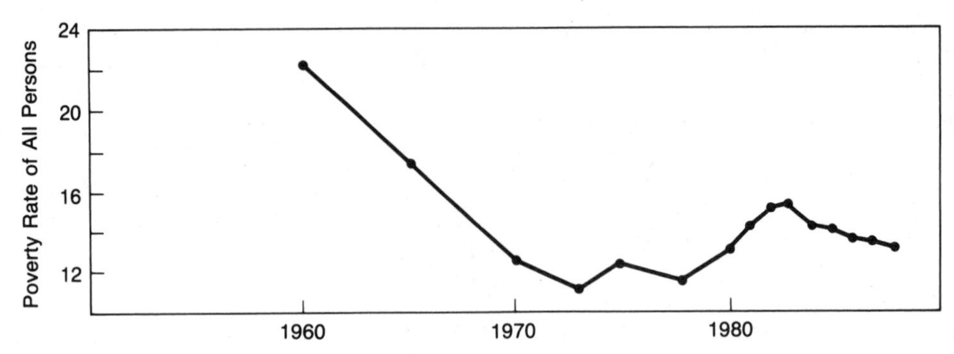

FIGURE 10.1 The Progress Against Poverty, 1960–1990 Poverty Rates (all persons) by Year

SOURCE: *Economic Report of the President 1990* (Washington, DC: U.S. Government Printing Office, February 1990), Table C–30.

The overall performance of the economy is measured in many ways. For our purpose a useful indicator is the constant dollar median wage of the full-year full-time worker (Figure 10.2).

When we look at both sets of numbers we see that they are systematically connected (Figure 10.3).

For the greater part of this century the real expansion of the economy, as reflected in the constant median full-time full-year wage, was the driving force in the reduction of the poverty rate. In recent years the rate of reduction of poverty has slowed. In part this is a function of the flattening of the rate of increase in the real wage of the median worker. The data also show that as real wages have gone up, the impact of that increase on the poverty rate has become less dramatic. The curvilinear relationship between the poverty rate and the median wage rate is shown in Figure 10.3.

FIGURE 10.2 Changes in Wages as Measured by Median Full-Time Full-Year Work in Constant Dollars (1988)

SOURCE: *Economic Report of the President 1990* (Washington, DC: U.S. Government Printing Office, February 1990), Table C–30.

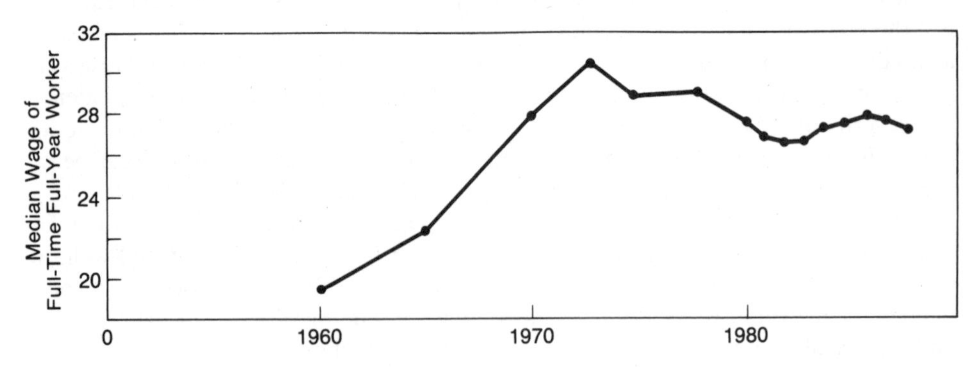

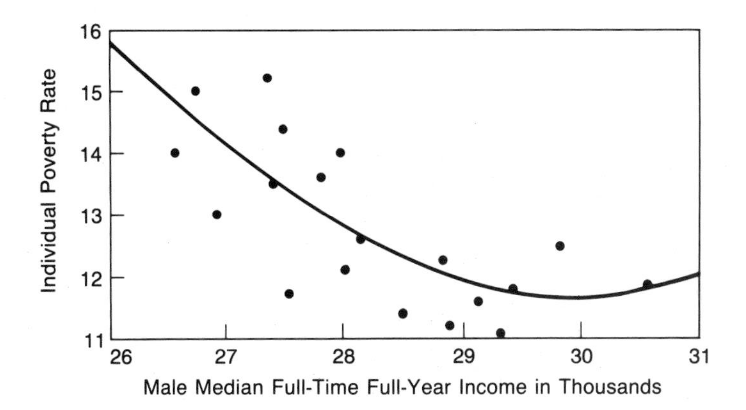

FIGURE 10.3 The Poverty Rate as a Function of the Median Full-Time Full-Year Wages, 1960–1990

SOURCE: *Economic Report of the President 1990* (Washington, DC: U.S. Government Printing Office, February 1990), Table C–30.

Critics from the liberal perspective and from the political right look at the same data, or at least the data from the same period, and reach diametrically opposite views, although both agree that the progress against poverty has been unequal. The conservative was quick to see the sharp relationship between real economic progress and poverty rates and to argue that the best defense against poverty is a strong economy. The liberal response is that the sharp relationship makes clear that increasing aid to the poor does not slow economic progress.[7] The liberals also show that spending on welfare does slow the poverty rate as seen in Figure 10.4.

During the 1960s, 1970s, and early 1980s, debates linked poverty and strategies of its reduction to strong world views that saw the poor as victims of their own culture or victims of social indifference. Policy critics now show a greater appreciation for the diversity of the poverty population. The poverty of the elderly widow differs

FIGURE 10.4 Share of Gross National Product to Direct Cash Assistance to the Poor

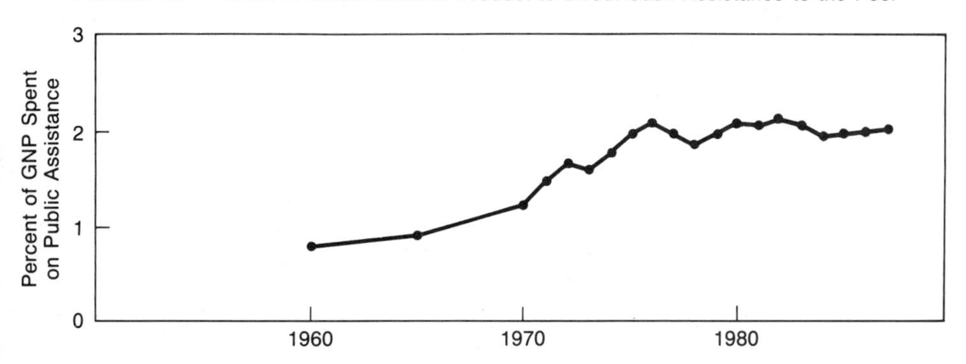

from that of the two-parent family where the adults seek full-time work but find it only sporadically, and both differ from the poverty of the second-, perhaps third-generation teen pregnant out of wedlock.[8] Macro data do not reflect what happens to particular groups; the overall rate of poverty may fall while the rate of poverty for a specific group might increase.

Among the lessons to be drawn from the War on Poverty is that what happened then was not preordained by structural/functional conditions. It is now clear that the programs being shaped by the Kennedy advisers were significantly different from those implemented by the Johnson administration.[9] Further, the structural functional predictions were flat wrong.[10]

THE CASE STUDY APPROACH

In philosophy and psychology a distinction is made between the nomothetic, or rule-seeking, and the ideograph, or individualizing, accounts of events. A policy history needs to show how the processes of problem definition and policy formation occur in specific historical contexts. This description demands a sophisticated awareness of standards, conditions, and circumstances that explain changes in social welfare programs.

Policy choices are consequences of the roles played by specific individuals in highly unique circumstances. Although general rules can be derived from numerous case studies, the real lessons are learned from the uniqueness of each case. In each case study, a wealth of detail, both organizational and individual, is available. From this detail a coherent story or explanation is fashioned. The details of the history show, presumably by both good and bad examples, the importance of timing, coalition formation, problem definition, and redefinition of the problem. A major dimension of historical context is the multitude of details. The case study approach, for example, shows that in the early 1960s mental health legislation to aid retarded citizens was surely shaped by the personal interest of both President Kennedy and the majority leader in the Senate, Hubert Humphrey—the president through his sister, and the senator through his grandchild.

Among other things, case examples help the student to appreciate the time and information constraints under which public officials and opinion leaders are forced to operate. They foster an awareness of the ill-defined central character of most policy decisions and the extent to which most policy decisions are folded into a much larger political and social context. The case examples illustrate the real-world tensions in policy choices, the trade-offs required, and the conflicts between the objective and the subjective as well as between the abstract and concrete. Studying cases helps the student to understand the interaction between the world of ideas and the world of actions. Case studies, sharply focused in their context, provide a reality screen of the intricacies that the individual policy actors must face. The development of a case history of a policy in progress helps political decision makers to understand their options better as the process moves forward.

The lines separating a political tract, a policy history developed during the course of a legislative campaign, and objective historical research are difficult to draw. Consider the sixteenth- and seventeenth-century histories of pauperism. Social commentaries about poor people were written by churchmen or those educated in theological schools. The effort was not to promote understanding; often the antithesis of understanding was the real goal. In nineteenth-century England the classical works of Charles Booth, Sir George Nicholls, and E. M. Leonard, and in the early twentieth century the works of Beatrice and Sidney Webb, were prepared as political tracts.[11] Though they were presented as historical accounts of conditions of the poor, their primary intent was to influence the perception of current events in a particular ideological way. In both England and the United States these political tracts in the form of histories were significantly powerful to influence the development of a liberal perspective among social welfare professionals.

In the United States histories of policy played a less important role. The studies of state poor laws sponsored by the University of Chicago between 1930 and 1943 focused on the administrative and institutional context under which changes could best be accomplished.[12] As objects of historical scholarship, however, they left a great deal to be desired. They were structured to prepare the future social work administrator to understand his or her options. Social welfare histories after World War II split into two not entirely distinct streams. One stream, influenced largely by the American Studies movement, was characterized by a sharp concern for particularities with regard to topic but they remained general in their focus. Thus histories of the almshouse, mental institutions, the abortion movement, child care, and such topics went beyond the legalistic and the administrative and focused attention instead on culture in all of its manifestations, including the arts, literature, and the media, as a confluence of factors generating social reform ideas.[13] As useful as this stream was, it did not enter social work education significantly below the level of Ph.D. training. In the professional histories used in schools of social work, the connection between mass culture and social policy simply was not made.

The second relevant stream included a number of works produced by historians with appointments in schools of social work. This genre of historical scholarship was as much concerned with the history of the profession of social work as it was with social welfare history. Its primary purpose appeared to be reinforcing the developing sense of professionalism among social workers. The critic Raymond Mohl has suggested that it was not a very good history. Like the University of Chicago project two decades earlier, it focused on administrative and institutional forms rather than politics and culture.[14] Neither the studies published in the American Studies tradition nor those published in the social work tradition paid much attention to the viewpoints and circumstances of the clients who were presumedly served by the profession and its institutions. This body of knowledge, to the extent that it was mined, was developed by the social anthropologist. Curiously, this material was not presented as history in welfare histories.

In the 1970s the professional social work/social welfare histories incorporated the American Studies traditions in their texts.[15] Politics and culture received as much attention as did obscure conference reports of social work professionals.[16] This advance was overshadowed, however, by yet another type of social welfare histories. Marxist histories became the hallmark for the teaching of history in American schools of social work.[17] Essentially, after a half century in which politics was neglected in social welfare history, this history was politicized. It was not until 1983 that a balanced set of arguments about the legitimacy of the Marxist tradition in social welfare history became generally available in the literature of social work.[18]

USES OF HISTORY IN POLICY STUDIES

If historic accounts are inevitably incomplete and less than objective, how then do we justify using for the historical statement anything other than propaganda and special pleading? A focus on selected facts, events, dates, and significant actors represents the too dominant (and too narrow) view of history in most social work curricula.[19] One of the questions that political scientists ask is how political actors have used history to reach decisions. Richard E. Neustadt, a political scientist, and Ernest May, a historian, combined their efforts at the John F. Kennedy School of Public Affairs at Harvard to teach a course on how political leaders use (or fail to use) historical experiences to make current policy decisions. The text resulting from that course[20] provides what I believe to be a useful focus for the development of historical statements of a policy.

Three critical assumptions lie at the heart of their book. The first assumption is that particulars matter. While ideology, *zeitgeist,* or the general forces of history are important, particular problems are presented and seen through the eyes of particular people in particular circumstances. If any of these variables were to change, the results would also change. The interaction between the general and the particular forces is not fully understood, but the critical importance of the particular cannot be denied. An important part of this assumption is that political actors are vital individuals and their actions are such that no one else would act in quite the same manner. Typically, actors are free to choose and their individual choices do make a difference. For example, it did make a difference that Wilbur Cohen was assistant secretary of Health Education and Welfare when Medicaid was sent to Congress and it did make a difference that Martin Anderson provided unique social policy guidance to President Reagan in Reagan's first term. Policy problems are a product of a socially constructed reality. They arise not only from events and circumstances, but also from the meanings that particular individuals in unique positions attribute to these events and circumstances.

Neustadt and May's second assumption is that marginal or incremental improvements in policy choice are worth seeking. Individual policy choices come one at a time but cumulatively their impact is fundamental. An examination of the evolution of social policy in any sphere reveals that change, for good or ill, comes a piece at a time. Cataclysmic events that help to explain the shape of a nation's foreign policy seldom have an analogue in domestic policy. Sometimes cataclysmic events such as the Great Depression force a set of social policy decisions, but each action decision is surely evolutionarily shaped.

Their third assumption is that historical sensitivity contributes to the rationality in the selection of available options. Political actors are compelled to act under conditions of uncertainty. They are not compelled to act with historical ignorance, though they often do so. The case studies presented by these authors were designed to demonstrate that a more sophisticated historical sensitivity would have led to more

	Conditions Similar	Conditions Dissimilar
What Facts Are Known		
What Motivations Are Presumed		
What Consequences Are Unclear		

FIGURE 10.5 Critical Conditions to Be Specified in the Case for Analogy

rational choices. Neustadt and May made clear that the use of history involves far more than reasoning from analogy. They illustrate the fundamental differences between using historic analogy as an instrument of analysis and using it as an instrument of persuasion in a specific policy debate.

In the first instance they attempt to classify analogies according to their allure. Some are *irresistible.* The irresistible analogy is one in which all observers see the events as a replay of an earlier story. Some analogies are merely *captivating.* In the captivating analogue some dominating similarities are used to make points for preordained ideas about how to act. Other analogies are simply *seductive,* where the appearance of similarity hides the reality of fundamental difference.[21] Neustadt and May suggest that in the analysis of a policy decision one should employ what they call their mini-method. This exercise requires that in the re-creation of the story of a policy choice one seeks to identify what was known, what was presumed, and what was unclear. If reliance is going to be placed on analogy, it is incumbent on the investigator to focus on the differences, as well the similarities, of the putative analogue. Completing the chart in Figure 10.5 can help the investigator in this task.

CONTENTS OF THE POLICY HISTORY STATEMENT

The contents of the policy history statement should tell a comprehensive story of the evolution of a social welfare problem and the responses to it, but this is only part of the purpose of the statement. It should also focus attention on each significant juncture of the evolving policy. These questions about events, ideas, and actors may be summarized as follows:

1. What significant events shaped the policy question so that it emerged at that particular time on some significant actor's political agenda?
2. What were the contending perceptions and ideologies used to define the problem and how are they different now?
3. Which significant policy actors defined the problem and shaped the options? There is a need to take note of the stakeholders in the choice. The focus should

be on both those who have taken action and those who have not; in social policy it is particularly important to know the latter. An association of nursing home owners will be clearly visible in a policy debate in their domain; user groups of nursing homes and their relatives are sometimes not visible. When relevant stakeholders do not play a role in the decisions made, the question of their absence needs to be explored; were they unheard, silenced, and unheeded or were they simply unaware that they were stakeholders in this policy issue?

Harry Eckstein has demonstrated that there are many forms of case studies.[22] Of interest in this context are three distinct studies of particular policy histories. The first is the truly ideographic form in which the interest does not stray beyond the facts and the circumstances of the particular case. Neil Gilbert's study of the transformation of the social service network by the 1962 Amendments is an example.[23]

The second form is the heuristic case in which a particular policy story is told to illustrate the working of some particular institution. Laurence Lynn and David Whitman's *The President as Policy Maker*[24] is an example. Their effort was to tell the story of the presidential role in the legislative process by using as an example Carter's failed welfare reform effort. In this way, the substance of the policy is used to illustrate a process.

The third form of policy history is the crucial case history in which the event itself is of such significance that there is an interest in the particular configuration of events and personalities involved. Ernest Witte's participant observer account, *The Development of the Social Security Act,*[25] is a prime example.

A fourth form of policy history not covered by Eckstein is the puzzle history in which the prime intent of the investigator is to provide insight into a particularly perplexing and unexpected event. Gates and Rather's[26] account of the Family Assistance Plan of 1969, when a conservative president proposed a liberal welfare reform effort, is an exemplary case. Perhaps soon we will see a story of the Family Support Act of 1988, when a liberal senator, Patrick Moynihan, was the key legislative actor in the passage of a conservative reform.

THE DEVELOPMENT OF A POLICY HISTORY

The questions identified previously are shaped in a historical context—the intellectual and cultural environment in which the events took place. The first task of the policy historian is to understand and interpret this context. The enormity of establishing a historical context has been well described by Jacques Barzun:

> Take this eye-catching paragraph from the announcement of a scholarly work:
>
> "The year the *Communist Manifesto* appeared, gold was discovered in California, *Vanity Fair* was published, Metternich resigned, the new French Republic elected Louis Napoleon president, Emperor Ferdinand abdicated."
>
> What these remarks are supposed to do is transport us back to 1848. In order to report intelligently about those six events (out of many more) an historian must be prepared to write about the following subjects, among others:

> For the *Communist Manifesto:* about Marx and Marxism, the history of economic thought, and Utopian Socialism. For the discovery of gold: about California geology, geography and settlement; the history of exploration and of western expansion. For *Vanity Fair:* about Thackeray and the English and Continental novel. For Metternich: about the Congress of Vienna, the Holy Alliance, Nationalism and Friedrich Gentz. For Louis Napoleon: about Napoleon Bonaparte, his empire, his brothers, their fate and their descendants. Also: the genesis of the Second French Republic, its constitution, parties and problems. For Emperor Ferdinand: about the house of Hapsburg, the Austrian Empire in the nineteenth century, its national and linguistic minorities and the rise of Liberalism.[27]

Timelines help the reader trace a particular policy as it goes forward and provide a corresponding listing of events that are concurrent with those under investigation. The reader must be given a sufficient number of events to get a "sense of the times." The task of the investigator is to avoid being captured by the twin seductresses of the historical context: antiquarianism, in which the investigator becomes hopelessly lost in the enormity of details that establish the verisimilitude of any event; and presentism, in which only those circumstances with direct links to the present are considered worthy of attention.

Although the policy history statement is not intended to compete with a product that would be prepared by a professional historian, the rules of evidence and the rules of inference that are employed by the professional historian do apply. Two sources are recommended to assist students who seek to prepare reliable policy histories. The first is *The Modern Researcher* by Jacques Barzun and Henry F. Graff. This is a classic, if not *the* classic, introductory work for the research and preparation of historical inquiry. The second is Richard Neustadt and Ernest Mays's *Thinking in Time.* Particularly in the third, sixth, and thirteenth chapters this work provides cogent advice on how to prepare a policy history "on the quick" with the skills available to those not trained as professional historians.

SOURCES OF THE HISTORICAL STATEMENT

In the preparation of detailed histories of a policy the following rules of evidence are useful. Three sources—the personal knowledge of participants, the archives of the relevant agencies, and the published accounts of prior investigations—are the points of reference in the development of a specific policy history.

Collecting Policy History Data from Participants

Because someone was a significant actor in a political event does not suggest that he or she is automatically a good source of what transpired. The bias of the vantage point is particularly strong for those who have been in the thick of the events as they occurred. In addition there is the problem of selective memory, a characteristic shared by all. Unfortunately, it appears that the more significant the event, the more selective is the memory. However, with participant-informants the most serious problem is the continuing agenda of those expected to recount the events. A former secretary of Health, Education and Welfare might, for example, have very useful insights into how a past political battle shapes a current political battle, but the secretary also has a current political agenda. Particularly for political activists, the memory of past events is shaped by the desire for future agendas. The activist does not necessarily fool himself, though this sometimes happens, nor does he or she deliberately distort the historical record, though this clearly happens also. The truth is that historical information about a policy's evolution is a political weapon and may be used as such.

In selecting a cast of activists to interview, the investigator must be satisfied on three points: (1) The respondent has firsthand information about the events, and the circumstance of the involvement can be verified by independent sources; (2) the respondent is motivated to cooperate with the investigator; and (3) the respondent's biases and vantage point can be identified and systematically neutralized by other sources or other interviews.

Before conducting the focused interview the investigator should develop a useful interview guide. By virtue of his or her professional training as a social worker, the investigator is likely to be a skilled interviewer; but while the clinical interview is structured to discover broad underlying feelings or motivations of the individual's involvement, the focused historical interview is structured to examine specific experiences. The focused historical interview guide is structured to obtain the respondent's subjective experience. The queries have been preanalyzed to obtain the respondent's perceptions and recollections of the event. It is the investigator, not the respondent, who should control the structure of the recollection, although this is often very difficult. By virtue of having been involved in public life, those who have played dominant policy roles are likely to be among the most verbally skilled persons one encounters. Many a scholar has walked away from a "wonderfully exciting interview" only to find on reconstruction that nothing of substance was said.

Accessing and Verifying Archival Data

The discussion in Chapter 8 on accessing congressional information is relevant to the discovery of materials available in archives that are not readily available in secondary sources. There is a significant difference in retrospective studies. In a retrospective investigation the investigator can rely more on secondary sources, and this is normally sufficient to satisfy the appearance and the reality of an impartial investigation. There will be circumstances in which the reliance on primary documentation is required. The *Federal Register* will indicate the location of primary records on federal questions. Most relevant public agencies will have their own librarian or archivist. The accessing procedures and the availability of online accessing aids vary so greatly from one facility to the next that talking to the librarian or archivist is highly advisable before beginning a search.

Archival reconstruction is a complex and demanding task. If the effort is strictly limited to obtaining printed documents whose authenticity cannot be questioned, then the interpretation of the records should be a straightforward task. Often, however, that is not the case. Again, it is useful to quote Barzun on authenticity:

> The historian arrives at truth through probability. This does not mean "a doubtful kind of truth," but a firm reliance on the likelihood that the evidence which has

> been examined and found solid is veracious. If you receive a letter from a relative that bears what looks like her signature, that refers to family matters you and she commonly discuss, and that was postmarked in the city where she lives, the probability is very great that she wrote it. The contrary hypothesis would need at least as many opposing signs in order to take root in your mind—though the possibility of forgery, tampering, and substitution is always there.[28]

A very useful short note on the procedures followed by one investigator in his use of personal interviews and the correspondence of the interviewee as well as the archival record is given in the appendix of Robert Caro's *The Years of Lyndon Johnson: The Path to Power.*[29] Caro shows how, in pursuit of Barzun's probability of truth, one must use both archival and personal interviews to reinforce one another.

Examination of Secondary Sources

In most cases the examination of the secondary source will precede archival searches and personal interviews. In virtually every subject area the investigator will want to supplement the materials that are collected from interviews and archives with accounts from contemporary journals and press.

Obtaining the best secondary sources is again a problem of access. There are many indexing and abstracting services that facilitate the location of articles appearing in major periodicals and reports from governmental agencies. The public documents accessing procedure has been previously discussed in Chapter 8. The two sources that policy history investigators use for general investigations are the *Social Science Citation Index* and *American Political Science Documents.* Both of these are available in both print and electronic form. For highly specialized investigation there are countless abstracting services by subject area that are best discovered by asking at the reference desk of a major library.

CONCLUSIONS

The preparation of a historical statement need not be an intimidating task. This is not to say that it is an easy one. The development of a specific social policy history is different from the development of history as history. It relies on social work skills as well as the knowledge and skills of the professional historian. The focus is on how the policy problems have been defined, how the processes and structures of the various relevant institutions were shaped by the political process, and specifically, how stakeholders have acted and/or failed to act in shaping the policy in its process.

NOTES

1. Richard Spano, "Creating the Context for the Analysis of Social Policies," in *Social Policy and Social Programs,* ed. Donald Chambers (New York: Macmillan, 1986).
2. Abram L. Harris, "John Stuart Mill: Government and the Economy," *Social Service Review* 37 (June 1963): 134–153.
3. For further discussion of the various streams of leftist thought on social welfare see Lionel Robbins, "The Economic Functions of the State in English Classical Political Economy,"

in *Private Wants and Public Needs,* ed. Edmund Phelps (New York: Norton, 1965). For a more recent perspective see Neil Gilbert, *Capitalism and the Welfare State* (New Haven, CT: Yale University Press, 1983).

4. For an exemplar of this argument see Frances Piven and Richard Cloward, *Regulating the Poor: The Functions of Public Welfare* (New York: Pantheon, 1971). For a critique of this approach see W. I. Trattner, ed., *Social Welfare or Social Control: Some Reflections on Regulating the Poor* (Knoxville: University of Tennessee Press, 1983).
5. John Schwarz, *America's Hidden Success: A Reassessment of Twenty Years of Public Policy* (New York: Norton, 1983).
6. Charles Murray, *Losing Ground: American Social Policy, 1950–80* (New York: Basic Books, 1984).
7. An increasing share of a growing gross national product went to poverty programs in the sixties and early seventies. The economy flourished for most of that period. The flattening of expenditure in the late seventies did not stimulate the economy.
8. For further discussion see Phoebe Cottingham and David Elwood, eds., *Welfare Policy for the 1990s* (Cambridge, MA: Harvard University Press, 1989), especially Chapter 2, Sheldon Danziger, "Fighting Poverty and Reducing Welfare Dependency."
9. Nicholas Lemann, "The Unfinished War," *Atlantic Monthly* (December 1988): 37–56; (January 1989): 52–68.
10. Barbara Gottschalk and Peter Gottschalk, "The Reagan Retrenchment in Historical Context," in *Remaking the Welfare State,* ed. M. Brown (Philadelphia: Temple University Press, 1988).
11. Charles Booth, *Life and Labor of the People of London,* 17 vols (London: Macmillan, 1891–1903); Sir George Nicholls, *A History of the English Poor Laws* (London: King, 1888); E. M. Leonard, *The Early History of English Poor Relief* (Cambridge: Cambridge University Press, 1900); Sidney and Beatrice Webb, *English Poor Law Policy* (London: Longmans, Green, 1910).
12. For an example of one of the best in this genre see Albert Deutsch, *The History of Public Welfare in New York State, 1876–1940* (Chicago: University of Chicago Press, 1941).
13. Exemplars of this genre of literature span three decades. The seminal example was Robert Bremner, *From the Depths: The Discovery of Poverty in the U.S.* (New York: New York State University Press, 1956).
14. Raymond Mohl, "Mainstream Social Welfare History and Its Problems," *Reviews in American History* 17, no. 4 (December 1979): 464–476. Cf. Samuel Mencher, *Poor Law to Poverty Program: Economic Security Policy in Britain and the United States* (Pittsburgh: University of Pittsburgh Press, 1967).
15. James Leiby, *A History of Social Welfare and Social Work in the United States* (New York: Columbia University Press, 1978).
16. W. I. Trattner, *From Poor Law to Welfare State: A History of Social Welfare in America* (New York: Free Press, 1974); June Axinn and Herman Levin, *Social Welfare: A History of America's Response to Need* (New York: Dodd Mead, 1975).
17. Frances Piven and Richard Cloward, *Regulating the Poor: The Functions of Public Welfare* (New York: Pantheon, 1971); Jeffrey H. Galper, *The Politics of Social Service* (Englewood Cliffs, NJ: Prentice-Hall, 1975).
18. W. I. Trattner, ed., *Social Welfare or Social Control: Some Reflections on Regulating the Poor* (Knoxville: University of Tennessee Press, 1983).
19. Richard Spano, "Creating the Context for the Analysis of Social Policies," in *Social Policy and Social Programs,* ed. Donald Chambers (New York: Macmillan, 1986).
20. Richard E. Neustadt and Ernest R. May, *Thinking in Time: The Uses of History for Decision Makers* (New York: Free Press, 1986).

21. Neustadt and May, *Thinking in Time,* pp. 48, 56, 66.
22. Harry Eckstein, "Case Study and Theory in Political Science," in *Handbook of Political Science,* Vol. 7, ed. Nelson Polsby (Philadelphia: Temple University Press, 1981).
23. Neil Gilbert, "The Transformation of the Social Services," *Social Service Review* (December 1977): 624–641.
24. Laurence Lynn and David Whitman, *The President as Policy Maker* (Philadelphia: Temple University Press, 1981).
25. E. E. Witte, *The Development of the Social Security Act* (Madison: University of Wisconsin Press, 1962).
26. Dan Rather and Gary Paul Gates, *The Palace Guard* (New York: Harper & Row, 1974), chap. 8.
27. Jacques Barzun and Henry F. Graff, *The Modern Researcher* (New York: Harcourt Brace Jovanovich, 1985): 13–14.
28. Barzun and Graff, *The Modern Researcher,* p. 122.
29. Robert Caro, *The Years of Lyndon Johnson: The Path to Power* (New York: Alfred A. Knopf, 1982).

BIBLIOGRAPHY

Axinn, June, and Herman Levin. *Social Welfare: A History of America's Response to Need.* New York: Dodd Mead, 1975.

Barzun, Jacques, and Henry F. Graff. *The Modern Researcher.* New York: Harcourt Brace Jovanovich, 1985.

Eckstein, Harry. "Case Study and Theory in Political Science." In *Handbook of Political Science,* vol. 7, ed. Nelson Polsby. Philadelphia: Temple University Press, 1981.

Galper, Jeffrey H. *The Politics of Social Service.* Englewood Cliffs, NJ: Prentice-Hall, 1975.

Harris, Abram L. "John Stuart Mill: Government and the Economy." *Social Service Review* 37 (June 1963): 134–153.

Leiby, James. *A History of Social Welfare and Social Work in the United States.* New York: Columbia University Press, 1978.

Mencher, Samuel. *Poor Law to Poverty Program: Economic Security Policy in Britain and the United States.* Pittsburgh: University of Pittsburgh Press, 1967.

Mohl, Raymond. "Mainstream Social Welfare History and Its Problems." *Reviews in American History* 17, no. 4 (December 1979): 469–476.

Neustadt, Richard E., and Ernest R. May. *Thinking in Time: The Uses of History for Decision Makers.* New York: Free Press, 1986.

Piven, Frances, and Richard Cloward. *Regulating the Poor: The Functions of Public Welfare.* New York: Pantheon, 1971

Rather, Dan, and Gary Paul Gates. *The Palace Guard.* New York: Harper & Row, 1974.

Spano, Richard. "Creating the Context for the Analysis of Social Policies." In *Social Policy and Social Programs,* ed. Donald Chambers. New York: Macmillan, 1986.

Trattner, W. I. *From Poor Law to Welfare State: A History of Social Welfare in America.* New York: Free Press, 1974.

Trattner, W. I. ed. *Social Welfare or Social Control: Some Reflections on Regulating the Poor.* Knoxville: University of Tennessee Press, 1983.

Witte, E. E. *The Development of the Social Security Act.* Madison: University of Wisconsin Press, 1962.

CHAPTER **11**

Qualitative Data Requirements

A popular government, without popular information, or the means of acquiring it, is but a prologue to a farce.

James Madison

The requirements of a policy paper are vast and varied. Social workers involved in the development of policy papers may be asked to prepare a monograph on the funding of Medicare on one day and on some aspect of programs for the homeless the next. Thus they cannot hope to become substantive experts on the issues about which commentary is required. Realistic time constraints compound the problem; the policy investigator often needs to obtain a useful perspective within days, sometimes within hours. What the policy investigator can hope to become expert in is the retrieval and use of information developed by others.

The one common requirement of all who write policy research papers is the need to formulate a clear plan for literature and information retrieval. The plan will vary from topic to topic and from assignment to assignment. The basic steps involved are (1) having a clear understanding of the primary purpose of the paper, (2) specifying topics properly, (3) developing and utilizing the seminal literature, (4) constructing a working bibliography, (5) identifying the prime sources of statistical and other information, and (6) acquiring supplemental information and commentary from persons in the field who can provide firsthand perspectives.

STATEMENT OF PURPOSE

Unlike research papers which, while often jointly prepared, clearly identify a principal investigator, policy papers are jointly produced products in which the various participants hold very specific responsibilities that are not always mutually consistent.

Policy papers are distinctive in their nature. Their primary aim is not discovery in the social scientific sense, nor is it elaboration and justification in the rhetorical sense. The useful, but elusive, distinction between advocacy and analysis needs to be kept in mind as in the development of an information plan for any particular paper. The principal aim is to use the methods of social research to provide a technique of reasoning and a system of acquiring and verifying information which, when consistently applied, will result in more rational decisions.

A policy paper is written to provide counsel for decision makers. The investigator must know who the client is to know to whom the counsel is to be directed. The investigator also needs to be aware of his clients' allegiances, constraints, and aspirations. A paper written to aid a legislator in sorting out a problem may be redundant or worse to a person in an administrative position, and vice versa. The potential morass of conflicting objectives is best resolved with a clear statement of the goals for the policy paper.

The aim of the counsel can be threefold: (1) to formulate the dimensions of the social problem and to isolate the dimensions of the uniqueness of the problem so that strategies of intervention can be appraised; (2) to clarify the implications of the options to the various political agents who will be called upon to act in the course of the policy process; and (3) to advocate selection in terms of a well-specified hierarchy of values in regard to a general vision of what is good for the community.

The realistic demands that are placed on a policy paper differ as a problem moves through the policy process. The paper must provide a construction of social reality that is useful to the reader in time, place, and circumstance. It is expected to meet the reader's intellectual needs for explanation and comprehension of the problem, provide him or her with a practical awareness of the political constraints that inhibit the various political agents, and yield a statement of value clarification. Few papers can do all of these things; thus, the first requirement for proper policy investigation is that the investigator and the client be aware of exactly what kind of paper is asked for and exactly what kind of paper they are producing.

Table 11.1 may be a useful guide in specifying the dimensions of policy papers. As this table indicates, there are fifteen different kinds of papers that can be written.

TABLE 11.1 Forms of Social Policy Paper Related to Components of Investigation

	Empirico/Normative Intent		
Stage of Investigation	***Problem Identification***	***Options Specification***	***Value Clarification***
Definition/ Formulation	1	2	3
Legislative Choice	4	5	6
Implementation	7	8	9
Evaluation/ Resolution	10	11	12
Termination	13	14	15

TOPIC SPECIFICATION AND THE INFORMATION RETRIEVAL PLAN

After the resolution of for whom and for what purpose the paper is being written, the next stage of planning for the policy paper is the development of a useful information base. Research topic specification is not the same as policy formulation. The latter is a dynamic action strategy whereas the former is a reflective plan structured to provide participants in the policy debate with the best relevant information. Topic specification that is too broad will overwhelm the investigator with a comprehensive list of literature too large to be examined in the time available. Topic specification that is too narrow will leave the investigator and client insufficiently informed and unprepared to engage effectively in the play of ideas that occurs as the policy process unfolds. The need for an optimal level of information demands care in establishing the parameters of the literature and information search.

A specific statement of a data and literature retrieval policy for each question should precede the actual search for literature. The investigator and the client should discuss the breadth of the search. Minimally it will include the following:

1. A generalized overview of the topic(s)
2. An identification of the various instruments to be used in accessing
   a. relevant data
   b. appropriate commentary
   c. descriptive information
3. A plan for the systematic identification and discounting of bias in the information stream that is to be utilized

The policy investigator does derivative rather than original research. The interest is in the creative play of ideas and data generated by others. The shape of the derivative investigation should be developed with the above-specified tasks in mind.

INSTRUMENTS OF ACCESS TO THE SEMINAL LITERATURE

Perhaps the most important need is for the investigator to become familiar with the seminal literature on the topic. Often he or she omits this important step thinking that this information is already part of the general knowledge of both investigator and client. Yet, unless one has been immersed in a particular topic area for an extensive period of time, the information at hand is at the same time both too random and too specific. Minimally, the policy investigator needs to establish that a systematic search for the seminal works in the area of inquiry has been done. This is necessary for three basic reasons:

1. The seminal works allow the investigator to become familiar with the information problems encountered by other investigations and to gain insight into what is known as well as what is unknown. With regard to the known, it is

important to ascertain the degree of consensus that surrounds the conventional information and scholarly research available on the topic.

2. They help the investigator to become aware of the unique vocabulary and terminology used in discussing the topic. This is particularly important as further data and information retrieval is dependent on precise specification of terminology in the use of printed index and abstracting services as well as electronic data retrieval of both public documents and previously published materials.
3. Most important, the background literature specifies the most significant streams of thought that appraise the actions and inactions of a government's or an agency's response to the social problem under investigation.

The literature and information search will include major books on the topic, the most pertinent journal articles, and the relevant public documents and statistical data.

Monograph Search

The investigator should begin the literature search by consulting a professional librarian who will provide assistance in using the various electronic and print searches available. The most important information the investigator can bring to the process is a knowledge of locator terms to be used and the data base to be searched. The search is a very tricky operation, but if the topic's parameters have been specified a competent librarian can guide you through this process. If time is not of the essence, the literature search can be done in two stages: first with monographs and books, then with journals, public documents, and statistical data.

The first step in accessing the background books and monographs is to identify the locator terms that will act as entry points to the relevant literature. The *Library of Congress Subject Heading Index* (LCSI) lists the topical terms used to classify the contents of books. Most printed and electronic systems adapt these terms to the particular format of a specific inventory of works available. There is a need for flexibility in the use of LCSI. For example, the term *welfare programs* is not available as a compound term, and the term *welfare economics* refers to a normative branch of the study of economics rather than to books dealing with economic considerations of welfare programs. The terms *public* and *welfare* have connotations far broader than social workers' use of these terms. For this reason, multiple locator terms may be required in most investigations.

Serials Search

"Serials" refers to magazines and journals that are published on a regular periodic basis, as opposed to books and monographs that appear at random and usually singly. The literature retrieval plan for each set of material differs in important ways. It is therefore a good idea to interrupt the search after the monograph stage and to use the materials collected to guide a more specific search into the serials literature.

As with the monograph search, the serials search requires careful consultation with a reference librarian. It is important at this point to understand the relationship between the specifics of your topic and the journals and magazines that typically produce articles and commentary suited to your specification. The *Social Science Citation Index* (SSCI) provides a term subject guide called Permuterm that functions much like LCSI. Other online searches likely to be used are *Public Affairs Information Service* and *United States Political Science Documents,* both of which provide an abstracting and indexing service across a broad range of literature sources. The *Reader's Guide to Periodical Literature* is useful for highly popular subject matter being treated in the vernacular. It is perhaps unfortunate but true that a reference to the vernacular literature for a complex concept could easily destroy the credibility of an otherwise well-done policy research paper.

The SSCI is the most comprehensive source of social scientific materials about public programs and policy actions. This is an international indexing service of journals of opinion, information, and research produced in English. It provides access to the literature through three paths: Permuterm, source, and citation. Permuterm is a contraction of permutation terms, which means that the key words from the title are arranged in pairs. Looking under welfare reform, one finds only the following:

WELFARE-REFORM

	▸STOESZ D
CONSERVATI.	▸SCHAPIRO MO+
REAGAN - - - - -	▸HAMILTON D
RHETORIC - - - -	▸LYNN LE
STRATEGY - - -	SCHAPIRO MO+
VICTIMS - - - - -	▸UDESKY L
YEARS - - - - - -	HAMILTON D

To locate the article selected one uses either a print form or an electronic search in the source file of SSCI to find the precise title and publication information. It provides a wealth of information, telling what authorities the author has cited and where those authors' works were originally published.

The citation index can then be used for each person cited by L. E. Lynn to find whom they have cited. Very quickly a citation pattern of the principal investigators will emerge and a small number of seminal authors can be selected who are doing pioneer work in the field.

United States Political Science Documents is both an abstracting and an indexing service. One could start a search here with a subject term or a specific author's name. The term *welfare reform* has no separate listing, but under *social welfare policy* one would note the potentially useful paper by Sawhill and others. To ascertain its utility we look up the abstract.

89002582• Sawhill, Isabel V. • *An Overview* • *PUBLIC INTEREST,* Iss. No. 96, (Summer, 1989), 3–15.

To ascertain its utility we look up the abstract.

89002582 AUTHOR(S): Sawhill, Isabel V.; **TITLE:** *An Overview.* **SOURCE:** *PUBLIC INTEREST,* Iss. No. 96, (Summer, 1989), 3–15. **ABSTRACT:** Underclass neighborhoods are characterized by welfare dependency, joblessness or irregular employment, large numbers of school drop-outs, female-headed families with children, and high crime rates. Although only a small proportion of those living in poverty are members of the underclass, increasing numbers of people are living in communities where poverty and social dislocation are pervasive and persistent. The underclass is growing because worsening conditions in the nation's inner cities are impeding escape through social mobility and are dragging formerly working-class families into the underclass. The objective of public policy must be to widen people's choices and reward those who want to become self-sufficient, self-respecting citizens. The government should support programs which serve children, help families, open up employment and educational opportunities, and offer incentives for young people to defer childbearing. **KEY SUBJECTS:** Public Policy Studies; Social Welfare Policy; Underclass; Poverty; Poverty Culture; Inner City; Ghetto Community; Social Deviance; **KEY GEOGRAPHIC AREAS:** United States of America;

Public Documents Search

The third important data source for information is public documents, which provide a maze of their own. The U.S. government is the largest publisher in the world, and if guidance from the reference desk is helpful in the monograph and serial searches, it is indispensable in the maze of public documents. Online searches that the researcher will likely consider are (1) *Government Publications Monthly Catalog,* an index source to records, reports, hearings, and so on published by all three branches of the federal government; (2) *Congressional Information Service,* which provides comprehensive information about the entire spectrum of congressional working papers; and (3) The *Federal Index,* which provides an indexing service not only to congressional activity but also presidential proclamations. Federal court rulings and executive branch actions are reported in the *Federal Register,* which is itself a source for federal regulations that are under consideration or have been promulgated for the implementation of federal social policies. CIS provides an annual abstracting and indexing service for public documents, as well as access information about major legislation.

AID
  see Agency for International Development
Aid to developing countries
  see Developing countries
  see Foreign assistance
  see Military assistance
Aid to Families with Dependent Children
  Child day care services improvement
    program estab, S181–32.2
  Child support supplement program
    replacement of AFDC program, S361–41,
    S363-3
  Child welfare programs background data,
    S362–10

An examination of entries listed by specific numbers in the abstract series provides the following example:

Ways and Means H781-28.3

H781-28 FAMILY WELFARE REFORM ACT.
Mar. 30, Apr. 1, 1987. 100-1
iv+435 p. GPO S2.00
S/N 552-070-04036-6
CIS/MF/7
*Item 1028-A: 1028-B.
*Y4.W36:100-38.
MC 88-14274. LC 88-601975.

Committee Serial No. 100-38. Hearings before the *Subcom on Public Assistance and Unemployment Compensation* to consider H.R. 1720 (text, p. 3–73), the Family Welfare Reform Act of 1987, to amend Title IV-A of the Social Security Act to replace AFDC with a new family support program (FSP). Includes provisions to:

a. Require each State participating in FSP to establish and operate a national education, training, and work (NETWORK) program for FSP recipients.
b. Provide for reimbursement of child care expenses for certain FSP recipients.
c. Revise FSP benefit calculation procedures to increase work incentives.
d. Revise requirements for States regarding child support enforcement and award amounts, and paternity determination procedures.

Includes submitted statements and correspondence (p. 425–435).

H781-28.1: Mar. 30, 1987, p. 93–133.

Witnesses: HEINTZ, Stephen B., commr, Conn Dept of Income Maintenance; representing Amer Public Welfare Assn.
COLER, Gregory L., sec, Fla Dept of Health and Rehabilitative Services.
PERALES, Cesar A., commr, NY State Dept of Social Services.

Statements and Discussion: Review of and general support for H.R. 1720, with recommended revisions; views on essential components of welfare reform legislation; importance of NETWORK program and work incentive provisions for FSP recipients.

Principal legislative histories, which are accessible by title subject and congressional law number, also provide an important source of retrospective policy information.

Statistical Information

William Alonso and Paul Starr's *The Politics of Numbers* and Harold Stanley and Richard Niemi's *Vital Statistics of American Politics*[1] provide excellent analyses of the issues relating to the collection, publication, and accession of the numbers needed for policy investigations. *American Statistical Index* (ASI) provides information about abstracts and indexes of all federal statistical information. ASI is an important source of trend data and should be supplemented with the special reports of the Census Bureau as well as the *Statistical Abstracts of the U.S.: Historical Statistics of the U.S.,* and the *Handbook of Labor Statistical Yearbook.* Economic statistics are available in the annual *Economic Report of the President.* International data are published in the United Nation's *Demographic Yearbook.*

Commentary on Public Documents and Official Actions

An indispensable source of information and commentary is a set of publications produced by Congressional Quarterly, Inc., a private information service and publishing company founded in 1945. Its *CQ Weekly Report* provides an exhaustive summary of the activities of Congress each week, including information about hearings and actions as well as commentary for the week. These are summarized in the *CQ Almanac* for the year, which provides a summation of each annual session. CQ's *Congress and the Nation* provides a compendium for each presidential term and is published once every four years, in the spring of presidential inaugural years. In each of its iterations CQ provides valuable clues to where to search for indices that will provide more detailed information. It provides a very quick, essential overview of the various policy topics that are likely to be explored in any policy paper with a federal governmental involvement.

Commentary on national political actions from a policy perspective is available in another private publication, the *National Journal.* This is a weekly publication monitoring the activities of the federal bureaucracy. It is particularly well indexed and provides comprehensive coverage of social policies. It acts as a quick source of information regarding significant events that shape social policy, including occurrences that did not officially happen, that is, rules, regulations, and law proposals that were only discussed and not formally introduced. The use of the *National Journal* along with the indexes of the *New York Times,* the *Washington Post* and the *Christian Science Monitor* will yield a wealth of information about the context of public actions.

A project may have to go forward for one reason or another without the assistance of a professional librarian. This is a condition to be avoided if at all possible. If it cannot be helped, the investigator will do well to consult printed substitutes for this advice. Two particularly useful sources are Joe Morehead's *Introduction to United States Publications* and the appendix to Jay Shafritz's *Dorsey's Dictionary of American Government and Politics* (Chicago: Dorsey, 1988).

NOTES

1. William Alonso and Paul Starr, *The Politics of Numbers* (New York: Russell Sage, 1987); Harold Stanley and Richard Niemi, *Vital Statistics of American Politics* (Washington, DC: Congressional Quarterly Press, 1990).

BIBLIOGRAPHY

Alonso, William, and Paul Starr. *The Politics of Numbers.* New York: Russell Sage, 1987.
Stanley, Harold, and Richard Niemi. *Vital Statistics of American Politics.* Washington, DC: Congressional Quarterly Press, 1990.

CHAPTER **12**

Quantitative Analysis

The relevant policy story can rarely be told with words alone. There are too many cases involved and the relationships among aspects of each case are too complex. We all know of "the horror" case in which a particular policy led to disaster and we all know of "the exceptional" case in which a particular policy produced spectacular results. We clearly need to have ways to recognize the horror, the exceptional, and the normal case. In short, we need to have ways to summarize our observations and to make inferences about them.

Statistics allow us to summarize data but they are also often used to distort data. Darrell Huff's *How to Lie with Statistics*[1] remains the classic about the ways in which deliberate distortions are used in statistical, graphic, and tabular presentations of data. However, our concern is not with how to lie or with the even more important skill of how to detect a lie. Our concern is the problems associated with the clear, concise, and precise presentation of quantitative information. Concise presentation refers to the effective summation of relevant data, while precision of presentation refers to the limiting of distortions that are associated with any summation.

Statistics is both more than a systematic collection of facts and less than some esoteric procedures that reveal the only truths about the data. Useful statistical presentations and the inferences derived from statistical procedures are based on the assumption that the original observations and measurements are both valid and reliable. Statistical analysis may be used for advocacy or analysis, but in both cases proper regard for the rules of evidence and the rules of statistical reasoning must apply. There is nothing inherent in the procedures that prevents the careless or deliberate distortion of the data. The purpose of statistics courses in most schools of social work is to ensure that students know the rules for presentation and interpretation that do not go beyond the limits of the data. This chapter does not substitute for such courses.

FUNCTIONS OF STATISTICS IN POLICY INVESTIGATIONS

In general and in policy studies in particular, statistics are used for two purposes: description and inference.

Descriptive Intent

Descriptive statistics are used to condense a large mass of information so that the policy decision maker can see the essential characteristics of the data and visualize their various associations. In a word, it is a process of summarization. Inevitably, by the process of substituting a very few measures for many, certain vital information is lost. Therefore, the limitations of each summarization procedure must be understood. In the analysis of a problem descriptive statistics are used as a systematic form of summarization. In an advocacy paper summarization may be used to draw attention to particular characteristics of the data. In both cases the procedure ought not give a misleading impression.

Inferential Intent

Inferential statistics are used to make inferences about a population based on the known characteristics of a sample. Statistical inference involves rather complex reasoning and is based directly on theories of probability. There is extensive and complex discussion concerning the use of tests of statistical inference when one is dealing with the total population rather than a sample.[2] In some cases the question involves moving from an observation of a sample to an observation about the population. We may know from valid and reliable observations that a disproportionate number of the youth in our sample fare well when given the benefits of a particular form of assistance. But can we generalize to the population at large?

On the other hand, much of the policy investigation involves estimation about association within a known population—all fifty states, for example. Suppose one finds a difference between, say, the mean duration of time on AFDC and the mean level of AFDC benefits. We are concerned, of course, with the validity of the observation: To what extent do the means in each case communicate a real circumstance? Ordinarily we are not content with leaving the question with a valid description. We would also like to make an observation about the statistical significance of the association. The focus of attention is on the statistical significance of association between variables. The problem of making statements about causal inference from either population or sample is far too complex for a single chapter. Nevertheless, there is a way of looking at significance that is useful for our more limited purpose. A parameter estimation is based on the level of confidence essential, or sampling error acceptable, to making a decision. A statement of a statistically significant association is based on the probability that the observed (or estimated) association could be explained by chance distribution. When an association, not merely by chance, is compatible with a theory of policy impact, we have indications of a valid policy

TABLE 12.1 AFDC Benefit Levels and Unmarried Birth for Whites, 1985

	Maximum Benefits	Unmarried Birth/All Births
Alabama	$118	8.1
Arizona	293	19.6
Arkansas	202	10.6
California	633	22.3
Colorado	356	15.2
Connecticut	601	15.2
Delaware	319	14.2
District of Columbia	379	16.3
Florida	275	13.9
Georgia	263	9.3
Idaho	304	10.2
Illinois	342	13.3
Indiana	288	14.3
Iowa	381	12.2
Kansas	409	11.2
Kentucky	207	14.3
Louisiana	190	10.0
Maine	416	17.7
Maryland	359	14.8
Massachusetts	510	15.4
Michigan	528	10.6
Minnesota	532	12.4
Mississippi	120	8.5
Missouri	282	12.9
Montana	359	12.4
Nebraska	350	11.6
Nevada	325	11.3
New Hampshire	486	13.3
New Jersey	424	13.0
New Mexico	264	22.1
New York	539	18.7
North Carolina	266	8.8
North Dakota	371	8.5
Ohio	309	14.3
Oklahoma	310	11.9
Oregon	412	17.6
Pennsylvania	401	14.9
Rhode Island	503	16.5
South Carolina	200	26.4
South Dakota	366	17.9
Tennessee	159	24.3
Texas	184	16.4
Utah	376	8.7
Vermont	603	17.2
Virginia	354	21.4
Washington	492	18.5
West Virginia	249	17.4
Wisconsin	517	18.1
Wyoming	360	13.3

SOURCE: Wellness Program for Families, p. 322. *House Ways & Means Report,* 100th Congress, 2nd session.

observation. Note carefully two things: The observation does not establish causality, nor is there any intent to generalize the observation beyond the population observed to, say, a community of nations. For inferential statistics as much as for descriptive statistics, the limits of the procedures must be understood.

At a minimum the reader should know whether the observations are based on population estimations or on actual observations. In a formal sense, population observations use Greek symbols while sample observations use the more familiar Roman symbols. In practice the Roman symbols are often used throughout. This leads to the useful pun about the data, "It doesn't look like Greek to me."

PROBLEMS OF PRESENTATION

The most common ways to present data are in tabular form by enumeration or by the more frequent contingency table. The most common graphic presentations are the bar chart, the pie chart, the line graph, and the scattergram. Tabular and graphic presentations, as we well know, can be used to mislead as well as to inform. The enumeration table is the most basic form of summarization. An enumeration is simply a tabular presentation of the data grouped in some fashion to focus attention on various aspects of the phenomena being considered. The contingency table (Table 12.1) presents "the evidence" about AFDC benefit levels and illegitimacy rates. Each column within the table is, strictly speaking, an enumeration of its own.

The data presented in Table 12.1 are complete, concise, and precise, but not very informative. In the scattergram (Figure 12.1) the data are presented graphically. The illegitimacy rate, which is the presumed dependent variable, is placed on the vertical axis while the AFDC rates, the presumed independent variable, are placed on the horizontal axis. The nearly complete statistical independence of the two variables is revealed in the scattergram in Figure 12.1.

FIGURE 12.1 Relationship between Out-of-Wedlock Births and AFDC Benefit Levels, 1985

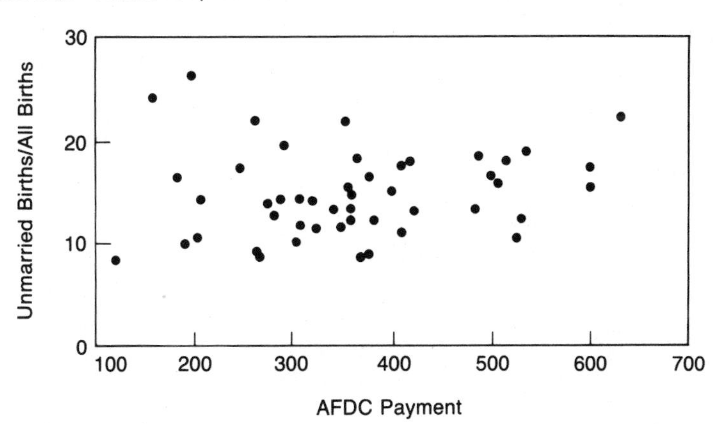

TABLE 12.2 Welfare Payments in 1986, in Comparison to Payments if Each State Had Adjusted Payments at the National Average since 1960.

	Actual 1986	1986 Normalized	Col 2/Col 3	Z score
West Virginia	3744	2347.108	1.595	2.688
Wisconsin	7788	5361.474	1.453	2.047
Michigan	7416	5239.988	1.415	1.876
Vermont	7812	5546.621	1.408	1.844
California	8376	6461.947	1.296	1.339
Rhode Island	6888	5425.112	1.270	1.222
Pennsylvania	5592	4584.260	1.220	0.996
New York	8472	6986.342	1.213	0.964
Maine	5868	4885.032	1.201	0.910
Washington	6936	5811.188	1.194	0.879
Oklahoma	4608	3918.296	1.176	0.798
Minnesota	7392	6463.202	1.144	0.653
Connecticut	7968	7110.717	1.121	0.549
North Dakota	5448	4971.863	1.096	0.437
Oregon	5784	5285.482	1.094	0.428
Kentucky	2952	2783.853	1.060	0.274
Iowa	5316	5049.265	1.053	0.243
Utah	5268	5073.797	1.038	0.175
Idaho	4128	4003.421	1.031	0.143
Louisiana	2808	2730.733	1.028	0.130
Arkansas	2688	2635.920	1.020	0.094
Ohio	4488	4449.644	1.009	0.044
Montana	5112	5101.318	1.002	0.013
Virginia	4920	5061.417	0.972	−0.123
Kansas	5400	5562.731	0.971	−0.127
South Dakota	4452	4625.064	0.963	−0.163
North Carolina	3228	3474.889	0.929	−0.317
Illinois	4620	4998.982	0.924	−0.339
South Carolina	2868	3122.345	0.919	−0.362
Missouri	3840	4191.990	0.916	−0.376
Nebraska	5040	5538.060	0.910	−0.403
New Hampshire	5304	5842.971	0.908	−0.412
Mississippi	1728	1907.330	0.906	−0.421
Massachusetts	6060	6765.479	0.896	−0.466
Indiana	3792	4230.255	0.896	−0.466
New Mexico	3756	4243.683	0.885	−0.515
Colorado	5040	5987.445	0.842	−0.709
Arizona	4236	5122.137	0.827	−0.777
New Jersey	5580	6812.992	0.819	−0.813
Georgia	3168	4006.928	0.791	−0.939
Maryland	4740	6163.185	0.769	−1.039
Florida	3576	4753.757	0.752	−1.115
Tennessee	2232	3155.289	0.707	−1.318
Delaware	4188	6028.426	0.695	−1.373
Texas	2652	3889.316	0.682	−1.431
Wyoming	4680	7080.928	0.661	−1.526
Nevada	4092	6197.378	0.660	−1.530
Alabama	1764	2818.439	0.626	−1.670

The graph makes a powerful inferential statement. One hardly needs to be educated about the complexity of social science to draw the obvious inference. The innate power of graphic presentations either to inform or to mislead should serve as a caution for the policy investigator. A useful tool for handling this is Smart and Arnold's *Practical Rules for Graphic Presentation of Business Statistics.*[3]

THE USE OF THE COUNTERFACTUAL

Often in policy debate there is a desire to create a "counterfactual condition." We know that states do not adjust AFDC payments in a random fashion. We might be interested in showing which states adjusted their payments more rapidly than the nation as a whole and which states lagged behind in their payments. Table 12.2 shows this information.

Counterfactual data do not fit nicely into the rules of evidence yet they are a powerful form of rhetoric. Rhetoric, as discussed earlier, has its place in both advocacy and analysis. As he or she does in using other procedures, the policy investigator who produces a counterfactual table has dual obligations. The first is not to present the table as if it were fact and the second, equally important, is not to push the created data beyond the limits of their assumptions.

RULES OF THE ROAD

This chapter serves as a very sparse introduction to the use of policy statistics. Descriptive statistics attempt to present an overview or summation of the conditions. In such discussions the focus is on the following:

1. What can be said about the distribution of the attributes of the variables that have been measured?
   a. What does a typical case look like? These are the measures of central tendency.
   b. How typical is a typical case? These are the measures of variation.
2. What can be inferred about the relationships between two or more particular variables?
   a. What is the direction of the association between the variables? Do they move in the same direction or the opposite direction, and do they do so in a linear or curvilinear manner?
   b. To what extent can we attribute a shift in one variable to a shift in the second, given the fact that many other observed and unobserved variables may also be in operation?
   c. Is the observed association between variables a function of chance?

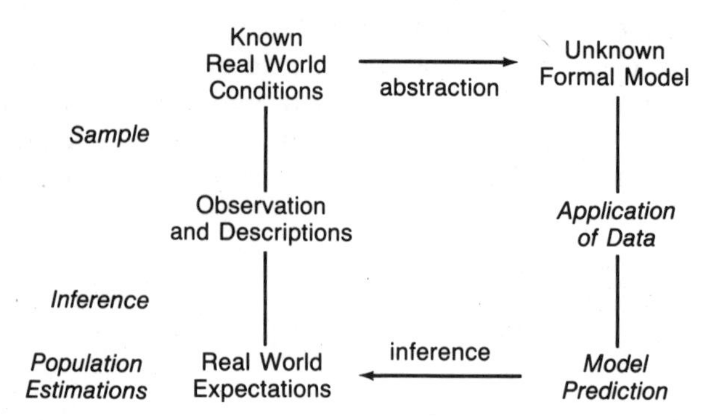

FIGURE 12.2

In the statistical model, estimations are based on a wide variety of formal models. It is not our intent to review most of these models. Our more limited focus is to show that the models are used to estimate, within a range of probability, the pattern of occurrence.

Figure 12.2 illustrates two ways of gaining information about what has happened and what is likely to happen when governments intervene in particular ways.

Each operation involves an understanding of the complex rules of statistical analysis. The rules are rigid, but when followed they allow for clear descriptive and inferential statements. This chapter does not teach all one needs to know about statistics, or even most of what one needs to know about particular methods. Its far more limited goal is to provide an overview of how the data need to be used in order to obtain their fullest benefit without distortion. We will begin with the essential rules of probability and proceed to a framework of understanding the uses and limits of the more commonly employed statistical procedures.

PROBABILITY

Probability is the expression of the likelihood that something will occur. Random probability is an expression of what is expected to occur when chance alone governs. The difference between observed occurrence and random occurrence provides the basis for much that we call science. The nonrandom occurrence of consequent events is one of the most basic presumptions about the impacts of policy intervention. In order to appreciate what occurs nonrandomly we must first understand what would be expected if chance alone were in operation.

Since probability is thought of as an expression of the likelihood of a particular occurrence under various conditions, it is possible to provide a limited number of fundamental rules of probability. Probability statements are about outcomes, the most fundamental of occurrences, or events, which are classes of outcomes. For example, the toss of a single six-sided die will yield one of six outcomes: 1,2,3,4,5, or 6. These are the possible outcomes. The outcomes can be further classed as events such as an even outcome, 2,4, or 6, or an odd outcome, 1,3, or 5.

The assignment of the probability value can be accomplished in one of three ways:

1. *A priori*—the favored outcome divided by the number of possible outcomes. In the example case 1/6.
2. *Empirical*—The number of favored occurrences divided by the number of options when the favored occurrence could have occurred. In the example this could be the number of times the six appeared in repeated throws of the die. If the six appeared every time the die was tossed in 100 tosses even the student with no formal familiarity with probability would conclude that the die was fixed.
3. *Judgmental*—This is the probability when the value is assigned on some best guess, a hunch or some highly complicated procedure, such as the race track tout's handicapping procedure.

As we shall see, each assignment procedure has a place in policy research and also, each procedure can be used nonsensically.

Basic Probability Statements

A probability value is the chance that something will occur. If a thing cannot occur it is assigned a value of zero; if it is certain to occur it is assigned a value of one. Outcomes that are neither certain nor impossible have probability values greater than zero and less than one, represented by $0 < P(A) < 1$. To calculate the specific marginal probability of any outcome we use the expression:

$$P(A) = n/(n + m)$$

where $P(A)$ = the marginal probability of outcome A

n = the occurrence of outcome A,

The occurrences are possible for a priori, observed for empirical, or estimated for judgmental.

m = the frequency of all other outcomes in the set of outcomes being estimated.

Notice that in the case of certainty, if only n can occur then $m = 0$, thus $N/(M + N) = P(N)$ or $1/(1+ 0) = 1$. The probability of a certain event is equal to one. In the case of impossibility $n = 0$ $N/(N + N) = P(N) = 0 + 0/(0 + 1)$. The probability of an impossible event is zero.

The value of the probability of mutually exclusive and exhaustive outcomes is equal to one. Thus $P(A) + P(B) + P(C) = 1.0$ where A, B, and C are distinct and separate outcomes and A, B, and C are the only possible outcomes. In a three candidate race where write-ins are not allowed, the sum of the marginal probabilities of each candidate's winning is equal to one.

In Texas, write-ins for presidential elections are not allowed. In 1988 there were eight candidates on the ballot, thus each candidate, including George Bush, had an a priori marginal probability of .125. In the 36 presidential elections held in Texas the Republican candidate has won six times; thus candidate Bush's chances were one in six if judged in strictly empirical terms. Most observers on the scene would have estimated his chances much higher.

Calculation of Probabilities

When the marginal probabilities are known the interest shifts to more complex outcomes. All such outcomes are easily calculated by the rules of probability. This is possible only when the events are not independent of one another.

What is the probability of *A* and *B* occurring?

If the outcomes are mutually exclusive, the probability value of *A* and *B* is the sum of $P(A) + P(B)$.

If the outcomes are not mutually exclusive, the probability value of either $P(A \text{ or B})$ is $P(A) + P(B) - P(A \text{ and } B)$.

What is the probability of *A* and *B* both occurring?

When the events are independent of one another and are not mutually exclusive, their joint occurrence is the marginal probability of *A* times the marginal probability of *B*. Thus

$$P(A \text{ and } B) = P(A) \times P(B).$$

If the events are independent of one another, the conditional probability of *A* given *B* is the same as the marginal probability of *A*. When events are dependent on one another, the probability of *A* given *B*, which is expressed as $P(A|B)$, is the quotient $P(A \text{ and } B) \div P(B)$. Thus

$$P(A|B) = P(A \text{ and } B) \div P(B).$$

When we compare the conditional probability to the marginal probability in the absence of the conditioning variable we see the impact of the conditional variable: $P(A|B) \div P(A|\text{non } B)$. The classic illustration is the probability of death by cancer if one is a smoker compared to the marginal probability of death by cancer if one is not a smoker.

AN EXAMPLE

The problem of intergenerational welfare dependency provides a useful case example of how probability concepts provide insight. Using data from the Panel Study of Income Dynamics (PSID) Hill and Ponza found the distribution over two generations (Table 12.3):

TABLE 12.3 Daughter's Welfare Experience Based on Mother's Welfare Experience (for whites, 1984)

		Daughter's Experience			
		None	***Low***	***High***	***Total***
	None	280	67	7	354
Mother's	Low	48	23	4	75
Experience	High	7	12	6	25
	Total	335	102	17	454

SOURCE: Martha Hill and Michael Ponza, "Does Welfare Beget Dependency?" (Institute for Social Research, 1984). Author's calculation from Hill and Ponza's data.

On the face of these numbers it appears that intergenerational welfare is not a serious problem. In only six of 454 families was there high experience of welfare for a daughter as both a child and subsequently as an adult and mother. If, however, these number are expressed as probabilities, the circumstance appears to change (Table 12.4):

TABLE 12.4 Daughter's Welfare Experience Based on Mother's Welfare Experience (for whites, 1984) By Subsets

		Daughter's Experience						
		None	***Low***	***High***		***Total***		
	None	.79	.19	.02	(1.0)	354	.780	
Mother's	Low	.63	.31	.05	(1.0)	75	.165	>.22
Experience	High	.28	.47	.26	(1.0)	25	.055	
		.74	.22	.04	(1.0)	454	1.0	
			.26					

SOURCE: Martha Hill and Michael Ponza, "Does Welfare Beget Dependency?" (Institute for Social Research, 1984). Author's calculation from Hill and Ponza's data.

Using the probability expressions reviewed above we can gain some new insights:

1. Addition and Subtraction Rules:

$$P(\text{M}) + P(\text{D}) - P(\text{M \& D}) = P(\text{Ever})$$
$$.22 \quad .26 \quad .10 = .38$$

$$P(\text{M \& D}) = \frac{23 + 12 + 4 + 6}{454} = \frac{45}{454} = .10$$

W (on Welfare)
P (Mothers) = .22
P (Daughters) = .26
P (Both) = .10
P (Either mother or daughter) = .38
P (Never) = 1.0 − *P* (Ever)
1.0 − .38 = .62

2. Changes in Probability
   A. $P(\text{D \& M}) \div \text{M(W)} = .10/.22 = .45$
   B. $P(\text{D}) = .26$
   C. $\dfrac{P(\text{D \& M}) \div \text{M(W)}}{P(\text{D})} = \dfrac{.45}{.26} = 1.73$

The probability expressions reveal that young women who grew up on welfare are 1.7 times more likely than the random household to be on welfare themselves. Further, while only six of 435 families have persistent two-generational welfare dependence,

1. $P(\text{D \& M High}) = \dfrac{6}{454} = .0132$

2. $P(\text{MOTHER High}) = \dfrac{25}{454} = .055$

3. $P(\text{D \& M High} | \text{Mother High}) = \dfrac{.0132}{.0555} = .240$

4. $P(\text{D \& M High}) | \text{Mother High} = \dfrac{.240}{(18/454)} = \dfrac{.240}{.0396} = 6.05$

Thus young women brought up in persistent welfare households are six times more likely than the random household to become mothers in persistent welfare families. While intergenerational poverty makes up only a tiny segment of the welfare population, this probability evidence suggests that intergenerational welfare is a serious problem. This does not mean that prior welfare dependency causes dependency.

MEASUREMENT SCALES

Variables must be measurable before they can enter into the discourse of politics. This is a bothersome concept for some persons. All it means is that if policy is made with regard to a phenomenon as we think we see it, then assignments of measurability of the phenomenon must occur.

Measurements and Scale Type

When variables are measured their attributes are measured on a *scale* that distinguishes the various attributes of a variable. Table 12.5 presents a representation of the various scale types encountered in policy research.

Measures of Inference

The scale type is essential to understanding the use of instruments of inference. The scale type in its turn determines the form of statistical number manipulation that is seen as valid. A basic summation is provided in Table 12.6.

TABLE 12.5 Types of Scales

Scale Type	Characteristic of Class Distinction of Attribute Being Measured	Example
Nominal	Attributes are clearly distinguished from one another and each observation fits into only one available class and all observations fit into some class	Party affiliation Democrat Republican Other No affiliation
Ordinal	In addition, the attributes can be ranked along a continuum	Social class
Interval	In addition, the intervals between ranks are fixed	Scores on most performance tests such as GRE
Ratio	In addition, the attribute being measured has a natural zero	Hourly wage

TABLE 12.6 Measure of Variability and Association Classed by Scale Type

Scale Type of Dependent Variable	**Scale Type of Independent Variable Inference About Association**			
	Descriptive Statistic	***Nominal***	***Ordinal***	***Interval/Ratio***
Nominal	Proportion Ratio Mode	Chi Square Difference of Proportions		
Ordinal	Percentile Mode	Correlation	Analysis of Variance	Regression (with dummy variables)
Interval/Ratio	Means, Medians, Standard deviation	Difference of Means	Intraclass Analysis and Correlation	Full Range of Procedures

The higher the scale type becomes, the more sophisticated are the statistical measures of association. Thus the investigator is under pressure to devise a more sophisticated measure of the variables under evaluation. The only known antidote to statistical misrepresentation is a mathematically literate citizenry. In the absence of that antidote it is imperative that policy investigators use statistics appropriately. Investigators fit statistical procedures to the level of the measurements used.

NOTES

1. Darrell Huff, *How to Lie with Statistics* (New York: Norton, 1954).
2. Hubert M. Blalock, *Social Statistics* (New York: McGraw-Hill, 1979), chap. 13.
3. Edwin Smart and Sam Arnold, *Practical Rules for Graphic Presentation of Business Statistics (Columbus, OH: The Bureau of Business Research, College of Commerce and Administration, Ohio State University, 1951).*

BIBLIOGRAPHY

Blalock, Hubert M. *Social Statistics.* New York: McGraw-Hill, 1979.
Huff, Darrell. *How to Lie with Statistics.* New York: Norton, 1954.
Smart, Edwin, and Sam Arnold. *Practical Rules for Graphic Presentation of Business Statistics.* Columbus, OH: The Bureau of Business Research, College of Commerce and Administration, Ohio State University, 1951.

CHAPTER **13**

Policy Presentation

The central purpose of policy research is to inform and/or influence decision makers about the options relevant to a particular problem. The first task in the formulation of the plan of presentation is to structure the presentation consistently with its primary purpose. A report that is designed to *inform* a decision maker has different structural demands from one that is structured to *persuade.* To confound the problem, often in the investigator's own mind the purpose of informing and the purpose of influencing are mixed. To disentangle them the researcher must clarify his or her values while at the same time providing a systematic method for reducing factual uncertainties. In addition, the links between action strategies and their probable outcomes need to be clearly specified. This division of policy research into its normative and empirical stances on the one hand and its analytic and factual components on the other places a strain on the integrity of the written report. The strain is but a reflection of the difficult choices to be made and the problems faced in the presentation of political advice.

THE POLICY RESEARCH PRESENTATION PLAN

Planning the printed presentation begins with the plan for the investigation. Nowhere is the interdependence of the various actors in the policy process more evident than in the considerations involved in the preparation of the written report. The shorthand communication available to a community of similarly trained scholars is not available to the policy investigator. The policy research statement must be clear in its two modes: normative/factual and analytical/factual. Yet in both forms the relevant concepts need to be presented precisely and the basic terms defined with clarity to an audience of readers with disparate educational and training backgrounds. This is a particular problem in political discourse where phrases such as "revenue enhancements" can be used but "tax increases" cannot.

THE STRUCTURE OF THE POLICY RESEARCH REPORT

Because of the range of topics and the different conditions that dominate the various phases of the policy process, it is clearly not possible to suggest a single template for the policy report. It is more useful to speak of the choices involved in the preparation of the report.

POLICY RESEARCH AS ANALYSIS

There has long been a debate over the question of social science as science. We can hardly open that important debate in the final chapter of this text. However, it is worthy to note in this context a first principle of the sociology of knowledge: "If men define situations as real, they are real in their consequences." The policy researcher plays a significant role in the definition of reality, scientific or not. Constant awareness of this aspect of the sociology of knowledge dictates that the analyst take great care when establishing the structure and content of policy research reports. The choice focuses on the ideal of science in relation to other ways of knowing. Specifically, it pits logical positivism, a philosophical elaboration of the scientific ideal, against its conservative and radical critics.

In the positivist ideal the investigator is essentially value neutral. The investigator strives to provide structured factual knowledge without regard for whom it benefits or the consequences for social norms. It is, according to this view, possible to use the instruments of quantitative science to specify, for example, a reasonably accurate estimate of the impact of capital punishment as a crime deterrent or the way a shift in abortion policy will affect the actual number of abortions demanded. It is not the purpose of the investigator to consider the value implications. The science model presumedly narrows the range of factors to be considered and requires of the investigator that he or she obey the various canons of scientific rationality and objectivity. The policy adviser must not allow personal values or beliefs to impact the data collection methods, the means of assessments, and the conclusions reached.

Critics to the right of logical positivism object to "value neutral" policy science because of its failure to incorporate the principal value assumptions of Western civilization. Critics of the left charge that the appearance of value neutrality means that the reports have unconsciously, or insidiously, incorporated these values without the required acknowledgment.

According to both the conservative and radical critiques, the elimination of institutional and personal bias is not only impossible but would be undesirable if it were possible. According to both positions, positivism is a futile attempt to externalize the relationship between knowing the subject and the object of knowledge. The positivists' response is that a useful level of objectivity can be achieved by a strict separation of

1. factual statements (those that are capable of empirical verification)
2. analytical statements (those that are valid by establishing canons of logic)
3. value statements (those that are capable of neither verification nor validation, except by reference to some specified system of beliefs)

The positivists admit that practical political privilege, the maldistribution of power, and simple malevolence may distort the kinds of questions asked or present false evidence. Positivists simply suggest that the responsibility of the investigator ends when he or she has specified the assumption surrounding the collection and the interpretation of the data. The investigator is not responsible for the ways the information is used or presented by others. He or she is responsible solely for the structure of the report.

There is a significant amount of disagreement about the extent to which policy analysis is or ought to be available for hire to whatever patrons can afford the investment. Advocates for and against the death penalty will each hire their own professional policy analysts. Does this mean that social science is silent on the saliency of the options that are open? We think not. Policy science can specify the conditions under which the death penalty deters; science can specify the conditions under which more women will seek (and/or secure) abortions. The knowledge ought to be available to anyone who feels political responsibility. This knowledge should be available to all voters who choose those who choose policies. The world of science, by its nature, is the world of ongoing discovery and change. All that policy science can say is that program Å produces a β probability of producing a Δ response under assumption £. The clear specification of Å, β, Δ, and £ is what policy science as analysis is all about.

POLICY RESEARCH AS ADVOCACY

Policies are pursued in conjunction with the values of various distinct belief systems. There is an infinite means/ends regression involved when policies are selected, but the ultimate criterion is some normative conception of the truly just society. It is a presumption of democracy that at a level of sufficient abstraction there lies a basic consensus about what a just society looks like. Without such a consensus democracy becomes a self-justifying instrument. It is not our intent in the closing pages to open a whole new discourse on political philosophy. Nonetheless, political advocacy must be placed in context. Choosing to be an advocate for or against the death penalty or the public funding of abortions arises out of personal beliefs about what effect that policy will ultimately have in the stream of events that generate or destroy the just society. When any particular policy preference is taken out of the stream and is justified or rejected as an end in itself, that end becomes more important than instrumental democracy.

At a somewhat more pragmatic level of policy advocacy a research report is simply one more instrument in political conflict. Advocacy research reports are like candidate advertisements: They are not structured to provide full information; they are structured to persuade. This statement involves a distinction between the policy investigator as political analyst and as political advocate. In the former role the quest is for effective and efficient instrumental solutions to specific problems. In the latter role the task is to present previously selected programs in their most attractive political cover. Academics are often critical of analysts who become too involved in the process of persuasion in the debate. There is a perception that such involvement demeans the scholarly standards of objectivity and impartiality. On the other hand, the suspicion is well founded that political actors, as advocates either of particular causes or of their own political careers, are interested in the policy investigation only to the extent that it supports positions they have previously adopted.

ETHICAL PROBLEMS FACED BY THE POLICY INVESTIGATOR

The choice between advocacy and analysis is not the only choice that must be faced. Earlier chapters discussed the structured process of policy choice and related it to the social scientific skills required to inform and/or influence policymakers. Clearly, explanations about the impacts of social policy must be understood in the context of basic beliefs about the ultimate goals of social policy. Social policy may be viewed in several ways:

1. As the efforts of control advanced by dominant elites who are reluctant to share economic or political power. In this view, the appearance of recipients sharing in welfare program decisions is but a sham to maintain dominance and control.
2. As the neutral political response of instrumental democracy to the demands of groups who see themselves as sharing certain problems.
3. As genuine expression of concern by the elites and powerful political coalitions about inequality and human suffering.

Explanation in the first mode will be essentially palliative to those who are seen as threats to the established order. Explanations in the second mode involve a search for some sort of negotiated, socially acceptable, or at least permissive consensus. The political marketplace of ideas about social programs is like any other marketplace. The most desirable social programs are the ones that produce the greatest profit, and in this case political equilibrium is the sought-after profit. This is not the same thing as domination by an elite. If one assumes that the political system itself is an open one, then a conflict between, say, the contradictory demands of child protection and the privacy of the family is possible. The political system, guarded by constitutional constraints, is the best way of resolving such a conflict.

Explanations of the third view are essentially technocratic and attempt to portray conflicts in welfare policy as being somehow outside normal political conflicts. There is an expression, "War is too important to be left to the generals." We know that generals often resent "the meddling politician"; so too does the professional social worker. Yet if one believes that war is too important to be left to the generals then one also needs to believe, in the name of consistency, that welfare is too important to be left solely to social workers.

Policy analysis at root is policy advice. It may be structured to inform, it may be structured to influence, or it may contain the unstructured and largely unexamined components for each. The advice must be seen as being offered in an environment dominated by economic and political conflict mediated by instrumental democracy, as that democracy is further constrained by constitutional protections.

This last chapter has sought to reveal the important overriding issues that shape the relationships between the individual or corporate authors of these policy research reports and the official audience of the reports. There may well be no single theme for social welfare policy analysis. The theme is established in the context of each unique political condition. The notion of policy analysis as counsel does not imply any specific value orientation, nor does it imply any specific civic commitment toward the goals of social welfare policy. The goal of policy analysis as counsel is to establish and present the dialogue between citizens and government officials in a manner that will ensure the inclusion of

1. explicit statements about and awareness of the various decision makers' preferences
2. a full exposition of alternative options available along with an understanding of why other options are not being pursued
3. sufficient information to facilitate the identification of efficient and politically feasible choices in their normative contexts

BIBLIOGRAPHY

Jennings, Bruce. "Interpretation and the Practice of Policy Analysis." In *Confronting Values in Policy Analysis,* eds. Frank Fisher and John Forester, pp. 128–152. Newbury Park, CA: Sage, 1987.

Appendix

Conformity and Diversity in State Responses to National Welfare Law Changes

The debate over welfare reform has involved two interrelated themes. The first concerns assumptions about the fundamental causes of poverty and the proper course and realistic capacity of government to reduce its magnitude and consequence. The second has to do with beliefs about the relative roles of each level of government and the best patterns of intergovernmental cooperation in a federal welfare system. Policy studies have contributed significantly to the understanding of both issues, but the second has been less thoroughly investigated.

Political folklore perpetuates a notion that policy shifts start in Washington and end in Pocatello. In fact, in an intergovernmental program each unit of government makes a decision predicated on the belief of what the other will do. The central concept of federalism is the existence of two sovereign governments with integrated responsibilities in one geographic area.[1] One of the characteristics of federalism is its aspiration to simultaneously generate unity and diversity. National standards adapted to local conditions is the ideal, yet between national and state officials there is little agreement on what the concept of federalism means in program design, program financing, or program administration.

The issues concerning the proper role of each level of government in providing for individual citizens' income needs and the most appropriate pattern of intergovernmental cooperation in a federal system go to the heart of welfare system design.[2] Federalism issues have seldom held center stage in welfare reform debates; however, beliefs held about federalism have fundamentally shaped the structure of the debate and defined the policy options throughout the evolution of American welfare policy. Shifts in beliefs about welfare have sparked debates about federalism issues, and shifts in attitudes toward federalism have altered beliefs about appropriate welfare policy.[3]

LEGISLATIVE HISTORY

The legislative history of the Family Support Act of 1988 provides the most recent example of how federalism and welfare policy are intertwined. In 1987 the National Governors' Association adopted a resolution calling on the federal government to accept the primary fiscal responsibility for financing income security programs.[4] Specifically, the governors called for the establishment of a national minimum level of assistance that was to be fully federally funded. The governors also wanted more federal fiscal participation in support programs geared toward education, training, job placement, and job retention among present and former AFDC recipients. Not surprisingly, the governors also wanted more freedom in designing employment assistance programs.[5] Congressman Ford's House Ways and Means Subcommittee on Public Assistance prepared the most costly and most national reform package, supported by the National Conference of Mayors. The administration responded with a legislative proposal that specifically rejected the concept of a federal minimum and went only partway in giving states the freedom to design innovative approaches.[6] The Reagan administration contended that the responsibility for redistribution lies with the state, though some transition funding formula needed to be defined. This approach was to become the Republican plan in the Senate. Senator Moynihan then introduced legislation that, while not establishing a national minimum, would retain the national government's fiscal participation while dramatically expanding state prerogatives in program design.[7] Largely through the creative efforts of Senator Moynihan and Congressman Downey, Moynihan's version of the law prevailed. Congressman Downey, also of New York, had succeeded Congressman Ford as chair of the House Ways and Means Subcommittee on Public Assistance.

During this century there have been eight reasonably distinct phases of federal/state relationships: (1) 1900–1928: Progressive Failure and Prelude to Reform; (2) 1929–1935: Depression and Relief Legislation; (3) 1935–1941: Establishment of a Federal Presence; (4) 1941–1950: Belief in the Doctrine of Wither; (5) 1950–1960: Federal-State Shared Responsibilities; (6) 1960–1972: Drive to Federal Supremacy; (7) 1972–1980: Period of Political Drift; and (8) 1980–1990: Return to the States. Since 1960 urban Democrats in the House, along with the Conference of Mayors, have pushed Congress to expand national control. Conversely, Senate Republican leaders and the National Governors' Association have encouraged restricting the national government's role in program design. Presidential leadership, or the lack of leadership, on the federal-state balance is far more complex. Beginning with President Johnson's War on Poverty and extending to President Nixon's efforts to introduce the Family Assistance Program, presidential leadership moved toward nationalization albeit of very different national programs. In part, Presidents Ford and Carter were ineffective in pursuing their separate welfare agendas because they failed to address the complex sharing responsibilities of a federal system.[8]

In December 1980, three men who had played significant domestic policy roles in the Republican administrations debated welfare reform in the pages of the Republican policy journal, *Common Sense.*[9] The men were Richard Nathan, who had a principal role in the design of the *Family Assistance Plan,* Paul O'Neil, who had served as deputy director of OMB under Ford, and Robert Carlson, former welfare administrator under Governor Reagan and destined to become special assistant to the president for human resources. The paper was remarkably prescient. O'Neil presented the classic defense of a dominant national role by observing that the needy population was unevenly divided among the states, while the fiscal capacities to respond are often inverse to the conditions requiring assistance.[10] Nathan offered the historical and political rationale for a national program, noting, "The fact that people and jobs move in a free society is the underlying reason why the burden of financing welfare benefits should be shared on an equitable basis by society as a whole."[11] Carlson gave no response to the intergovernmental issues but suggested that shifting welfare programs to the states would hasten the end of the safety net social welfare programs.[12]

Reagan's federal reform efforts took place in two steps. In the fall of 1981 the Omnibus Reconciliation Act established a number of procedural reforms that would require the states to modify their own programs in such a way that national fiscal participation in the safety net would be reduced by a significant amount.[13] For the record at least, the administration expected a devolution of national responsibility would be matched by an expansion of state responsibility.[14]

When Reagan introduced the new federalism initiative in the State of the Union message of 1982 the centerpiece was a swap of welfare responsibilities. As originally crafted by the administration's own planners the entire exchange was to be revenue neutral. The national government would assume responsibility for Medicaid while the states would have responsibility for AFDC and food stamps. An expected windfall profits tax on oil would be used to finance the transition so that no state government would be a fiscal loser in the exchange. The administration's proposal failed to achieve legislative support and was never debated on the floor of the House or Senate as a legislative act. It died early in committee considerations. The legislative failure was due in part to falling oil profits, which would leave no windfall to finance the programmed exchange. Equally important, individual state projections did not agree with federal estimates.[15] Neither government trusted the other, and the administration quietly withdrew its proposal. Nevertheless the administration continued various efforts to reduce the national government's contribution to public aid programs.[16]

In the last three decades federal policies of national assumptions, drift, and a retreat from national responsibilities have all been in place. Simultaneously with the shifting national/state responsibilities, there has been a shift in state economic circumstances. From 1960 to 1972 economic diversity as measured by per capita income and by tax income decreased. From 1972 to 1984 state diversity stabilized, and since 1984 there has been a resurgence of greater interstate diversity. This change is reflected in Figure A.1.

If it is true, as suggested by the voluminous literature,[17] that welfare choices made by governments are a function of both economic and political circumstances, it appears reasonable to assume that a trend toward or away from conformity among the states would relate to both circumstances. Thus during a period of greater economic conformity and greater national incentives, state welfare performances would become more similar. Conversely, during political periods of incentives for diversity and a weakening of national economic homogeneity, intrastate diversity would reassert itself. During a period of political drift and economic stability among the states small changes would occur (Table A.1).

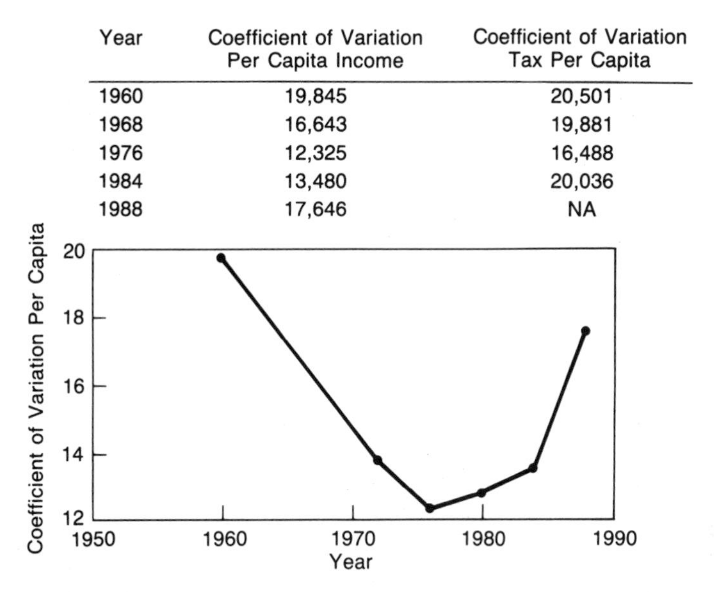

Year	Coefficient of Variation Per Capita Income	Coefficient of Variation Tax Per Capita
1960	19,845	20,501
1968	16,643	19,881
1976	12,325	16,488
1984	13,480	20,036
1988	17,646	NA

FIGURE A.1 Variations in Per Capita Income and Taxes Collected Per Capita in the 48 Contiguous States

Observations do not confirm the expectations. When AFDC benefits are viewed as a proportion of per capita income in each state the dynamic is nearly opposite the expectation (Figure A.2).

If the states had adjusted their benefit structures to changing economic resources, the shift toward and away from homogeneous economic conditions would have moved the coefficients of variation downward and then upward again in the expected directions. If the logic applied concerning the power of the national government to establish national goals or return prerogatives to the states, as suggested earlier, the trends would have been even stronger. A partial explanation for this counterintuitive finding is that the individual states have distinct historical cultures regarding welfare. Further, they use the power residing in the states in a federal system to thwart the national government's objectives. Finally, the national government's capacity to use fiscal carrots and sticks to promote collective state spending and more homogeneity among the states has not been effective.

TABLE A.1 National Political Incentives

	National Responsibility	**Drift**	**State Responsibility**
Economic Shifts			
More Alike	Decreased Coefficient of Variation		
Stable		Small Change	
Less Alike			Increased Coefficient of Variation

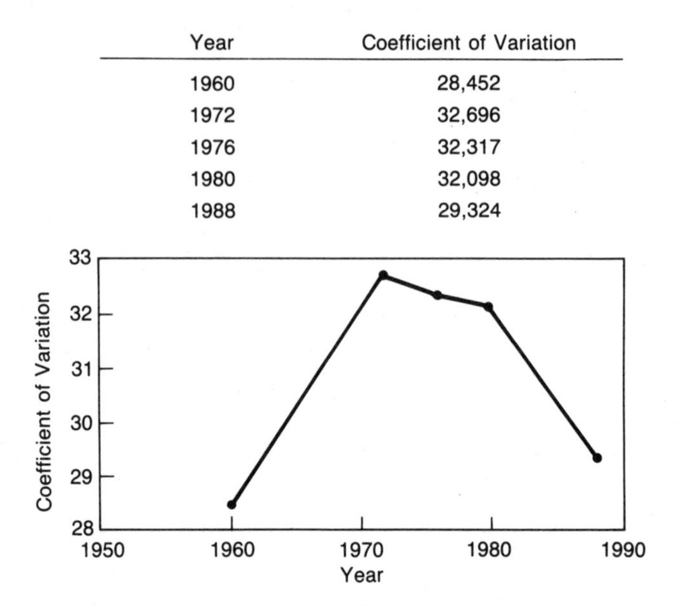

Year	Coefficient of Variation
1960	28,452
1972	32,696
1976	32,317
1980	32,098
1988	29,324

FIGURE A.2 Variations in AFDC Benefits as a Proportion of State Per Capita Income, 1960–1988

To evaluate the first argument one has to look at both present and historic practice among the states. In Table A.2 each state's welfare benefits are recorded and then compared to estimated welfare benefits as indicated by a cross-sectional regression procedure. This is the benefit that would be in place if each state set its welfare benefits in terms of its available resources and the demands faced in exactly the same way as every other state. This procedure is similar to the method used to establish tax yields if all states had identical tax laws. As with taxes, welfare benefits would still vary, as states have differing capacities and different demands.[18]

These deviations from national norms have been persistent over the past thirty years, the period for which there are reliable data. When states are ranked by their standardized residuals a few states have had remarkably generous programs and a few states have had remarkably stingy programs (Table A.3).

The second argument is that the states use their power in a federal system to at least slow, if not disrupt, national objectives as specified by Congress and the president. Evidence of this is shown with both expansions and reductions in national responsibility and fiscal participation in welfare programs.

In 1962 the service amendments provided the state with nearly free federal dollars to establish service programs. The 48 contiguous states took advantage of this opportunity at very different rates, as shown in Table A.4.

Twenty years later the Reagan administration's Omnibus Budget Reconciliation Act regulations pushed the states to restrict their levels of eligibility for welfare

TABLE A.2 Observed and Expected AFDC Benefits, 1988

	Observed	Expected	Standardized Residual	Deviation
California	633.000	447.785	2.379	185.215
Utah	376.000	214.503	2.074	161.497
Vermont	603.000	459.877	1.838	143.123
Michigan	513.000	379.583	1.713	133.417
Washington	492.000	397.662	1.212	94.338
Wisconsin	517.000	424.148	1.192	92.852
New Hampshire	486.000	413.506	0.931	72.494
Minnesota	532.000	467.196	0.832	64.804
Oklahoma	310.000	258.978	0.655	51.022
Louisiana	190.000	141.580	0.622	48.420
Connecticut	601.000	552.697	0.620	48.303
Rhode Island	503.000	467.828	0.452	35.172
Colorado	356.000	321.677	0.441	34.323
North Dakota	371.000	337.275	0.433	33.725
Arizona	293.000	264.322	0.368	28.678
New York	539.000	513.844	0.323	25.156
Kansas	409.000	386.869	0.284	22.130
Idaho	304.000	282.545	0.276	21.455
Virginia	354.000	333.308	0.266	20.692
Maine	416.000	395.504	0.263	20.495
Oregon	412.000	392.355	0.252	19.645
Pennsylvania	402.000	388.378	0.175	13.622
Wyoming	360.000	355.531	0.057	4.469
West Virginia	249.000	246.833	0.028	2.167
New Mexico	264.000	269.195	−0.067	−5.195
Montana	359.000	365.711	−0.086	−6.711
Mississippi	120.000	133.401	−0.172	−13.401
South Carolina	200.000	219.379	−0.249	−19.379
Florida	275.000	294.580	−0.251	−19.580
South Dakota	366.000	389.596	−0.303	−23.596
Georgia	263.000	291.315	−0.364	−28.315
Massachusetts	510.000	541.162	−0.400	−31.161
Arkansas	202.000	236.666	−0.445	−34.666
North Carolina	266.000	301.960	−0.462	−35.960
Alabama	118.000	155.680	−0.484	−37.680
New Jersey	424.000	478.181	−0.696	−54.181
Ohio	309.000	369.738	−0.780	−60.738
Nebraska	350.000	412.561	−0.803	−62.561
Kentucky	207.000	270.122	−0.811	−63.122
Iowa	381.000	450.326	−0.890	−69.326
Tennessee	159.000	236.030	−0.989	−77.030
Indiana	288.000	367.373	−1.019	−79.373
Texas	184.000	267.601	−1.074	−83.601
Missouri	282.000	371.821	−1.154	−89.821
Illinois	342.000	442.757	−1.294	−100.757
Nevada	325.000	430.566	−1.356	−105.566
Maryland	359.000	472.137	−1.453	−113.137
Delaware	319.000	481.358	−2.085	−162.358

TABLE A.3 States with Standardized Residuals Less than or Greater than 1: 1960–1988

	1960	1970	1980	1988	Significance
Wisconsin	+	+	+	+	sig. <.0005
South Dakota	+	+	+	0	sig. <.02
Idaho	+	+	+	0	sig. <.02
North Dakota	+	+	0	0	sig. >.10
New York	+	+	0	0	
Connecticut	+	+	0	0	
Washington	+	0	+	+	
New Jersey	+	+	0	0	
Montana	+	0	0	0	
Vermont	0	+	+	+	
Pennsylvania	0	+	0	0	
California	0	0	+	+	
Minnesota	0	0	+	+	
Utah	0	0	+	+	
New Mexico	0	0	0	0	
Michigan	–	0	+	+	
New Hampshire	0	+	0	0	
Massachusetts	0	0	0	0	
North Carolina	0	0	0	0	
Oregon	0	0	0	0	
Kentucky	0	0	0	0	
Wyoming	0	0	0	0	
Iowa	0	0	0	0	
Mississippi	0	0	0	0	
Kansas	0	0	0	0	
Oklahoma	0	0	0	0	
Virginia	0	0	0	0	
Ohio	0	0	0	0	
West Virginia	0	0	0	0	
Arkansas	0	0	0	0	
South Carolina	0	0	0	0	
Rhode Island	0	0	0	0	
Colorado	0	0	0	0	
Nebraska	0	0	0	0	
Maine	0	0	0	0	
Arizona	0	–	0	0	
Illinois	0	0	0	–	
Alabama	0	0	0	–	
Georgia	0	0	0	–	
Tennessee	0	0	–	–	
Maryland	0	–	–	–	
Louisiana	0	–	–	0	
Missouri	–	–	0	–	
Indiana	–	–	0	–	
Delaware	–	–	–	–	sig. <.005
Nevada	–	–	–	–	sig. <.005
Florida	–	–	–	–	sig. <.005
Texas	–	–	–	–	sig. <.005

Guttman's coefficient of reproducibility = .901

TABLE A.4 1962 Social Service Conformity of Contiguous States

	1961 AFDC Benefits		
	High	*Moderate*	*Slow*
Speed of Conformity			
Fast	5*	1	0
Moderate	5	20	4
Slow	0	10	3#

*Wisconsin, New York, California, Minnesota, and Michigan
#Texas, South Carolina, and Mississippi

programs under threat of loss of federal dollars. The states responded to the restrictive regulations at distinctly different rates (Table A.5).

The third argument is more complex. National policy and state policy intertwine to make federal policy but no group of legislators sits to formulate federal policy. Rather, legislative bodies at both levels make compromises, pass laws, and seek to shape the implementation process as it affects what the federal policy accomplishes at the street level where social worker and client interact. Often the action of one sovereign legislative body frustrates the intent of the other. Texas, for example, has several times used a nonrecurring special grant to AFDC recipients, the intended advantage of which is that it is not counted as income in the determination of food stamp benefits.[19] Not only legislative bodies but also the bureaucracies at both levels use a form of doublespeak. Many devices are created by inventive bureaucrats, sometimes enacted into law, which serve no purpose other than to affect the share of payment by one or another unit of government. During the Nixon and Carter years the national government made efforts to reduce interstate differences in benefits through establishing the food stamp program and then eliminating the purchasing requirement. As the value of the food stamp benefits declined in proportion to AFDC levels, in any cross-sectional analysis interstate variation in total benefits obviously fell. As it is a "counterfactual" one can never know how state benefits would have changed in the absence of the food stamp program. We do know that the variations

TABLE A.5 1982 Omnibus Budget Reconciliation Act Conformity of States

	1981 Benefit Levels		
	High	*Moderate*	*Low*
OBRA Regulations			
Slow	4*	2	1
Moderate	3	19	6
Fast	1	9	3#

*California, Vermont, Minnesota, and Connecticut
#Texas, Georgia, and Louisiana

TABLE A.6 AFDC Payments for a Family of Three in Current Dollars and Constant Dollars

Variable	Mean Current $'s	Standard Deviation	Minimum	Maximum	Fixed Mean 1982–84 = 100
AFDC 1960	1829.96	627.41	600.0	2861.0	6183
AFDC 1972	2651.50	972.89	720.0	4332.0	6342
AFDC 1976	2881.17	1014.40	976.0	4728.0	5063
AFDC 1980	3454.75	1240.77	1152.0	5904.0	4191
AFDC 1984	4377.46	1600.69	1416.0	7920.0	4212
AFDC 1988	4375.75	1568.32	1416.0	7596.0	3912
AFDC 1990	4446.50	1639.00	1416.0	8328.0	3525

in state payments have not responded in the expected directions and the cash benefit has fallen in constant dollar terms. This effect gives rise to the contention that although food stamp changes created more equal final benefits, the increase in total value occasioned by food stamp supplements may have been more than matched by a reduction in state payments (see Table A.6).[20]

The extent of "creative federalism accounting" and the final street-level impact of each unit's adjusting to the other is nearly impossible to know because the process is often structured so each unit of government is able to deny its real intent. Once one unit of government has acted, it is impossible to know what the other would have done in the absence of that action. It is, however, possible to track overall spending by the national government and by the states both individually and collectively. This is done in Figure A.3.

During the onset of new national programs in the sixties, amounts of national and state spending increased relative to the economy as a whole but were stable in relationship to one another. After 1972 the relative increase in national spending was not matched by a larger state effort. Further, the retreat from a national effort in the Reagan years was not matched by an increased state effort. The Family Support Act of 1988, seen by some as "the most sweeping overhaul of the nation's welfare

FIGURE A.3 National and State Expenditure for Public Aid as Percentage of Gross National Product

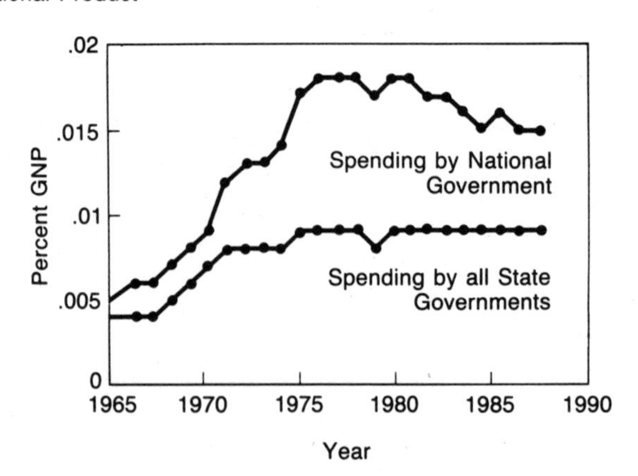

system in half a century,"[21] has now moved past its initial implementation phase. Irene Lurie's examination of program structures and implementation in New York shows that the states will march to their own political drums rather than a nationally prescribed consensus.[22]

Advocates of national efforts to establish and enforce national standards and advocates of greater state freedom have both used national/state spending data to further their respective ideological goals. It is clear that both nationalists and states' righters are able to frustrate one another. Conceptually and constitutionally, a purely national program could be put into place, but that, so far, has not been politically feasible. Whatever the next turn in the welfare reform debate, conflicts in state and national agendas will surely have a major place.

NOTES

1. D. J. Elizar, *Exploring Federalism* (Tuscaloosa: University of Alabama Press, 1987), p. 64.
2. Thomas A. Ault, "Federal-State Relations and Income Support Policy," in *Income Support: Conceptual and Policy Issues,* eds. P. G. Brown et al. (Totowa, NJ: Rowman & Littlefield, 1981).
3. Joseph Heffernan, "An Historic Preface to Welfare Reform" and "Welfare Reform, 1935–1968," in *Introduction to Social Welfare Policy* (Itasca, IL: F. E. Peacock, 1979). See also James T. Patterson, *The New Deal and the States* (Princeton, NJ: Princeton University Press, 1969).
4. National Governors' Association. Press release, 17 February 1987, p. 23.
5. National Governors' Association. Press release, 17 February 1987, p. 23.
6. White House Legislative Summary, 30 January 1987, pp. 2, 4.
7. S 1511, 100th Congress, 1st session, 21 July 1987.
8. Lawrence Lynn, *President as Policymaker* (Philadelphia: Temple, 1983).
9. R. Carlson, P. O'Neil, and R. Nathan, "The Future of Welfare," *Common Sense* (Winter 1980): 4.
10. Carlson, O'Neil, and Nathan, "The Future of Welfare," p. 27.
11. Carlson, O'Neil, and Nathan, "The Future of Welfare," p. 10.
12. Carlson, O'Neil, and Nathan, "The Future of Welfare," p. 15.
13. Joseph Heffernan and Wilbur Cohen, *Welfare Reform: A View from the States* (LBJ School of Public Affairs, Austin, Texas, 1984.)
14. Cited in J. Heffernan, "New Directions in the Welfare Reform Debate," *Journal of Sociology and Social Welfare* 15, no. 4 (1988): 10.
15. A. J. Davis and Kenneth Howard, "Perspectives on a New Day for Federalism," *Intergovernmental Perspectives* 8, no. 2 (Spring 1982): 9–21.
16. Paul E. Peterson, *Welfare Magnets* (Washington, DC: Brookings Institution, 1990).
17. Thomas Dye, *American Federalism: Competition among Governments* (Lexington, MA: Lexington Books, 1990); especially chap. 2.
18. A stepwise regression based on per capita income, percent black, mean Democratic vote, and percent of unemployed. Together they explain 75.5 percent of the interstate variation in welfare benefits. The justification and explanation of my procedure is spelled out in William B. Fairley and Frederick Mosteller, *Statistics and Public Policy* (Reading, MA: Addison-Wesley, 1977), part II, pp. 51–87.
19. Anthony Champagne and Edward Harpham, eds., *Texas at the Crossroads* (Bryan, TX: Texas A & M Press, 1987), p. 287ff.

20. Paul E. Peterson, *Welfare Magnets* (Washington, DC: Brookings Institution, 1990).
21. *Congressional Quarterly Weekly Report,* 8 October 1988, p. 2825 and previous CQ citations cited there.
22. Irene Lurie and Mary Bryna Sanger, "The Family Support Act: Defining the Social Contract in New York," *Social Service Review* (March 1991): 43–67.

Index